# SERMONS ON MICAH
## BY
## JEAN CALVIN

# SERMONS ON MICAH
# BY
# JEAN CALVIN

Translated by
Blair Reynolds

Texts and Studies in Religion
Volume 47

The Edwin Mellen Press
Lewiston/Queenston/Lampeter

BS
1615
.C28
1990

**Library of Congress Cataloging-in-Publication Data**

This book has been registered with the Library of Congress.

This is volume 47 in the continuing series
Texts and Studies in Religion
Volume 47 ISBN 0-88946-839-7
TSR Series ISBN 0-88946-976-8

A CIP catalog record for this book
is available from the British Library.

Copyright©1990 The Edwin Mellen Press

All rights reserved. For information contact

The Edwin Mellen Press
Box 450
Lewiston, New York
USA   14092

The Edwin Mellen Press
Box 67
Queenston, Ontario
CANADA   L0S 1L0

The Edwin Mellen Press, Ltd.
Lampeter, Dyfed, Wales
UNITED KINGDOM   SA48 7DY

Printed in the United States of America

GENERAL THEOLOGICAL SEMINARY

# ACKNOWLEDGEMENTS

This translation of 28 sermons on Micah delivered in French by Jean Calvin in Geneva, Wednesday, November 12, 1550 through Saturday, January 10, 1551, was made possible by a Research Assistance Grant from the American Academy of Religion.

# TRANSLATOR'S PREFACE

Although for some years complete texts of sermons Calvin delivered in French have been available through the *Supplementa Calviniana*, English translations have yet to appear. My translation is taken from *Sermons sur le Livre de Michée* (*Volumen* V of *Supplementa*), which is the original, handwritten transcription set into modern type with modern punctuation, capitalization, and accent marks. I believe that my translation provides a valuable asset to Calvin scholarship in English-speaking countries in the following four ways.

First, Calvin was not only a theologian but a prolific preacher who delivered an average of 286 sermons a year. It is, then, a serious omission in Calvin scholarship to overlook his sermons. It is time that the voice of Calvin the preacher be heard.

Secondly, the question arises whether Calvin the theologian is also Calvin the preacher. I think that the reader will agree his sermons on Micah answer the affirmative. Although they were intended for relatively uneducated laity, they contain a very high level of theological content. All his major doctrinal concepts are to be found among them, and in a language simple and to the point.

Thirdly, these sermons center upon two interrelated issues that are just as important today as they were then: Since Christians have the Gospels, do they need the Old Testament? And if so, how is the vengeful, wrathful God of Old Testamental prophecy to be reconciled with the Christian God of love?

# CONTENTS

[*]Calvin's Geneva began the New Year on December 25.

# SERMONS ON MICAH
## BY
## JEAN CALVIN

(1) Wednesday, November 12, 1550

The Word of the Lord given Micah Morasthite in the days of Jotham, Ahaz, and Hezekiah, kings of Judah, whom he saw about Samaria and Jerusalem, etc. Micah 1

How hardened is man that he stubbornly refuses to obey God, despite all His prodding. Worse yet, God cannot insure that His Word will be received as certain truth, although He has provided sufficient proof and witness. Because God has given us such ample confirmation of His Word, we will be so much the more inexcusable before Him and His angels if we refuse it. True, men now care little about the Word; but on Judgment Day, God will show that He has not spoken in vain, that His Word is too precious to remain idle. So much the more responsive, then, must we be when God calls us to know His truth as sure and certain. Let each of us submit to the Word; let us not be as wild horses; let us bow our heads and bear His yoke.

Now, here is a good example of what I mean. Micah's prophesies were publicly proclaimed during the reigns of three kings, Jotham, Ahaz, and Hezekiah. Isaiah also lived during these times. Jeremiah came later, when our Lord sent other prophets, such as Amos. Micah, then, proclaimed nothing that had not already been said by Isaiah. Was it not sufficient that only one prophet spoke the Word of God? Well, yes, but as I have said, our Lord wished to render the Jews and all of Israel so much more inexcusable, when He ordained Micah to succeed Isaiah.

1

Those two spoke as from the same mouth. Their messages were so alike that it seemed only one man spoke.

The prophets served well their times; but, as Saint Paul says, their teaching is also addressed to us today. He even goes so far as to say that they regarded our time as special, as the perfection of all things. Indeed, it is not without reason that Christ is said to be the goal and end of the Law. This does not mean that the teaching contained in Moses and in the prophets is over and done with, that all recollection of it may not be abolished. On the contrary, he says that we today are in a position to better understand the Law and the prophets than those who lived before the Gospel, that we can profit from this knowledge better than they. Mind, we are without excuse before God. So let us listen carefully to Micah and be further strengthened in the knowledge we have already received from Jeremiah and Isaiah.

Micah came at the same time as Isaiah (although the latter outlived him), whereas Jeremiah came later, as we have seen. It is safe to assume from our passage for today that Micah exercised his office of prophecy, by which he reproached and admonished his people, for a very long time. It speaks of three kings, of which the second, Ahaz, reigned for sixteen years. If we divide the reigns of the other kings into halves of comparable time spans, we can assume he prophesied for about thirty-eight years.

We see so much the clearer, then, how rebellious the men of his time were against God and His Word. Micah served his people

2

faithfully, but to what avail? Did they amend their ways? No, not much, except at the time of Hezekiah. Indeed, his reign makes so much the more obvious the maliciousness of the world. Here was a king whose only desire was to lead all the world to God. He devoted all his efforts to this end, he looked to the honor of God in all matters, and yet he never succeeded in winning over enough people that iniquity did not reign everywhere. He employed all his might to abolish all idolatry and superstitions. But, oh, how the Devil dominates man's nature until God steps in! If there ever was a prince who strove to put the Church in order, Hezekiah is a shining example above all others. Indeed, he even destroyed the brass serpent made by Moses, for fear it would become an idol. Though he struggled very hard to root out everything contrary to the honor of God, he failed to render his people obedient to Him.

Micah was to some avail, but only to a very slight degree. The Jews of his time refused to accept his teachings, and we can say as much for ourselves today. Understand that what Micah has to say is also directed against us, that we are among the ranks of those headed for even greater condemnation. Since the world is no better today than it was then, our Lord wished His condemnation of the Jews to be made public and to be remembered until Judgment Day. As I have said, if we act as they did, we also share their fate. If we ignore God's call to repentance, if we refuse God and show ourselves rebels against Him from the very start, we will surely bear the punishment we so well deserve.

Micah struggled long and painfully to exhort his people. This was as God had so ordained in order to render sinners inexcusable and therefore unable to plead ignorance. In this way, God convicted them for their manifest rebellion against Him. No matter what obstacles were thrown against Micah, he followed only God's commandments. He rose above whatever resistance he encountered in men. When the world becomes as wicked as it can be, let us remember that God wants His Word to be preached. Let us face all difficulties squarely on. Although men may resist with all their might (as they did at the time of the prophet), we must surmount all such evil, as the prophet did. Do not attribute such patience and fidelity to Micah himself. These came to him through the Holy Spirit. However hardened, perverse, and incorrigible remained the people, he never once abandoned his vocation.

We should come to appreciate what grace God shed upon us when He ordained that so much preaching be collected into such a small book, so that we are able to read in merely an hour what Micah preached in the space of thirty-eight or forty years.

What ingrates we are! Micah devoted his whole life to the exhortation of his people; God wished us to have a concise summary of his preaching; and yet we pay it no heed, will not even take the time to glance at it. Our ingratitude is not directed against a merely mortal man, but against God, who used Micah as His instrument. The Holy Spirit spoke through his mouth to save the Jews. All this has been brought to light for us today. The blame rests squarely on our shoulders, then, if we do not profit from the prophet's labors and the grace of the Spirit. If we are not moved to read this book and engrave its teachings upon our hearts, what excuse have we for having failed at our calling?

To say that the prophets no longer have any value and that the Gospels alone are sufficient is an inexcusable blasphemy. It is for us that prophesies were written down. Saint Paul says that they apply to our time when he says that "all doctrine is useful to reproach, correct, and instruct." He does not say that doctrine _was_ useful; he says it _is_ useful today. There is no doubt he is referring to the Law and the prophets. At another place, he says, "All these things were written down to teach us by example." Elsewhere, he says that these things were written down "in order that the man of God be rendered perfect in all good works." Let us receive, then, Micah's teaching, which is presented to us today in the name of God. Do not think for a minute that Micah was wasting words, because he preached for such a long time and yet the whole of his teaching can be summarized in two or three pages. The prophet exhorted at great length, for we are the greatest slackards and so must be continually goaded and prodded along. Indeed, an ass has not as much need to be prodded by blows of the whip as we have for God to goad us along.

Our Lord wished us to have a concise, written summary of Micah's teaching. However, we must not confuse its brevity with the notion that a quick glance will suffice for our instruction.

5

What goes in one ear, as they say, comes out the other.  If we are told some fable or fib, we will remember it all our lives. It will be well received by us, since it is in accord with our nature, which pleases us.  But if it is a matter of learning in the School of God, we forget our lesson as soon as it has been taught.  Therefore, it is necessary for God to repeat our lesson many times over to us.  The ears of men are always attuned to novelty.  Many will say, "Look!  Day and night, we hear about God, Jesus Christ, and the grace shed on us by His death and passion.  Now, is it not enough that we hear but once that our sins are forgiven?  That we put all our trust in His sacrifice can be said in very few words.  Once it has been said, that is enough."  Indeed!  But consider how we put our faith in Christ. On the contrary, we are so unfaithful that although our ears be thrashed thoroughly by this teaching, we forget it soon enough. When we are exhorted to carry out our office, how many take up this task?  Very few, indeed.  When we put God's teaching into practice, we can well say that we have been lectured enough.  But that will never happen as long as we are in this world.  God must speak often to us to strengthen us in what we have learned.  He remonstrates us at great length in order to engrave deeply into our memory and spirit all that He has to say to us.

Let us turn now to Micah's teaching, which consists of revelations against Jerusalem and Samaria.  This is a very difficult task for us.  If the prophet were merely speaking of the grace God shed on Jerusalem and Samaria, ah, what desire we would have to read his prophecies, as they would then bear us the message of God's love and our salvation! But what message do we really receive from Micah? God rages against us all. Who can take pleasure in such a message? It seems that the Holy Spirit rejects us all, for what is said here is not at all to our liking. But we have great need for God to reproach us; so God reveals through Micah the evil that will befall Jerusalem and Samaria, in order to correct their iniquitous and sinful behavior. I say that if we are to taste God's love and infinite bounty, we must be wounded to the depths of our hearts and feel the wrath of God upon us. In short, our Lord wishes to prepare us to receive His grace, when He reproaches us for the vices by which we provoke His wrath against us. As long as men remain hardened and continue to take pleasure in evil, it is impossible for God to enable them to taste His bounty. Whatever grace God sheds in abundance upon the world, if we remain hard as rocks, we will taste nothing of it. If it were to rain night and day on rocks, would they be capable of producing fruit? No, for the water would run off and flow into the earth, which, because it is soft and moist, would receive it in order to bear fruit. Likewise, unless God has softened our hearts, the grace He sheds upon the world will be of no benefit to us. But by making our sins manifest to us, God brings us to a true displeasure in ourselves for having offended Him, as we are then well on the way to receive His grace. Have we only a little remorse in ourselves, it will be as a small drop of dew that bears fruit,

7

and we will come to sense its efficacy for our salvation. All this must be borne in mind when we read in Micah that God condemned Samaria and Jerusalem.

It is astonishing that the prophet speaks of Jerusalem and Samaria in the same breath. Samaria, we know, was the source of all the abominations that reigned during this period. There was a temple there, but it was full of idolatries and superstitions. God was blasphemed rather than honored there. Ever since Jeroboam erected his golden calves in the temple, nothing but abominations were to be found there. How, then, can Micah identify Jerusalem with Samaria when in point of fact the former was the place the Lord has chosen for His Temple and to be the center of His cult? Why does he put it on a par with Samaria, which was like a whorehouse full of all sorts of filth and infections? He has good reason to do so, for he says, "If there is corruption in Judah, it comes from Jerusalem." Although God's Temple was in Jerusalem, this does not mean the inhabitants were sanctified. Indeed, they polluted themselves by all sorts of abominations. God's Temple may have been sacred territory; but those who entered it polluted it by their filth and villainy, as the prophet Haggai says. If men are of an unclean conscience, they pollute everything around them. Even what has been sanctified in the name of God will be spoiled by their iniquities. Such was the case with the inhabitants of Jerusalem. This teaches us that we cannot glorify God unless we put His teachings into practice. Today, we have the Gospel, which is

8

preached in purity to us. However, there are the Papists, who wander about like poor, misguided beasts without an ounce of solid teaching. We would pay a dear price for true doctrine, were it not for the fact that we can profit from it by putting into practice what the Gospels teach and we preach. We should not be surprised, then, that the prophet lumps Jerusalem together with Samaria. Our Lord says that Sodom and Gomorrah will have an easier time than we. Although they were destroyed by thunderbolts, they will receive even greater condemnation on Judgment Day. But our fate will be even more grievous and horrible yet, for we have heard the Gospel preached and yet continue to rebel against God. That is why the prophet identifies Jerusalem with Samaria.

Our human pride and arrogance can easily lead us to assume that Micah's condemnation of the Jews was a very harsh, unfeeling act, especially as they were the Chosen People. Indeed, at the time, many said of him, "Cannot he distinguish between Jerusalem and Samaria? What he says is totally offensive." How men wish to be flattered! We simply cannot tolerate the slightest reproach from God, although we have greater need of this than I can say. We are so wicked. The instant we receive something for our benefit, we throw it away.

But good King Hezekiah did not refuse to be reproached; indeed, he endured some of the harshest and severe reproaches possible, being told by Micah that Jerusalem will be plowed under like a field, the Temple would be destroyed, and Mt. Zion would

9

become so overgrown that no one would ever recognize that there were ever any buildings there. When Micah thus spoke, the people cried out against him; but good King Hezekiah said, "We must hear God's threats. We must throw ourselves at His feet. We must not be stubborn asses, for that will get us nowhere. We must humble ourselves before the majesty of God and beg Him to pardon our sins, for we have offended Him. Then, He will lift His hand from us, the prophesies will change, and He will treat us gently. Whereas He had previously made up His mind to punish us severely, now we will know only sweetness in Him."

This is, of course, clearly spelled out for us in the 26th chapter of Jeremiah, as we have seen. Drawing upon Micah, Jeremiah says to the people, "Do you think that in the long run God will tolerate the enormous iniquity within you? It may seem to you that it is enough that you merely say that you are the People of God; but in the end, that will serve you nothing. I proclaim and reveal to you the judgment of God that is upon you. Do not think that your clever facades can shield you against it!" For having so spoken, he was brought to trial by the priests, prophets, and governors of the people, who all thought that he deserved death. But, as I have said, in the end he was able to rescue himself by making them face the fact they were confronted by a prophesy made earlier by Micah: "Beware," he said, "for in the time of King Hezekiah, Micah proclaimed what must come to pass." He was careful to mention Micah's name and quoted him word for word (later we will explore this prophesy in detail) in order that they would know he was speaking genuine prophesy. Also he reminded them of what had come to pass between Micah and Hezekiah: Micah had spoken out strongly against Jerusalem; but Hezekiah was not angered. He humbly accepted Micah's sentence. This, of course, was not easy for him, as he and his people were humiliated before God. But he knew that God's punishment is always just. Because they so humbled themselves, our Lord did not execute the sentence He had pronounced upon them.

Hezekiah's example teaches us that whenever God threatens us, we must come to fear Him and to humble ourselves before Him. Then, He will take pity on those who have so subjugated themselves. A contrary example is the situation of Urijah, who preached under the reign of Jehoiakim. Urijah exercised his charge faithfully. What did he have to say? The same as Micah and God's judgment was then much closer upon them. Now, Jehoiakim, who was wicked, wished to capture and kill Urijah; but the prophet fled to Egypt. So Jehoiakim sent his ambassadors to the King of Egypt to bring Urijah back and kill him. Well we know how princes enjoy tormenting the poor faithful ones! What came to pass? What did it profit Jehoiakim to put Urijah to death? Our Lord gave him a dose of his own medicine. He was stripped of his kingdom, bound and gagged like a common criminal, which was exactly how he deserved to be treated. Whereas our Lord had given him a position of great dignity among men, now he was shamed and embarrassed before all the world. That is what

Jehoiakim gained for himself when he went to war against Urijah, for he was in point of fact fighting against God.

The example of Jehoiakim teaches us that there is no real way to prevent God's judgment from befalling us, save that when He brings our sins to light, we willingly condemn ourselves, bow our heads, and ask for pardon with a truly repentant heart. That, I say, is how we must appease the wrath of God; for if we are a people with necks as stiff as iron or brass and therefore too proud to acknowledge our sins, His wrath will be so much the more augmented against us. Do not doubt for an instant that God is far harder than we, that in the end we will succeed only in breaking our arms, legs, and necks if we hurl ourselves against Him.

Samaria and Jerusalem are mentioned, instead of lands, because the great cities are the source of all the corruption in the world. Men, however many there may be, are by nature inclined and given to evil. Men do not have to go to school to learn to do evil, for each is his own master and doctor. Those who are supposed to be a shining example to all others are the most evil of all. When they abandon themselves to evil, others take them as an example and do likewise. That is how it goes in the world, which is why Micah says, "What are the high places of Judah, save Jerusalem? What is the sin of Jacob, save Samaria?" Jerusalem was supposed to be a lamp to light all the lands of Judah to provide them with true doctrine. God had established the seat of His Law there. If anyone had any sort of legal difficulty, he went to Jerusalem to resolve matters. But Micah says that it is the source of all idolatry: "Behold, you have infected the city and all the lands by your iniquities; you are an abomination before God and His angels; evil can be blamed on none other than you." God exalts us in order that we be an example to all others, an example, I say, of all goodness. That is why Christians are told that they must lead the way and be the Light of Life to the poor blind souls. If we fail at this task, certainly our laxity will be remembered. Indeed, today, many are astonished to hear us say that Geneva has a calling to profess the Gospel. We must demonstrate to others that we put God's calling into practice. Our life must be a light for those poor blind souls, so that we win them over to the knowledge of His truth by our shining example. Let them be so inflamed by our light that they wish nothing but to come to God and humble themselves in total obedience to Him. But, on the contrary, we have amply tempted others by our scandalous behavior. Know, then, that Micah's warnings are addressed to us. God spoke not only to Jerusalem but to us in order that we might profit from His teachings. We, whom God has given a privileged position and exalted above all others, must devote all our energy to serving God. We must be a shining example to inspire men to honor and glorify God. In this way, we will avoid Micah's condemnation, which will be spelled out further now.

Micah says, "All peoples, give ear; listen, earth. May the Lord God be your witness, the Lord from His holy Temple; for He

13

will depart from His holy place and go to the high places of the earth." Why is it that Micah, sent only to the Jews, calls upon all peoples of the world? Why is it that he is not even content with that, but calls yet upon all insensible creatures, who have no intelligence? Does he not seem to have totally disregarded his God-given calling, which is to minister to the Jews? No, he has not forgotten his God-given calling, which is to minister to the Jews. Because his people turn a deaf ear to him, he wishes his voice to reach the ends of the earth, so that not one small piece of land or sky will fail to witness against the wickedness and unfaithfulness of his people. This is also why Isaiah says, "Earth, give ear; sky, hear me." Our Lord did not wish Isaiah to speak to the earth and sky, for they cannot profit from his teaching. We know that God gave no intelligence to the earth or sky; they cannot understand anything. When Isaiah speaks in this way, he means that the voice of God has such great power that it touches earth and sky, that all creatures are moved by it. As it says in another passage from Isaiah, "'Behold, I will move the earth,' says the Lord." Although the earth has no intelligence, the Word of God has such power that it will be recognized there. So when men reject the Word, what else can they say for themselves, save that they are without excuse?

Micah, here, is comparing the Jews to the Pagans. True, this is not expressly stated, but it is strongly implied in his words. Although the Jews were unfaithful and rebelled against God, they did not hesitate to glorify themselves in His name:

14

"Are we not the people God chose to be His heirs? We are His chosen people, for we are of the sacred line of Abraham. We have the priesthood, we have the kingdom God established, and we have the Temple, in which He wishes to be worshipped. The Pagans are nothing but dogs, for God did not reveal Himself to them as He did to us." How conceited were the Jews! "What are we?" they ask. "Do you think you can bridle us like cattle and beasts?" The stubborn pride of these people is condemned by the whole of Scripture. The prophet says to them, "You really believe that the Pagans are damned, for God does not spare them, and you believe well; for they are all damned. But because they are witnesses to your unfaithfulness, you will be damned with them, as you so well deserve." By this comparison, the prophet bursts their bubble. He says, "You know that your God has shed great grace upon you, but do you think that this will go on forever? Because you are unworthy, God will give the damned the honor of judging you. He will hear them as witnesses against you."

It would be a trifling matter to be judged by others, save that God gave them that authority. This is why Micah adds, "May God be a witness against you, the Lord from His Temple." By these words, he shows that he is not speaking through his hat but that he has been sent by God. All our teaching must be grounded in God alone, who alone has complete and total authority over our souls. His Word alone must govern us. Each must submit to it, from the least to the most important among us. If men look only to themselves, all will be in vain and rejected by God. Indeed,

15

there is no foundation to our faith, save that we know God has spoken. Our business is not with mortal men. If we support ourselves upon them, our faith will be very weak. But if we ground ourselves in God, our faith will be steadfast, for He is immutable. Those who are called to proclaim the Word of God must follow Micah's example and say nothing other than what they receive from God. They must testify to the truth: "Behold, God commissioned me; I speak nothing other than His Word." We must all submit to their teaching, without the slightest waxing or waning. We must all become students with God as our teacher.

God has revealed himself to us for our salvation. If we do not profit from this grace of God, we will be rendered inexcusable for having refused it. The Word of God did not descend to earth to work in vain. Although it sometimes seems that the Word is ineffective in our lives, the truth is that it is continually empowered by God to damn or save us. One or the other of these two things must come to pass. There is no middle ground here. Let us, then, accept the salvific teaching sent us. Let us not be so foolish as to refuse this grace acquired for, and revealed to us by, Jesus Christ. If we refuse this very good thing, it is certain we will be deprived of it.

Because the Jews boasted of their Temple, Micah says to them, "The Lord will be your witness, the Lord from His Temple," as if to say, "God's curse be upon you! You rise up against God because of the grace He has shed upon you. You think it is enough that you possess the Temple and that this gives you free reign to do evil. But I say to you that He will depart from this very Temple to condemn you!" Isaiah says that idolaters use God's name to cloak their wicked practices. This is precisely Micah's point, as if he were saying, "You think that because you have the Temple it can be disfigured to resemble you, who are full of nothing but iniquity. But you will come to know that the Word preached to you has real power and will convict you, you will be without excuse, for you have been warned more than enough." So let us look upon ourselves and realize how much more grace God has shed upon us than He did upon the ancient fathers. Christ has been revealed to us and He wishes us to share in all the blessings of God, His Father. So I emphasize that if we refuse God's grace, we will come to know this salvific power is the very power which condemns us.

Following this holy teaching, we prostrate ourselves before the face of our good God, acknowledging our sinfulness. We pray that it please Him to touch us with true repentance. May we know His judgment against us. May He receive us in mercy in the name of our Lord, Jesus Christ. May he give us the grace to obey Him throughout all our life. May we strive for nothing other than to serve Him and educate our neighbors. May we, who have turned the unlearned from the Path of Righteousness, take pains to instruct them and lead them to the knowledge of the truth of God. May in this way the Kingdom of our Lord, Jesus Christ, be augmented more and more. May God shed this grace not only on us but upon all the people and nations of the earth, etc.

* * *

(2) Thursday, November 13, 1550

Behold, the Lord will leave His dwelling. He will come down and walk on the high places of the earth. The mountains will flow under Him, and the valleys will melt away as wax before fire and as water pouring down, etc. Micah 1

Yesterday, we learned that God, through His prophet, reveals His judgment against all infidels. In this way, we said, God testifies to the power of His truth to save us, provided that we do not erect stumbling blocks. Although it is merely a mortal man who announces God's promise to be our Father, we can rest assured it is true; for God fully guarantees whatsoever is said in His name. Do not doubt that the Gospel has the power to revive us and to ransom us from the death and danger upon us, provided that we walk by a faith higher than our corporal senses. Let us not become boastful when God gives us more than the others, when God is close to us. Let us not make this an excuse to abuse God's name, as did the Jews, who were given to all iniquities under the pretext they were God's people. "We have the Temple of the Lord! The Temple of the Lord!" they shouted at Jeremiah. But they were sharply rebuked for taking for granted the privileges they had received from God; for in this very Temple God sat in judgment against them. Today we have no material temple of which to boast; but because God has revealed Himself to us through His Gospel, we will feel His hand upon us to our shame and bewilderment if we do not serve Him as we should.

That is why Micah says that God will depart from His Temple to tread upon the high places of the earth. True, God does not come and go to do His work, for He fills all things. Why, then, does Micah say that God will depart from His Temple? It is for the benefit of men who think that God is confined to a certain place or that He is far away in the heavens above and so pays no attention to anything on earth. For if we know that God watches over us, that all things are present before Him, that all our works and even our thoughts stand before Him, will we not have so much the more respect for His majesty? What man would wish to do evil, when he realizes God stands before him as his judge? Human pride leads men to the foolish opinion that they hold God enclosed in some rickety, tumble-down place, for they can conceive of nothing that they cannot see with their eyes. Scripture has God moving from one place to another, I say, because men are so entrenched in their vices that God seems very far away from them. "Do not think," says Micah, "that God will always turn a blind eye to you, as He has done. True, He has spared you, but not because He is blind. You hope that He will not depart from His dwelling; that is, it seems to you that He cannot punish you unless He comes to you. Well, He is on the way." In order that this condemnation not befall us, pay heed to what Scripture says so often: God inhabits the sky such that He sees everything going on down here. He cares for those who humble themselves before His majesty. On the contrary, if we rebel and raise up against Him, we will most assuredly feel His

19

hand fall upon us so heavily that we will be totally crushed. Let us have the presence of God so ingrained in our hearts that whenever the Devil tempts us, we can say, "Alas! I fear mortal men and do not wish to offend them. Should I do no less for the honor of my God? Even if I do not fear men, I have such respect for my honor that I would do nothing wicked before them. Should I, then, profane the honor of God? Behold how wicked is my ingratitude, if I fear more what I do before men than before God and His angels!" Although the prophet is rebuking the Jews, he is pointing to a common-enough vice among men. Indeed, there is not a man among us who will not find this vice in himself if he looks hard enough.

Micah speaks to men because of their unfaithfulness. When we are afflicted, we lose faith, we come to think that God has forgotten all about us and pays no attention to what is going on down here. It is to arm us with hope that Micah says God will depart from His place. Although at first glance it seems God does not wish to aid us, let us continue to rely upon Him and invoke His name until He reveals Himself as He promised.

Our passage for today makes two important points. The first is that it awakens us from our foolish opinion that God does not see the evil we do, by which we give ourselves license to do all sorts of evil things. The second is that whenever we are afflicted, we become impatient and bitterly complain if God does not aid us at once. Nevertheless, the Lord afflicts us to nourish our faith and to keep us fearful of Him, in order that we

20

do not give free reign to evil, under the guise that God does not see what we do.

Micah says that God will trample upon the high places. By this, he means powerful men; for they are full of pride and conceit. They believe that they do not have to humble themselves to God. It is quite easy, I emphasize, for us to overlook the poverty of our own being, which is a natural tendency. Kings and princes come to stand as idols. They are so conceited that they feel grievously wronged if one considers them to be a member of the human race. They commit villainous acts on an enormous scale, they attribute these acts to their own outstanding sense of righteousness, and they will tolerate no criticism whatsoever. They forget that they are merely human. This condition is not unique to outstanding princes; it also holds for those who have an intermediate level of power. Not a day passes that they do not abuse what little power they may have. They are totally obsessed with their own authority. They consider their subordinates unworthy of any real degree of consideration. In brief, we are all so terribly prideful that we totally refuse to humble ourselves, as God commands. The instant we see an opportunity to better our status, we disobey God. That is why Micah says that God will trample down the high places of the earth.

So I wish to emphasize that the main point of today's passage is that the high and the mighty will be the first to be destroyed and embarrassed, for they have rebelled against God.

Pride is a much stronger vice among the rich, powerful, and famous. True, a man with no one to govern but himself will not fail to offend God in many ways. Even if we were to flee from all the evil temptations of the world, our nature is fertile enough that it would provide more than ample opportunity for evil. However, those empowered over us offend so much more because of the greater number of tempting opportunities that befall them. We should not be surprised, then, that Micah says that God will trample down the high places of the earth; for he is not only speaking of princes or powerful persons but also of cities and peoples. If a people is puffed up with pride, first it will be chastised, then the cities, and finally individual persons, as we have already seen. If there is some little town totally abandoned to evil, the source is the big cities; for they commit the most enormous crimes. Blasphemers, perjurers, murderers, traitors and all other wicked persons come from large cities. All scandals and other stumbling blocks can come only from areas where there is a large multitude of people. The greatest cities are the most chaotic, evil places on earth. So we must realize that we have committed enormously grievous offenses against God. Instead of being a lamp unto the world, we have done the complete opposite. We have abused the good things that God has given us. The more freely God sheds His grace upon us, the more we conspire against Him. God is really going to work us over, for Micah says He will trample down the high places. Our Lord will render judgment against kingdoms and principalities, according to their status among others. Then He will turn to the cities, as I have said, and from cities to persons. Let us look to ourselves as a whole, and then let each look to himself. Let us get it into our heads that either we humble ourselves before God or He will trample us underfoot, as Micah says. The reason why Our Lord fights against men is that they are inflated with pride. God cannot bear this, for He is the sworn enemy of all those puffed up with pride. Let us humble ourselves before His mighty hand if we do not wish that of which the passage speaks to befall us.

You might be wondering whether or not God judges only the high and mighty, for the lowly can be just as puffed up with pride as anyone else. True, the high and mighty are so drunk on their own power that they think of nothing else. True, they go to far greater extremes and extort far more, for they have the means to do so. But the lowly are also full of evil machinations, an ill will, and many other damnable things. If you look inside a lowly man, he is no better a soldier than anyone else; and our Lord looks only at the heart. Why, then, does He not punish the little as well as the big? Micah does not wish to exempt the lowly from God's punishment when he says that God will trample down the high places. Rather, he wishes to say that God starts working over the high and mighty first and then turns to the rest of the world. The lowly must not assume they have escaped punishment, just because the high and mighty lead the parade; for they are next in line. Micah is not saying that

God will judge only a part of the world, but that He has made a general threat against us all: Since the kings and princes extol themselves to the skies, God will start with them and then trample down all others in their turn.

Consequently, Micah says that "the mountains will flow before Him, and the valleys will melt away in His presence, as wax before fire and as waters falling from a high place"; for the majesty of God is so much the more exalted to the extent He destroys His enemies. It is not without reason, then, that God is said to depart from His dwelling; for we could not conceive of God as our Judge unless He were to exercise this office. The high and mighty are so conceited and puffed up with pride that they defy both God and man. They are like a fir tree or a cedar, as they are compared to in Psalm 37. The lowly do not seem worthy to walk among them. The high and mighty seem so well rooted that they can never be shaken. Judging by appearances, it seems very far-fetched that we will ever see them melt like wax. But that is only because God has spared them for a time. So the point here is that we must not judge God according to our standards, that is, according to our physical senses. Our faith leads us to know what is hidden and unknown to man. Remember that! For what is the real reason we do not walk in fear of God and are totally incorrigible, except that we mistakenly assume that God is far from punishing us if He does not do so at once? So let us wait patiently for God to carry out Micah's threat, namely that He will melt down the evildoers like wax, destroy all their pride, violently pound them into the dirt, as if a fast-flowing torrent of water suddenly fell to the ground from on high.

Scripture uses such metaphors to represent things that are important to know but that we poorly understand. Here, these metaphors are trying to tell us that we have not learned to fear God. We fear more a mortal man than the living God. One man has no great power, yet we will behold him in fear and anxiety. If he threatens us, we will always be on our guard. But if God reveals to us His wrath and vengeance, we sleep undisturbed. Where does such stupidity come from, save that we have not learned to fear God? That is why Isaiah and Jeremiah say, "Why do you shout, 'The Temple of the Lord! The Temple of the Lord!'? You will find it a hot fire ready to consume yourselves." God is not terrible to behold to those who put all their trust in Him, for He is kind and gracious to them. However, Scripture makes God's presence seem something horrible and quite frightening. In this passage, the Holy Spirit is addressing idolaters, or those who are given to all evil and care for nothing else. Insofar as these men have been blinded by the Devil, they have no more regard for God than they do for an inanimate object. That is why Scripture uses such violent language. We are well appraised of our condition, when we are compared to wax or to a torrent of water falling violently. There metaphors signify that in ourselves we have no power at all against God. We are far too weak to resist God. When God visits us, who can stand up against

His fury?  Nevertheless, even if our arms and legs were broken and we could not even move our little finger, still we would somehow signal our revolt against Him.  Therefore, our Lord warns us we are nothing but a wind, that is, nothing but vanity and lies, so that all we think to possess is merely so much smoke.  The instant God lays a hand on us, we are finished.  Indeed, it is not really necessary at all for God to lay a hand on us.  All He has to do is blow on us and we vanish like the wind, for we are only powder.  So let us humble ourselves and acknowledge our fragility.

God knows the infirmity of men and provides them the needed support, as it says in the Psalm, "He knows that we are but a passing breeze, that we are nothing but a herb which blooms." That is why He takes pity on us.  At the same time, it is a common-enough teaching in Scripture that we must humble ourselves and confess we are merely nothing.  Since we will not make this confession willingly, it is necessary for God to withhold His support from us for a time in order to force us to acknowledge our own fragility and dependence upon His aid.

Our situation is like that of a poor man who is unable to pay his debts.  If he humbles himself and offers to pay when he can, who would be so inhuman as to not patiently wait upon this man and accept whatever he can pay without overburdening himself? But if there be a debtor so ungrateful and stubborn that he refuses to pay up and also insults his creditor, who would tolerate such ingratitude?  The same thing holds for our Lord's dealings with us. If we willingly acknowledge that we are in debt to His majesty, He will pity us and lift His hand from us. He will be content that men come to Him to humble themselves. But if we persist in our malicious hardness against His Word and rebel against Him, He will carry out the prophet's threat. Let us guard against this condemnation befalling us, by which we will be convicted before God when He departs from His dwelling, that is, when He will make manifest His judgment against us, which is now hidden. Let us not wait upon God's judgment. Let us recognize our fragility. Let us pray to God that He strengthens us more and more, so that when we feel His hand upon us, we know it is for our own good and bear patiently all that it pleases Him to send upon us. That is the warning we must heed from Micah's teaching.

Micah says that whenever and wherever God's judgment might befall, it will come to pass because of the rebellions of Jacob and the sins of Judah. In order that the Jews could not accuse God of excessive punishment and therefore have cause to complain, Micah shows that God's punishment is always just. This practice is quite common among all the prophets; for when men see they can do nothing but submit to God, they gnash their teeth and become quite vexed with Him. They are like a condemned criminal who says, "Alas! I must go to the gallows," and becomes quite angered against his judge and enraged that he cannot escape. So it is that men rebel against God. For this reason, it is necessary that, on one hand, God warns us of His power, which we cannot resist, even if we had all the power in the world. On the other, we must come to realize that God does not punish without good reason, that we have merited His heavy hand upon us, and that none can resist it. That is what Micah means when he says God's punishment was due to the sins of Judah and the rebellions of Jacob.

Micah is compelled to appear unfeeling towards them; for he is not alluding to the sins of one or two individuals, but is speaking to the Jews as a whole. True, some Jews in Israel and Judah did in fact fear God; but if the whole body is infected and yet the little finger remains healthy, you cannot say that the whole body is healthy simply because of the little finger. Micah is addressing everyone when he says that God will battle against them because of the sins of Jacob and the rebellions of Judah. This means that our Lord does not wish to be a tyrant and torment us without just cause; for He would rather treat us in all sweetness, even though we have provoked Him against us. The sun is a creature without sense or reason and yet its heat warms the earth so all it produces comes from the sun. Now, we do not praise the sun, but God, who put this creature there to multiply His grace upon us. We know that it is our Lord who breathes strength and substance into us by way of the sun. Now, if our Lord has put such power into one creature, think what we will receive when we come to Him! Do we think that He created us only to abandon us? When Scripture says that God is angered against us, this does not mean that He wishes to destroy us:

Insofar as we are so evil that we alienate and turn our backs on Him, we must be rigorously punished to be shamed and humbled. Otherwise, we would not return to Him.

That is exactly what Micah means when he says that God will punish them for the sins of Judah and the rebellions of Jacob, as if he were saying, "You should not accuse other men of the evil about to befall you, for it will come from nothing other than your own iniquities." We must not blame God for the bad things that happen in the world; for insofar as our nature is totally perverse and corrupt, God must subdue it by many afflictions. Let us, then, accept our own culpability and not place the blame on God. When the sky or the earth menace us, when we think upon our miseries, let each meditate upon his sins. The sky and earth are ordained to serve us; and God will see to it they exercise their proper function, provided that we recognize God as our Master and Savior. Whatever wickedness there may be in us, the sun does not cease to illuminate us daily and there is continual order in nature. Now, what is the reason for all this, save that God surmounts our sins? If we were not as wicked as we are, all creatures would be better disposed towards us to multiply God's grace. Whenever some famine, pestilence, or war befalls us, or whenever particular individuals are afflicted by illness, poverty, or some wrong done them, rest assured that the hand of God is on us because of our sins. True, men are always quick to criticize and accuse God of injustice or unjustifiably harsh punishment; but in the end they will be shut up.

Micah asks, "What is the sin of Jacob, save Samaria? What are the high places of Judah, save Jerusalem?" Here, as we noted yesterday, the prophet is showing how corruption moves from the great to the small. Here is Jerusalem, royal seat of Judah; here is Samaria, capitol of Israel; yet it is said that these are the two gates to Hell, that they are full of enough filth and infection to poison the entire earth. What is said of these two cities goes for all the world. Today, if we look all around, what is it we really see? The greatest and the most renown cities are full of all sorts of filth and villainy. They produce nothing but scandals and licentiousness. Next we see that the small towns are also infected by this poison. The whole world is perverted today. If you want to find really evil cunning and craftiness, you do not have to go to the big cities; for the country folk are yet even more evil. But if you look closely enough, you will find that evil originated in the big cities and then spread elsewhere. Do not be surprised that evil continues to grow more and more, for not one person with the know-how is willing to apply it to eradicate evil. Know, then, that insofar as God has given us the means to advance His Kingdom and we have not responded, our offenses will be so much the more grievous. Since they are so great and enormous, our punishment will be so much the more horrible, especially because we abandoned ourselves to all evil when we were supposed to be a shining example to the others. Let the lowly know they are afflicted because they refused to submit to God. Let the high and mighty know that

30

because all evil originates with them, they will be punished more horribly than the others. Micah's intention is to exhort both the big and the small to return to God, beg pardon for their offenses, confess they have well merited the punishment inflicted upon them, and acknowledge that they are without excuse. That is the key point to bear in mind if we wish to profit from this passage.

Micah is speaking of a specific kind of evil, namely idolatry, when he says, "What are the high places of Judah, save Jerusalem?" But he does not wish to reproach only this particular sin. He uses this sin as an example of all forms of sinning, as is common in prophetic writing. He does so because once we stray from the knowledge of God and the pure doctrine of the Lord, we fall into an abysm of iniquities and abandon ourselves to evil beyond measure. He speaks specifically of idolatry also because it is the root of all evil. If the Jews had returned to the pure doctrine of God and had not made idols, they would never have fallen into such bad times. But they rejected the doctrine and true service of God, and so they fell from one vice to another until they reached the heights of all iniquity. All of this happened because of Jerusalem. Therefore, today, when God has so graciously given us His Word, let us be a shining example to lead all the others to the truth and doctrine of God. Otherwise, we will lead the weak astray and it is certain that the judgment pronounced against Samaria and

31

Jerusalem will befall upon us. There is more to be said here, but that will have to wait until tomorrow.

Following this holy teaching, we prostrate ourselves before the face of our good God, acknowledging our sinfulness. May it please Him to open our eyes so that we, recognizing our malicious, sinful nature, learn to arrange our lives according to His commandments. May it please Him to so strengthen us and charge us by the Holy Spirit that, whereas we had been puffed up by pride and conceit, we now humble ourselves and pay homage to His majesty. May His grace so reform us that our good life and conduct attracts others to the path to salvation. May the world glorify His name. May we all together reach the Kingdom, to which He beckons us. May He shed this grace not only on us but upon all the peoples and nations of the world, etc.

* * *

What is the sin of Jacob, save Samaria? What are the high places of Judah, save Jerusalem? I will turn Samaria into a field of rubble and plant there a vineyard, etc. Micah 1

We have begun to explore the meaning of true leadership according to Micah. We have seen that those in positions of great power and respect must be very circumspect in their actions, lest they be the cause of scandals. God intends them to be shining examples to the others, burning lamps to light the Path of Righteousness. Furthermore, God is not more sparing of the big than He is of the small, for God is no respecter of persons. Leaders will be condemned so much the more grievously than those who had no real authority in matters of state.

We also saw that Micah identifies Jerusalem with Samaria, although one would think there is a vast difference between the two. Samaria was like a whorehouse, full of all abominations, whereas Jerusalem was the place of God's Throne. The Temple, in which He was to be worshipped in all purity, was there. In short, it was The Holy City. Micah, then, seems to do it grave injustice when he says that the high places of Judah come from there; for in the time of Hezekiah, there was no civil corruption or superstition in the city of Jerusalem. One sacrificed there, as God had so ordained. Why, then, is it said that the high places come from there? From the time of Solomon to the reign of Hezekiah, there had always been some idolaters in Jerusalem. King Ahaz, during whose reign Micah prophesied, introduced many practices against the true worship of God, including the burning of infants as sacrifices. Although for some time Jerusalem had been purged of idolatries, it brought about corruption in the land of Judah. So it is not without reason that Micah asks, "What are the high places of Judah, save Jerusalem?"

If ever we wrong someone, we must take pains to correct the situation; otherwise, he who is wronged will go to God to demand vengeance upon us. This is something we hardly ever think about. Whenever someone makes a big mistake that results in a scandal corrupting many men, he thinks it sufficient to acquit himself before God by merely confessing in a few words that he is responsible and then touching his mouth to signify that he is not culpable. But do we really think that God will forget his sin? Micah warns us that if we lead our neighbors into sin, as Scripture says we do, then we should strive to return them to God, so that their sins may be forgiven and they may be led to the truth. Although what they do is their own business, we are the ones who put them in a very difficult situation. That is the main point to bear in mind.

God's punishment will be carried out wherever it is merited, for God is no respecter of persons or places. Scripture makes this point quite strongly, and it is particularly relevant to our situation today. On one hand, we are continually up against men who are so puffed up with pride that they cannot bear the slightest reproach. On the other, those who would call themselves the Church are the source of many abominations which one dare not reproach. Today, the abominations of the Papists continue to multiply. Do not expect there to be any remedy for this situation. If anything, it will worsen, for they have at their disposal all sorts of excellent facades to hide behind: the Holy Church, the Holy Apostolic See, and many others. Rome is a glutton for iniquities. It is completely controlled by the Devil himself. His filth and infections are spread from there to the end of the earth. Yet one dare not utter a single word against Rome, for only good things are supposed to come from there.

If Rome and Jerusalem are compared, which is be found the more holy and precious? Our Lord chose Jerusalem from among all the others to there be served and honored by men. The Temple was built there, as God had so commanded in a vision. Prophesies verify that the city was given to David by God. Our Lord witnesses that it is His resting place forever, that He wished His Throne to be built there, and that there will always be some sign of His majesty and presence there. Yet Micah compared it to Samaria. When he says that it is the source of all the abominations and idolatries in the lands of Judah, what does that make of Rome today? Since it is totally corrupt, God will punish it as severely as He did the city of His Temple and Throne. If our Lord, through Micah, raged against Jerusalem, will not Rome necessarily be subject to the same condemnation, as it is the very reason why the world is going to Hell and damnation? True, the Pope tries to extract passages from

Scripture to cover up his turpitude and to show his diabolical throne is approved by God. But this is mere balderdash that even small children can mock and know to be a fib. Granted, the Pope may cook up all sorts of arguments that God once had His Throne in Rome. But the truth of the matter is this: Those who go against the Word are condemned as devils, despite the fact they were heretofore like angels.

Look how Micah condemned the Jews, although they had no intention whatsoever of rejecting God. What's more, they were not content with one temple and so built many chapels and altars. There was not one small corner without some sign of devotion to God, and talk of serving God was everywhere. But Jeremiah said: "Did God request these things from your hands? No, for He does not wish to be served according to man's fancy." If we bring to God that which we have found good, do not expect Him to accept it; if He had no hand in our work, we must go to Hell for our wages. Let us not be as blind as we were in our time of ignorance. As we are so strongly inclined to such a vice, so much the more must we pay heed to those passages in Scripture which make it plain that our Lord rejects everything made according to man's fancy.

If we do not look to the Word but follow our own inclinations as to what seems good, all that we produce will be in vain and an abomination. If today the Papists put up such a beautiful facade, certainly the Jews were not inferior in this regard. Papists claim that they wish to serve God when they built a chapel or an altar to the honor of some saint. The Jews had their Baalims, which served as their patrons and advocates before God. They thought they were serving God, whereas in point of fact, He had rejected and condemned them. If today the Papists try to mask all the evil they spew out, the Jews did no less. If our Lord condemned the Jews, He will surely condemn the Papists. Know that our Lord has universally condemned and sentenced all that man invents and introduces into serving God. All these things He rejects as abominations, for He did not request them, as we saw a while ago in Jeremiah.

Certainly Micah makes it plain how deeply our Lord hates idolatry, how contemptible He finds all that men make under the pretext of honoring Him. Micah says that idolatry is the wages of a whore; he warns that Samaria is a whorehouse and that God will destroy all of it.

Although men must not abuse God's name by serving Him according to their fantasies, they are continually prone to idolatry. Just look at the Papists! They think that it is pleasing to God that they go on pilgrimages, mumble before an idol, abstain from eating meat for a day. They hold masses in honor of saints, attend matins, and celebrate holidays. Those are the ways of serving God that the Papists have invented. Does it not seem, then, that they have made God a carnal being very much like themselves? When we examine these matters closely enough, it is obvious that men wish to serve God by vain things, that they think God is a small child who will delight in all this tomfoolery, that they believe an infant's rattle is all that is necessary to appease God. Are we capable of transfiguring God by our imaginations? No, no, but as I have said, we certainly try to forge new gods. Without ever having been to school, we know all too well how to be idolatrous. No sooner will a man slacken the bridle on his senses than he will invent at least a thousand superstitions; for our soul is an abysm of evil that can invent superstitions beyond measure, save that God draws us to Himself and we come to live according to the teachings of His Word. We know all this by experience. What confusion reigns in Papism! That should not surprise us; for if there were no idolatry in the world, as soon as we would turn our backs on the purity of God's Law and Gospel, we would see the world instantly corrupted and infected by all sorts of idolatries heretofore unknown. What would produce them so fast? Our nature, which is all too fertile for idolatry.

So much the more, then, must we heed the Lord's warning that God rejects everything invented by men. Let men puff themselves with pride at their own inventions, let them use their ignorance as their shield, saying, "O, I thought I was doing something wonderful!" Our Lord, who has passed sentence upon them, will not budge an inch. So let us condemn all the works for man; let us honor God holding to His teaching as sure and profitable, without adding anything of our own. Otherwise, not only will everything we do be an abomination before God, but we will be severely punished as fools and pompous asses for having presumed to add something to His Word.

Look at how Papism is a perfect example of such abomination. What Papists call serving God is not approved of by one single word of Scripture. They do not serve God at all the way He wishes. They have abandoned the purity of the Gospel, allowing each to have a say in how God is to be served. That is why confusion reigns everywhere among them. They are like a woman who surrenders to her villainous impulses and becomes a whore. Whore! That is the badge of honor they deserve before God and man. But it is very difficult to convince them of this truth, just as Micah, who was a very sincere, hard-working preacher, had a great struggle with his people.

Look at the poverty we had to endure before our Lord enlightened us by knowledge of His Gospel. Although it seemed that we did good deeds and were enraptured among the angels, the truth is, I say, we served only the Devil and were nothing but shameless adulteresses, polluting and contaminating our bodies by all sorts of filth and abominations. Remember the abysm from which our Lord extracted us. Remember the evil we did by thinking that we were doing the right thing. Let us groan and pray to our good God that we never fall again into such abomination. Since He wishes us to be His true temples, may we be totally dedicated to His glory, we, I say, who are only poor laborers. May we receive the grace He sheds on us, to glorify His holy name.

It should come as no surprise that Micah equates idolaters with adulteresses. We have encountered this several other times in Scripture, in Jeremiah, for example. The Lord has warned that the superstitions of men are nothing but spiritual adultery, whatever facade they may put on and however they may believe themselves to do good. Although they may refuse to condemn themselves, nevertheless, they are condemned to the hilt. The reason is that our Lord has entered into a marriage contract with us, so we must be as faithful and loyal to Him as a wife must be to her husband. Therefore, let us remain chaste before God and not break this contract by committing adultery.

We remain chaste, according to Saint Paul, when we cling to the simplicity of the Word: "I have wed you," he says, "to Jesus Christ." He makes it clear that preaching the Gospel is a marriage ceremony intended to liberate souls from the Devil's tyranny so they may become brides of Christ. "Take care," he says, "that you do not become seduced by some clever lie, as Eve was seduced by Satan. How? By being diverted from the simplicity of the Gospel." He emphasizes the word "simplicity." He does not say merely, "from the Gospel"; he says, "Whenever you abandon the simplicity of the Gospel, you have been seduced by Satan. When men who are the instrument of Satan whisper something into your ears, you abandon the purity of the Gospel and cleave to their lies. You are like a poor woman who has been seduced into breaking her marriage vows." So remember, as I have said, all men who turn to idolatry are irrevocably sentenced to be polluted and spoiled by spiritual adultery.

It is no surprise, then, that Micah speaks of idolatry as adultery; for if we do not cling to the pure teachings of God when He puts us on the right path, we are nothing but adulteresses who have broken our spiritual marital contract with Him.

Micah says that God will destroy all the abominations which reign in Samaria, that He will smash down their idols, that their offerings are nothing but the wages of whores, which shall be returned to the whoredom from whence they came, that their buildings will be levelled, that rocks will fall upon their dwellings, and that all will be thrown into total chaos. Certainly this makes it plain enough how detestable the Lord finds idolatry; for He does not go to excesses in punishing men. We know the enormity of our offenses by the way God chastises us. If His punishments are terrible, we have grievously offended Him. Note well what is said here: A city which was a kingdom was completely destroyed. Know, then, as I have said, that idolatry is so detestable to God that He will not tolerate any form of it.

It might be argued that the ignorance and good intentions of men are a suitable defense, that God should not be so offended by what men do in their ignorance. But if we find ignorance good, God certainly does not. It is shameful for us to say, "O, I didn't know that." We are ignorant only if we willingly close

41

our eyes. True, men like to think they are doing good in whatever they do. They are prone to say, "I serve God and therefore please Him." But let us never make this claim, for it can not be said in all honesty. When Judgment Day comes, men will feign excuses such as ignorance; but if God condemns us, we can say only, "Amen!" For God's condemnation is always just and we have well merited it. There is no point in making up excuses, for God will show them to be of no value in hiding our turpitude. Adam tried to make up all sorts of excuses when he sinned, but where did that get him? He could not escape standing before God's judgment. The same thing is true of us. We like to think that we are well hidden and fortified by all sorts of good excuses when we are far from God. But the mere sound of God's voice is enough to unmask us.

Samaria willingly turned its back on God! The inhabitants of Israel were the descendants of Abraham. God revealed His Law to them and showed them how He wished to be served. They were united into one body, so it was necessary for each to come to the Temple of Zion. Yet to please Jeroboam, the people turned to idolatry. From the time Samaria was built and made the capitol, there were more and more abominations. It was not ignorance but manifest rebellion against God that led them to turn their backs on the Law. This teaches us that we are so much the more condemnable if we do not follow the right path once we have been taught how to please God. Those who fall by the wayside must not be considered among the ranks of the ignorant. There is no ignorance which is not condemnable before God and His angels. However, our condemnation will be so much the more grievous when God proclaims to us, "Behold how I wish to be served" and we pay no attention to it, preferring to obey men rather than the living God. That being the case, let us be on our guard; for God has introduced us to the Path of Righteousness, that we pursue our course and be not deterred by whatever may come to pass.

When Micah says that what came from whores will be returned to them, this signifies that everything will be in total chaos. It is a universal truth that whenever goods have been acquired illegally, God will melt them down and they will be to no avail, as we know by experience. For where does all the change come from that we see? When a rich man dies, his children exhaust all his wealth. Why? It is the curse of God upon us because the world is full of only usury, rape, extortion, adultery, and the like. Are not the upheavals in the world today greater than they have ever been? For a hundred years, things seemed to follow a definite course, but now all the world is in chaos. The reasons: Iniquities are now greater than they ever were. There is less loyalty to God today that there was a hundred years ago, however ignorant were our forefathers. Everywhere one finds only traitors, rapists, and the like. God certainly will hand down a sentence upon us more grievous and horrible than we have ever imagined.

So whenever God gives us some good thing, let us not make it an occasion to rebel against Him, as if we no longer had any need of His aid. Each day let us ask Him for our daily bread, to confess that all that we have we receive from His hand, that He alone makes efficacious the grace He sheds upon us. Otherwise, we will not rejoice in His grace. Let us not worry about amassing great wealth, as the majority of those who do, do not care about anything else or how even their wealth is acquired. As I have said, we must content ourselves with what God has given us, without wishing for more. Indeed, we should be more content with what God has given us than with the greatest riches of the world. Those who rest content with His goodwill will profit more from a mere penny than will a criminal with a hundred dollars acquired illegally. Why? The criminal has far, far less than he thinks. Indeed, this is a good example of how God's judgment becomes stronger and stronger against us in proportion to our own hardness.

Micah has revealed a universal truth: All ill-gotten goods lead only to chaos. Specifically he is speaking of the profits acquired from sacrilegious acts, namely adultery and idolatry, which go hand in hand. A whore can enjoy great fame and profit. Such is the case with the courtesans in Italy, where adultery is tolerated and taken not half as seriously as it should be. God has so cursed this land that it is without law and order and tolerates all forms of mischief. Lands become so cursed because men are so prone to spiritual adultery; indeed, it is esteemed throughout the world. You cannot enter into the temples of the Papists without becoming more polluted than if you entered a whorehouse.   The most honored and adorned temples in the world today are nothing but abominable whorehouses before God.   If a prince donates an armoire there, he might as well have gone and stuck it in some whorehouse, as if he wished to vex God by acting totally contrary to Him.

So remember how deeply the Lord detests idolatry.   Remember that not only will God condemn it before men but that Micah says, "I will turn all your offerings into the wages of whores, so that each will know that, despite their facade of devotion, honor, and zeal for God, they are nothing but an abomination before Him."   Micah makes it plain God will not tolerate any form of idolatry.   He will rain down such horrible vengeance upon all idolaters that all will know this is not the way He wishes to be served.   Everything that we do on our own is nothing but shit and abomination before the eyes of God.   Although we have taken great pains to serve idols, this is all in vain.   All we have succeeded in doing is to provoke greatly the wrath of God.   Think hard on this!

Our Lord is bitterly angry against Samaria; He will let this place remain in desolation forever.   Let us, then, so much the more glorify the grace He sheds on us today; for we have served idols, and our temple here was a whorehouse whose altars were just so many witnesses to our infidelity.   Now God wishes that the temples where there here only abominations be dedicated to His glory.   How merciful He is to us that we are now assembled in His name to hear His Word, whereas heretofore we were full of

45

lies and false doctrine. We invoke His name of common accord. He and His angels are in the midst of us now. When we see what a great privilege He has granted us, although we so grievously offended Him, do we not have good reason to glorify Him, especially as He never took such pity on Samaria?

It is not just today that our Lord has shed such grace on the world as He does upon us. Look at what Isaiah says about Tyre. He says that Tyre, a trading city, is a whorehouse and that all the merchants are adulterers who have cunning ways of extorting money from people, just as a whore will sing a sweet song to seduce the poor passers-by. But he also says that God will see to it that this city, whose wealth heretofore consisted of ill-gotten goods, will be dedicated and consecrated to His name. That came to pass through the Gospel. We see how our Lord has used it with us. Let us credit everything to His bounty. Let us not be so stupid as to wish to jump back into the abysm from which He has rescued us; let us make it the principal goal and intention of our life to serve Him in all purity. Well we know how careful we must be to serve God in all purity, when we see the horrible vengeance He delivered upon Samaria for turning its back upon Him.

Micah says consequently, "I will wail and mourn like the owls, I will howl like the dragons. It is not enough that I cry like a human being, for my scream must be like that of savage beasts." However, he says that he will not go to Gath, a Philistine city, as if he were saying, "Let us hide our

46

destruction from the infidels. Otherwise, when our Lord punishes us, they will mock and laugh at us and be ready to blaspheme God's name." But this is all in vain, for it is necessary that the punishment be known by all and that he mourns openly, covering himself with ashes and dust. Therefore he is told by God, "Go, roll yourself in the dust at the house of Aphrah." Now, Aphrah signifies powder, for this village was a powder maker. Regarding Saphir, whose name means beauty, it will, he says, be stripped naked and thrown into such chaos that it will be a shame to behold. Note that the prophet here speaks in ways that strongly emphasize God's vengeance. He does so for a good reason: We are often reproached that although God has spoken to us out of great anger, we are not moved by His words, and His threats seem absolutely nothing to us. Therefore, the prophet strives to make us really feel the terrible ferocity of God's anger, so that we can only gnash our teeth and be vexed with Him. This manner of speaking is common to all the prophets, as we have seen in Isaiah and Jeremiah. More will be said about this, tomorrow, at the pleasure of God, as matters continue.

Let us turn to an important and seemingly contradictory point here. God says to Micah, "Do not proclaim my punishment, in Gath." Then He says, "Go, roll yourself in the dust." Micah says, "I will go upon my way stripped totally naked." God seems to be contradicting Himself, because He wants His punishment kept secret and yet made public. However, the point here is not that God wished to conceal His punishment but that Micah wishes to better express how God will punish Israel and put it to shame. It is as if he were saying, "poor men, today you think you can hide your filth and the punishment of God upon you because of your sins, but your shame will be known by all the world. You will be mocked by all. Since you have not honored God as is fitting, it is just and right that you be held in abhorrence by all the world." If we wish God and His angels to approve of us and do not want men to mock us, we must honor God. It is not without reason that God shames us before men, for we have dishonored Him. We experience this daily, so we know well that God does not threaten us in vain through His prophets. But we must come to actually feel the power and efficacy of His Word. More needs to be said here, but that will have to wait until tomorrow.

Following this holy teaching, we prostrate ourselves before the face of our good God, acknowledging our sinfulness. We pray that it please Him to pardon our past faults. May we, who heretofore turned our backs on God, be given the grace to profit more and more from Gospel teaching and from the bounty He has shed upon us. May we, convinced of our salvation and the good God wishes upon us, never waver in our total and complete trust in Him. May we follow the holy vocation to which God has called us, until we come to our immortal glory. May God shed this grace not only on us but upon all the peoples and nations of the earth, etc.

All-powerful celestial Father, you are pleased to continually shed your grace upon perverse and rebellious people. You incessantly exhort them to repentance and lead them by the hand through your prophets. Give us the grace that your Word may resonate today in our ears. May you not reject us if we do not profit immediately from your teaching. May your Spirit so subdue our passions that we are truly humbled and glorify your majesty. May we, allured by your love and paternal favor toward us, totally subjugate ourselves to you. May we so receive the bounty you offer us through Lord Jesus that we never come to doubt that you are our own Father, until the end we share in the celestial heritage acquired for us by the blood of your Son, our Lord, Jesus Christ. Amen.

* * *

(4) Saturday, November 15, 1550

Pass on by, O inhabitant of Saphir naked in your shame. You will find no rest; for the inhabitant of Zaanan would not come forth for the mourning in Bethezel, and the inhabitant of Maroth hungers after goods because the evil of the Lord befell upon the gate of Jerusalem, etc. Micah 1

Micah makes it very obvious here in whose name he speaks, by virtue of the power and authority he attributes to his words. He does not speak of merely what might come to pass; but in fact ordains what will come to pass, as if he had the execution orders right in his hand. He is seated as a judge who peaks with total and complete authority. He sentences rebels to punishment. He orders battle plans and battle alerts. He commands sieges against villages and castles. In short, he would appear to be the executioner of God's judgments.

The prophet's role is to make us realize that God speaks in earnest and therefore to be so much the more responsive the instant He threatens us; for His Word never has the authority over us that it should. We know how poorly we have received God's promise of our salvation. We well know how unable we are to cling to it and put all our trust in God. God has said to us enough times: "Trust in me, I will not fail you, I will treat you as your Father." Yet we are always doubtful and say, "Well, suppose I get in such-and-such a jam. How will I be able to get out of it?" Because, men incessantly strive to defy God, they find absolutely no assurance in His promises. The same is true for His threats. When He reproaches us for our sins and reveals His judgment against us, it seems to us that this is nothing whatsoever to worry about. It never fails that whenever God warns men, they go astray, as if they wished to rebel against Him. Although He reveals His judgment and determination to punish us, we pay no attention. Yet we should react to prophetic warnings as if the punishment were already upon our heads. God's punishments are not, as some will say, idle threats to frighten babes. Saint Paul says that those whom God has charged to preach His Gospel will take vengeance on those who rebel and hold the Gospel in contempt. Note, then, that whosoever refuses to accommodate himself to Gospel teaching and to receive it in all humility will suffer precisely the punishment which it pronounces against him. Our salvation or eternal death lies in the voice of the Gospel.

Let us turn now to the punishments Micah ordains at the command of God. "Pass on by," he says, "O inhabitant of Saphir naked in your shame. The inhabitant of Zaanan would not come forth for the mourning in Bethezel." Now, Saphir means beauty, and so he is saying that God will render the city destitute and chaotic. If we do not honor God, it is just punishment that we be dishonored, shamed, and made contemptuous before men. Should those who refuse to honor God be themselves honored? Know that this threat is aimed at us, unless early on we come to praise the name of our God and exalt His glory. When we do this, God will restore us to order and power, whereas heretofore we were in shame and chaos. But if we were the most excellent people in the world, so that it seemed all honor dwelt among us, we would fall into shame and terrible chaos if we did not honor God as we should. Micah is saying in effect, "There is no honor or dignity in the world that cannot be turned to shame when God's honor is there trampled under foot." Think hard on Micah saying that the inhabitant of Saphir will be naked and stripped of all beauty. When Micah commands him to go to foreign lands, it amounts to saying that God does not wish to be worshipped in Saphir. No matter what part of the world we may live in, our Lord gives us sanctuary in order that we pay Him due homage for our life as well as for the nourishment and dwelling place He provides for us, for the earth belongs to Him. If we are so evil that we dishonor Him, we must be deprived of the goods he has given us, for we are unworthy of His grace. That is what Micah means, as if he were to say, "You have not glorified God for the grace He shed upon you, so now you must be deprived of His gifts."

Our Lord can well move about His people to teach them that there is no rest in this world, that they must not search for their comfort here. But Micah here is speaking to those whom God has driven from their homeland because their evil and rebellion deprived them of it. This serves as an example that those who refuse to dwell in God and are led astray by their evil appetites will by tormented by God. When our Lord reveals His will, He means for us to no longer toss and turn this way and that, as our nature subjects us to do. This is especially relevant to infidels. Since they refuse to rest in God, they are in continual turmoil. They can only wander about and never settle down. On the contrary, our Lord says, "Here is your rest!" when He gives us His Word in order that we find all our assurance in Him. Whoever does not wish to rest in God will be subject to continual agitation. After we have gone off on enough side trips, God will put us on the main road once again; but this comes to pass only by the force of blows upon us, for we will not willingly bend ourselves to Him. That is why Micah speaks to the inhabitant of Saphir.

Micah adds that "the inhabitants of Zaanan would not come forth for the mourning in Lachish," that they would not trouble themselves over the sufferings of others. He means that there will not be one place on earth where God will not execute His judgment, so that all lands polluted by idolatry will be destroyed and each will share in the punishment that will come to pass. "Behold," he says, "there will not be one who is not so fettered by his own punishment that he will be able to give consolation to the others." When evil befalls a certain place, others strive to give it aid and comfort. But Micah says this will no longer be the case, for "each will be too fettered by his own punishment, as the wrath of God will be manifested everywhere." Note that the inhabitants of Lachish did not mourn as a sign of their compassion or humanity. He adds that Maroth will be sacked. This means that the strongest and the richest do not always have the best time of it, for all they do is further incite and make crueler their enemies. If a city holds out well against its enemies for some time, they become all the more enraged and willing to put all to fire and the sword. Those who do not resist receive some degree of mercy; and traitors, even more. In sum, Micah is saying that if you do not surrender at first blow, your punishment will be redoubled as so much the more grievous.

Micah provides us here with a very useful teaching. We are prone to think that we have somehow escaped the hand of God if He sustains us for a time. Although He calls us to repentance and gives us the leisure to gather our thoughts together, we take this as an opportunity to harden ourselves; for it seems to us that the matter is over and done with, and that we are quit of God. That is how we commonly abuse the mercy and patience of God. On the other hand, if God were to punish us at once and we were to see that others remained at their ease, we would bitterly complain, "What's going on here? What's the meaning of all this? Are we more wicked than so-and-so?" That is what we do all the time. Therefore, let us pay heed to this passage, where it says that if for a time our Lord does not execute His judgments against us, we must not rest on our laurels and become nonchalant about God's chastisement. Always bear in mind that if we seem to avoid His judgment, that is, if He defers punishing us, this is a very great grace God has shed upon us. Also, if He punishes us first, let us not be envious towards those who remain prosperous; for they will have their turn.

Micah says next that Maroth was in chaos because it had been deprived of goods, for the evil of the Lord had befallen it. This is in regard to our previous point, namely that God's punishment is universal. God does not punish everyone at once, nor must He. God waits for the opportune moment, for iniquity is not always ripe enough. As we learn from Micah's threats against Israel and as sacred history teaches us, God worked from the premise that Samaria and all the rest must be punished before Judah. Why? Idolatry began there, not in Judah. The iniquity of Israel remained unpunished for a time, until it is necessary for God to take matters in hand. He delayed in punishing, to see if Israel might mend her ways. But, as we shall see, Micah's words proved true, namely that God doubles His punishment on those such as Israel who abuse His patience.

Micah says that "evil will befall upon the gates of Jerusalem," adding that Maroth, which was another city, will also be destitute and in total chaos. Know, then, that whenever God gives us good things, we must not count on having them forever. Know that we would not enjoy the good things that we have, save that God maintains them in our possession. Those with an abundance of goods must pray to God every day for their daily bread. Why? We confess, and the truth is such, that were we to have all the world at our disposal, God can well deprive us of everything. We would die of hunger and misery, save that God blesses us. How is it that God will continue to give us good things? We must receive with thanksgiving that which He has given us. We must remain mindful of His goodwill towards us, so that we accept patiently what He sends us. Then there will be no doubt that God will augment more and more the grace He sheds upon us. But if we are ungrateful, our ingratitude must be punished. Let us learn to use good things in such a way as acknowledges that we have received them from God. Otherwise we will share in the condemnation of the infidels, who put all their trust in creatures. There is no way they can rest in God when they have abandoned Him. It is necessary, then, that they suffer immeasurable torments forever.

Micah says that the evil which will befall upon the gates of Jerusalem is a just punishment of God. He also says that it is not enough that each suffers his own punishment, for each must also come to know the hand that strikes him. He says "upon the gates of Jerusalem," to emphasize that the small villages of the kingdom will be pillaged by the enemy, or else that they will deteriorate to the extent they suffer ruination greater than if the enemy had entered them. In short, when Micah speaks here of Jerusalem, it is as if he were saying, "If such things as these happen when the wood is green, what will it be like when it is dry?" Indeed, these are the very words of our Lord; for if there was ever a place in the world that God wished to spare, it was Jerusalem. Micah, however, says that evil will befall it. He means, by this, that God's judgment must befall upon wherever iniquity reigns. He says that there will be no exceptions based on privilege or place, for our Lord judges impartially. Be advised accordingly that if we are exalted above all the others and if God sheds more excellent grace on us than upon the others, we must take care not to overlook His great bounty. Let us be so much the more inflamed to serve Him. Let us be so strengthened by His love that we continually fear and obey Him. Otherwise, we will not escape the fate of Jerusalem.

Micah continues, "You also, daughter of Lachish, hitch up horses to your chariot, or dromedaries or other swift beasts." He means that however firm Lachish may stand, it will not escape God's judgment. The reason: "You are the poison that has infected the lands of Judah; you are the source of Israel's iniquities." Lachish was in Judah, not far from Jerusalem. Micah says that the land has been ruined by idolatry that first began in Lachish before it came to Jerusalem. That is why he proclaims that more severe punishment will befall Lachish. As we noted yesterday, if we tempt neighbors to sin by our scandalous behaviors, not only are we responsible for our own actions but we are also responsible for the souls which perished by following our example. Those poor souls badly instructed by the others cannot say, "behold, I have failed by virtue of my instruction. Must I be damned because of that?" All such excuses are to no avail before God. But he who has tempted his neighbors will be held accountable by God for all those he has led astray. Note well that Micah, speaking here to lands and to Lachish, says specifically that idolatry spread from there to all the lands of Judah and that consequently Mt. Zion has been corrupted and polluted. We see here how men are inclined to evil rather than to good; for although Lachish abandoned itself to all sorts of superstitions and idolatry, was it necessary for Jerusalem to have done likewise? Was it not intended by God to instruct all the other lands? When all the rest of the world was in darkness and Judah had abandoned itself to evil, Jerusalem was supposed to hold to the pure doctrine of God and therefore to have been a lamp unto the world. God built His Temple on Mt. Zion, His Throne was there, and He wished to be honored and worshipped there. Once Lachish had gone astray, it was the responsibility of Jerusalem to lead it back to the Path of Righteousness. Instead, it went along with all the idolatries and superstitions of Lachish. Here we see the natural inclination of men, by which absolutely nothing is required to make us turn our backs on God and become contaminated by idolatries and other superstitions. Nothing, I emphasize, is required to make us turn from God, for our nature has already predisposed us to be quit of God. So much the more, then, must we be on our guard. When we see that Lachish has so infected Jerusalem that idolatry reigned there, we must strive so much the harder to walk in fear of God. Let us pray that we are not diverted from serving God, that we do not stray from the Path of Righteousness, no matter what obstacles Satan may put in our way.

Micah says next, "You will send presents to Moreshethgath. The house of Achzib will be a lie to the kings of Israel." As we have already noted, he describes God's judgment as a universal event. This is important to note; for however God threatened Jerusalem, Lachish, Nazareth, Maroth, and all the other villages we have heard mentioned, each firmly believed that God's judgment was not against them, saying, "True, the others will be punished, but we stand separate and apart from them." Men are never willing to believe that the hand of God will befall upon them, until they feel its blows. True, we are sometimes quick to believe beyond our experiences; but this is not the case when it comes to taking seriously God's judgments in order that we become displeased with ourselves. We would do nothing of the sort unless God were to lay His hand on us in all earnestness. Otherwise, we will not be sufficiently moved by any of His remonstrances. Suppose one speaks to us in a wishy-washy manner. How would that move us, when God cannot touch us deeply, although He cries out after us night and day? Micah had to go from city to city to reproach each in particular to summon them before God's tribunal, as if he had their indictment in hand. This was necessary because men do not worry about God's judgment until they are threatened by it. Even as they feel the blows of God's hand upon them, they deceive themselves into thinking they can escape it. Our Lord judges the world in whole, not in part. There are no high places nor depths of the world that do not fall under His jurisdiction. Therefore, when we hear that God is angry with us, let us think upon our sins. Let us not be so foolish as to assume that the hand of God will not befall upon us; for it will land on us so much the harder if we have thought

59

to avoid it. Here Micah speaks in ways we cannot translate into our language, as when he says, "The house of Achzib will be a lie to the kings of Israel," that is, a false hope. He makes reference to the new masters of Israel when he says, "I will send an heir to Mareshah." Now this name means "he who inherits," as if Micah were saying, "I will send you new masters to usurp your inheritance." But all this is a play on words by him and so was much more meaningful and efficacious to those whom it was addressed.

Micah says, "You shall send presents to the people of Gath," that is to say, to Philistines. This means that Israel will be a tributary to its enemies and unbelievers. Because Israel defied God, it must bear the pain of this defiance and send presents to appease its enemies. Take care this same fate does not befall us today. God demands that we be His people, that each and every one of us accommodate himself to Him. If we will not accept God governing us, if He sees that He cannot make us His people, what will happen to us? We will become subjugated to others, indeed to our enemies. Who among us will deny that it is just punishment that God will hand us over to tyrants who will torment and molest us if we do not wish to be governed by Him? If we will not submit to the hand of God, is it not fitting that He deliver us to our enemies, who well know how to subjugate us?

Although Micah speaks to the people of his time, his message is addressed to us today. What must we do? Since our Lord had given us the grace to govern ourselves, let us subjugate ourselves to Him, since He has revealed that He will care for us. When God offers to be our leader, can we do any less than this? Is it not reasonable that we subjugate ourselves to Him? If we refuse His offer, what will happen? We will be deprived of all good things, because we are evil ingrates who refuse to recognize God's blessings. True, for a time, the infidels, who hold all God's judgments in contempt, will triumph in this world. However, in the end, God will strip them of all the good things He has given us for our physical existence in this world; but let us not expect to find anything permanent down here. Let us live such that we always look to God. Let us pray that it please Him to govern us by His grace; for we know that if we are faithful on our part, He will never default on His.

When Micah says that the House of Achzib is a lie for the kings of Israel, he shows the result of putting all our faith in creatures: We end up only deceiving ourselves with vain hopes. True, we do not wish to be deceived. Indeed, we protest against it. But there is not one person who does not deceive himself and is not a deceiver. Although we do not intend to deceive ourselves, God will nevertheless punish us for having done so, deliberately or otherwise, and make us bear the pain we have merited for putting our trust in creatures. God has revealed that there is no rest, save that He is our foundation. It never fails that we wander aimlessly about, dreaming up I don't know what all, and saying to ourselves, "I've got to carry out this really clever scheme for such-and-such that just popped into my

61

head." We are prone to creatures rather than God. But what will come of this? It is all nothing but deceit, and yet we will not stop fooling ourselves. Think hard on this point; for if we walk according to the ways we invent in our own heads, we deprive God of what properly belongs to Him.

At the end of this chapter, Micah says that "The glory of Jerusalem will come to Adullam"; that is to say, Jerusalem will be abolished, for Adullam means valley. Israel was extolled beyond the skies; it was put on a pedestal above all other kingdoms; indeed, it was chosen by God Himself. But Micah says that God will pay no attention to all this, that He will strip away all its glory, however it seemed that Israel should be respected everywhere. This teaches us that if God multiplies His grace upon us, we must not puff ourselves up with pride and abuse our greatness; for God can well strip away all our glory, although we are admired by all the world. All God has to do is blow a little on us, and our glory is snuffed out, just as one extinguishes a candle flame. Note well how that is exactly what happened to Israel's glory because God was not honored there. Let us not slack off in anything that is to the glory of our God. Above all, remember Jeremiah's admonition: Do not trust in your own power and virtue, but in God alone. Let us be glorified in God and not seek glory from the world. Then, we will enjoy radiant, eternal glory. As long as we are in this world, we will be mocked and shamed; for we must be like our Chief, who is Jesus Christ and who sustained the jeers and insults of evil persons, as Saint Paul says. But God will not permit us to remain in eternal shame, provided we seek our glory in Him. Then, all the disgrace and shame we suffered will be more honorable than all of the honors we could have had down here. Bear in mind a distinct affinity exists between ourselves and the people of Israel; for they, like ourselves, were prone to a false sense of security, believing themselves to be exempt from God's curse, because they were descended from the sacred line of Abraham.

Micah says that "the kingdom of Israel must shave off all its hair," which was a custom at that time. We must pay close attention to these ancient customs, or we will not properly comprehend what the prophets are saying. Micah means that there will be mourning and lamentation everywhere, for the people will be totally destitute. Israel's glory will be extinguished. The end of Judah will be at hand. None will escape the hand of God, which will land great sorrow on those who felt it was beneath their dignity to be instructed by His grace. True, the faithful are sometimes afflicted by God. Even our Lord treated His children harsher than He did strangers. God weans us off our evil cravings by the afflictions He sends upon us. He transforms our miseries into something good and sees to it that they serve our salvation. That is why the children of God can rejoice in the midst of all their suffering. But those who turn their backs on God will suffer double torment, with no hope of relief: Our Lord was a source of consolation and joy to the faithful who were among these doomed people. Micah is referring to them, when, after threatening the people, he says, "God has pity and is merciful. He is always ready to receive you in all mercy. Rejoice, fear not; for you have His promise to be your Savior." At present, however, He thunders and roars at the people because they lack reverence for God and are so hardened that they must be awakened to Him by force of blows upon them. Neither great nor small, he says, will escape God's judgment and there will be chaos everywhere.

Next Micah says that the kingdoms of Judah and Israel will be destroyed and that their children will be led into captivity. So let us hold fast to what God commands. Let us realize we will gain nothing by rebelling against Him. Let us serve God according to His will, not our own fantasies, as we are want to do. True, sometimes it seems that we can invent and make good things on our own. But they do not last. After we take great pains to make such-and-such, it proves to be of no value whatsoever and we end up merely worn out, embarrassed, confused.

Following this holy teaching, let us prostrate ourselves before the face of our good God, acknowledging our sinfulness. We pray that He touch us stronger and deeper than ever before, in order that we become totally displeased in ourselves and wish only to be renewed, not only in body, but in spirit, so that the Devil is no longer able to divert us from truly serving God. May we, standing upon His promises, put all our trust in Him, so that, whatever temptations may befall us, we do not abandon our vocation, to which He has called us in order to lead us back to

Himself, however we were separated in the past. May God shed this grace not only on us but upon all the people and nations of the earth, etc.

All-powerful God, celestial Father, you have given us so many warnings of your great wrath and vengeance, which you wish to be remembered forever. Give us the grace to learn from them that you are the redoubtable, terrible Judge of the obstinate and hardened. Give us the grace to hear your prophet and to apply all our energies to appease you. May we turn aside from all men and go directly to you. May your merciful promise in Christ alleviate all doubt that you are our true Father. Grant us the spirit of true repentance. If we have been a bad example and led others astray, may we now be their ensigns or guides to direct them to the Path of Righteousness. May each of us help the other to lead a happy, well-ordered life, that together we reach the blessed celestial life, which your only Son, our Lord Jesus, purchased for us so dearly by His blood. Amen.

* * *

## (5) Monday, November 24, 1550

A curse upon those who dream up evil schemes in their beds. When morning breaks, they will carry them out; for they have the power in their hands to do so. They covet the possessions of others and steal them away by force. They oppress a man, steal his house right out from under him, and usurp his inheritance, etc. Micah 2

We have heard Micah threaten most especially Judah because idolatry and consequently corrupt practices of serving God reigned there. New he turns to the crimes men commit against one another. God has given us two basic rules to live by, as there are two tablets of His Law: The first is that we honor Him. The second is that we treat our neighbors justly. Our Lord could have well written the Law on only one tablet if He had so desired. Why, then are there two? The Law is easier to read that way. Our Lord said everything we need to know about sanctity and justice in just ten simple, straightforward commandments. If we do not walk as we should, the fault is purely ours; for we are told how we are to live, in concise, easy-to-grasp terms. Ignorance is no excuse. God presented His rules to us in a format that really makes things stand out: He used two tables with a clear-cut distinction between themselves. Nobody, then, has any reason to get mixed up as to what's what. No one can say in all honesty, "I don't know what God wants of us. I just don't understand what we are supposed to do." Our Lord gave us two tablets, to make it perfectly clear we have two basic tasks: We must honor God and we must do unto others as we would have them do unto us. If we build all our laws and institutions upon these two principles of natural charity, we will walk in all righteousness, wrong no one.

Whereas Micah previously rebuked the Jews because they have strayed from true doctrine, serve God according to their own whims, and are possessed by evil superstitions, now he adds that they are also quite wicked in their dealings with one another.

Micah says first, "A curse on those who think up evil in bed, indeed during the rest period God gave us, which is night." David says that savage beasts, who chase their prey all day long, enter their caves to rest at night. It is contrary to the natural order if the night is used for other than rest. If God puts the sun to bed in order that we may rest, should we use this time to think up ways to harm our neighbors so they are unable to rest night or day? Is that not a thing completely contrary to God's ordinance? Micah, then, in speaking of those who plot evil schemes against their neighbors, had good reason to mention the specific time, as if he were saying, "Poor fools! Behold what the savage beasts have to teach you. Although they are quite cruel and wish to devour everything they encounter, they follow the natural order and go rest in their caves at night. They cease preying on men, in order that you can get some rest. God has ordained night as the time for rest. Yet you defy Him by using night as the time for you to think up torments. Compared to savage beasts, your cruelty is far more exorbitant. In brief, you go against nature, when you refuse to recognize that you must rest during the time God gave man, beasts, and all other creatures to do so."

Our Lord so well ordained all things that He provided for all the necessities of man. Let us see, then, how he wishes us to work for our neighbors. Does not the sun shine to arouse us and get us going about our tasks of helping neighbors while we have the needed strength and capability? We are frail creatures who need a time to rest. Let us, then, recognize what a great blessing night is and not use it as an opportunity to bedevil our neighbors. It is intended to strengthen us to better aid our neighbors and must not be used to molest them or cause them further difficulties. If we wish God to be with us when we sleep, let us pray when we go to bed that He give us the grace to rest with a clean conscience. May the body be retired from all work. May He purge us of all evil impulses and unfounded anxieties. May the Lord give us such spiritual rest that we are not tormented by evil thoughts. May God give us the grace that our soul is so in harmony with the body that it rests with it. May we sleep in such purity of conscience that we give no occasion for anyone to be harmed by us. That is the kind of rest we must seek.

Micah says, "those who concoct evil schemes in their beds will execute them in the morning because the power is in their hands to do so." He is not speaking against the lowly here, although they will not be exempt from God's judgment. Both the

68

high and mighty and the lowly will be summoned before God; for each and every one of us will be tried and sentenced without regard to persons. But Micah targets here the high and mighty because they have more opportunity to do harm by devouring and tormenting the lowly. They dream up evil schemes at night and execute them in the morning, for they have the power. They have no more wicked impulses than anyone else, but they have more power and opportunity to do evil. The lowly have very limited means to do evil and so refrain from it. This, however, does not render them just or innocent before God; for the seeds of iniquity are so deeply rooted in their nature that they would do evil if they just had the means. Man converts all the riches and opportunities God has given him for good into evil. That is why Micah focuses most especially upon the high and mighty.

Micah's words are not idle, for he is reproaching the vices that reigned at his time. He does not spare those in high positions of authority over others. He does not turn first to the common people, but to the princes of Sodom and the governors of Gomorrah, that is, the officers of the king who were responsible for the administration of justice in the holy city of Jerusalem. They share the limelight, when it is a matter of reproaching the people. He does not spare a one of these officials, crying out, "You who are responsible to see that each receives his due, you who hold the baton of justice, you are nothing but thieves. you incessantly concoct evil schemes against those you are supposed to defend. God gave you the power

69

to see to it that none are treated unjustly. Yet you have corrupted this power into something completely contrary. You dream up evil schemes in your beds; and because you have the power to carry them out, you do so as soon as you have dreamed them up."

Because men will never confess their sins, save that God were to force them, Micah now enumerates their crimes: "You have oppressed men in order to usurp their goods and their inheritances." What is the source of their sins and crimes? What does Saint Paul say is the root of all evil? Avarice! Of course there are other forms of sinning that seem to come from different sources. Adultery seems to have its own unique root, so too do pride and ambition. But Saint Paul says that there is not one form of evil that does not stem from avarice. Whenever a man is possessed by insatiable greed, he falls into one vice right after the other. There is no limit to what he will do, until finally he reaches the heights of all iniquity. That is what Micah means when he says, "A curse upon you who covet the riches and possessions of others, and who oppress men to usurp them," as if he were saying, "What makes you dream up evil schemes against your neighbors, during the period God ordained for rest? It is your insatiable desire to enrich yourselves. You usurp house after house, inheritance after inheritance. Yet you will know no contentment." Now, the desire to acquire possessions is not something evil in itself or something condemned by God. What is evil, however, is this insatiable

70

greed, by which men will find no contentment or satisfaction. In themselves, riches are very good things. Indeed, they are God's blessings upon us. But a soiled conscience will infect the most holy and the best the world has to offer. How? The buying and selling of land is a crucial part of human society. But if a man is so possessed by greed that he cannot content himself with his purchase of some acres of vineyard, he is condemned before God. Why? Our Lord does not judge by external appearances, as we do, but by what feelings are in a man's heart. True, of course the high and mighty wear their hearts out on their sleeves. Their hands and hearts are one. Their hearts are full of greed and restlessness, so their hands reach out to grab up a house, put the squeeze on some poor soul, snatch away his inheritance and all that they can from him. This unity exists between the hearts and hands of all the high and mighty simply because they have the capability and the opportunity to do evil.

Micah is saying that the root of all evil is avarice. We cannot rest content with what God has given us. We are totally unable to say, "Ah, well, God has given me such-and-such. I can live with that. If He gives me but a little, I do not worry, knowing that His grace will sustain me so that I can live well. If, however, God gives me a lot, I must carefully attend to how it can best be used to aid my neighbors." If ever we had such contentment, we would totally abstain from all evil towards our neighbors.

Avarice, as Saint Paul says, is the root of all evil! If our hearts burn with insatiable desire, we will give in to all forms of cruelty and inhumanity. If we wish to lead a well-ordered life, we must do what Saint Paul said to Timothy and what Saint Peter said in his first letter: We must put all our worries and cares into God's hands, knowing that He will provide us abundantly with what we need. Whenever infidelity takes possession of a man's soul, avarice follows right behind. If we lack faith, it seems the world will fail us; for we know not Him who sustains us. But if we are assured that our Lord cares for us, nourishes us, sustains us now in the world, if we truly believe that He will care for our children after our death, if we, I say, hold all this as sure and certain in our hearts, divine providence will prove to be far more a source of support for us and we will find our contentment in God's grace alone. But if we do not recognize that God cares for and nourishes us and will look after our children, then a terrible anxiety burns within us that nothing can extinguish. If men anguish with desire for this or that, they should stop and realize that God put us in the world to care for us. As God has taken special care of us, so He will care for our children.

Once we have so resolved to put all our trust in God, we will be content with whatever it pleased Him to send us. But how? There are very few truly content people. Furthermore, it often seems that God permits His people to languish in poverty. How can we trust in God, when we see that the only people who

72

enjoy the wealth of the world are usurers, and other vicious gluttons who grab up the world's wealth from all directions by evil and illegal means? What can we hope to gain if we live in all modesty and righteousness? These thoughts are what tempt us to sin. We fail to realize that when God nourishes His people in poverty, He cares for them far more miraculously than if He had given them goods in abundance; for He nourishes them as if by manna from the sky. If we had goods in abundance, we would become blind and no longer see that He sheds His grace upon us. Furthermore, it is a good idea that God holds back on the good things He gives His children, for fear they will become addicted to the world's riches. When we find ourselves in need, this must not deter us from putting our total and complete trust in Him.

Avarice is the root of all evil, for we never seem to have enough and are not content merely to have our needs met but always wish to have more, without ever really knowing why. Do not ever try to put a bridle on a man who is ambitious to become rich; he will follow his lust, no matter how one tries to rein him in. True, in the very beginning, the avaricious soul will say, "If I just had such-and-such, I would ask for nothing more." But when he gets it, he becomes more than ever greedy and would not be satisfied if he had all the goods in the world. What is to be done? We must root out this evil, or it will continue to produce its fruits. We must root out our lust for goods, I say, or we will be incessantly tormented by insatiable desire, "Will I ever have more than I already have?" That question will continually burn in our minds. But, as I have said, the remedy is simple enough: We must put all our trust in divine providence and we must come to accept what it really means to say the words of the Lord's Prayer, "Give us this day our daily bread." If we accomplish that, it is certain avarice will no longer reign in us, as it has. When we ask God for our daily bread, this means we receive it from His hand and according to His own good pleasure. We speak of our ordinary or daily bread, to signify that God does not wish us to be troubled by our necessities, that He knows what is expedient for us, and that He sustains and nourishes us every day. If that is what we truly believe, God will multiply the little He has given us. But look how we strongly resist God's will, lusting after this or that. Because we look out purely for our own interests and completely disregard God, there is only hypocrisy, idleness, and infidelity in us. Furthermore, we have no rest, neither in body nor soul. We toss and turn, night and day; for our insatiable desires will not let us sleep.

When Micah speaks of men coveting and stealing the possessions of others as well as oppressing a neighbor to grab up his house and inheritance, he is showing how avarice turns men into insatiable gluttons whose lust knows no limits. The avaricious man is never satisfied to grab up house after house, although he is only one body. If he has snatched up enough property to support a dozen or more persons, still that is not enough for him. He is always on the lookout to grab up more possessions and inheritances. Most often, this glutton has no offsprings to leave his ill-gotten gains to. Yet, he will never be satisfied, even if he were to have enough property to support more than a dozen persons. "How do I know," he says, "that I might not run into tough times and need to sell every inch of land I've got, just to barely get by?" Isaiah speaks about the avaricious man, in Chapter 5: "A curse upon you who join house to house, field to field, and extend your boundaries! Do you live alone in the midst of the earth? Do you wish to chase away your neighbors, as if the world had been made solely for you?" Some men are so greedy that they would shut up the sun in their coffers if they could. They are so envious of their neighbors that they are enraged the sun shines on all. A river flows so that each can use it according to his needs; but the avaricious man is so jealous that others can use it that he would dam it up and control it if he could. The Devil so blinds men that there is nothing more horrible than their avarice and insecurity.

From what has been said, it is clear that God wishes us to surrender ourselves to Himself and His providence. When He gives us goods in abundance, He does not want us to use them as if we expect to possess them forever. If He gives us joy today, we must not expect it tomorrow. But we can be certain that God will never fail us, as will the pleasures and delights of the world; for God's aid is continual. We must be totally grounded in Him. A man must not let his family make him burn with avarice. As I have said, just as we must put total trust in God to care for each and every one of us, so, too, we must commend our children to Him and doubt not that He will watch over them after our death.    True, some men will try to excuse their avarice by saying, "If I had only myself to look after, I wouldn't bother to amass so much wealth; but God does not forbid me to care for my children."  This may seem a good excuse; but, in point of fact, it abuses Scripture, to cover up evil.  A father who pillages and robs will try to excuse himself by saying that he has to take care of his children.  "Did not our Lord, Jesus Christ Himself," he will say, "wish a father to support his family?"  Christ wishes us to care for our families, but not by stealing from our neighbors.  A father can leave his children only what he has received from the hand of God.  Only these gifts will benefit them.  Whatsoever has been acquired dishonestly will not endure, as we will see.  That is the main point to bear in mind from Micah's passage.

Micah shows that avarice always leads to oppression, cruelty, extortion, and violence against the neighbor.  That is why he says, "You oppress a man to usurp his inheritance."  We see this happen every day.  In short, avarice is the root of all evil.  The reason is simple:  The avaricious man is self-centered, and he who is enraptured by self-love has no concern whatsoever for his neighbors.  This is true not only for matters of this world but also in regard to instructing neighbors in the doctrine of God.  It's not surprising that Scripture forbids avarice; for it brings all other sins with it, as we know from experience.  Did our Lord put us in this world to be crueler to one another than are savage beasts?  We are all created in the image of God, so I cannot look at a man and not see there God's image.  Should we not, then, love one another and not fight like cats and dogs, as the saying goes?  Very few men today stop to consider this point.  For the most part, men close their eyes when it is a matter of treating neighbors justly.  They will say, "I don't give a damn what happens to my neighbors.  I don't give a damn either where or how I get my goods.  All that matters to me is that I have them."  So much the more must we heed Micah's teaching and become aware of the image of God within ourselves, for the vast majority of men today think that Screw Your Neighbor is truly the motto to live by.  It seems to them that a man cannot be respected unless he amasses great wealth.  How does not matter.  Vice becomes virtue.  Avarice becomes more honorable than the contentment God wishes for us.  When God curses avarice, we better tremble in our boots that we are not included. If a man curses us, we are frightened.  But consider what happens with those so possessed by unbridled passion that they do not care to what extreme they must go to grab up wealth, those who have no scruples whatsoever about resorting to violence and extortion.  Whenever God curses them, that does not frighten them in the least.  Must we, then, renounce all faith in God's words? No, we must rest assured that God has not spoken in vain.  Those who do not fear the sentence Micah pronounced on them will nevertheless feel God's hand land heavily upon them.  Although they scoff at Micah's sentence, it will be executed upon them despite themselves. Let us humble ourselves before the mighty hand of God as soon as possible, so that He does not curse and punish us out of His great fury. And exactly how do we go about humbling ourselves to appease Him? By treating our neighbors justly, as I have already said.

Next Micah says, "The Lord says, 'Behold me as I do evil against this generation, from which you will be unable to remove your necks. You will not walk haughtily, for this time is devoted to evil.'" Our Lord says, "behold me," to emphasize that he does not speak in vain, that His mouth is ready to pronounce sentence upon us, that His hand is poised to execute it upon us, "Behold me!" He says, for His judgment is truly upon us. True, however, He does not execute His sentence at once. He wishes to give us ample opportunity to come to the realization that He alone is the Judge of all our works and to amend our ways so we come to walk in fear of Him. If we have these words engraved in our hearts, we will know God is present and not only sees all that we do but all that we think, even though the rest of the world thinks that God is far away. Let us not be like the infidels, who think that God does not see a wink of what we do. Let us stand up and shout, "Behold, God is among us!"

To believe that God is among us is to have true faith in Him, as it is said that He is in the midst of those who invoke His name in truth. On the contrary, those who think that they can escape from God will feel His hand in hot pursuit, even if they hid themselves in the depths of the earth. God will pursue them wherever they go. Isaiah says, "A curse upon those who dig underground caverns!" He is speaking against those who put on a facade of innocence, saying, "What in the world could I have possibly done that the prophet cries out so after me?" Many, at that time, thought they could somehow escape God's judgment. "You burrow," he says, "to try and bury your hypocrisy from the eyes of men. Also you think you can hide from God. But He can well find you. Your efforts at clever subterfuges are to no avail." We are admonished then, that God is present, as if He were saying, "I must reveal myself to be present among men; for it seems to many that I take absolutely no interest in their affairs, which they use as an excuse to give free reign to all sorts of evil." If we behold God standing before our very eyes, He who sees all and knows all our thoughts, we will not be so quick to relax the bridle upon our sinful impulses. If, however, it seems to us that God is far away, we have no inhibitions whatsoever about giving in to all sorts of evil impulses. All this simply goes to show that we do not sufficiently respect God. We find it far more difficult to do evil before men than before God. We fear men more so than God because we do not truly believe that He pays attention to us. We mistakenly assume that we can keep God off our track by hiding behind some sort of veil. But, on the contrary, our Lord warns that He is present, indeed as adversary, among those who think to have escaped Him and who use this as their pretext to pillage, treat cruelly their

79

neighbors, and steal all their sustenance. They will well feel the hand of God upon them because they did not believe His words.

The Lord says, "I think up an evil device against this house or generation," as if to say that He will spare none who have harmed their neighbors. Indeed, Micah is speaking against those who live by violence and extortion, those who care for nothing, save that they amass great riches. God is the sworn enemy of all avaricious souls, who acquire goods by evil means. They are all sentenced by the prophet's words.

Next He says, "You will not be able to remove your necks." Here, He is passing sentence on the high and mighty, who think they are a cut above all the others and therefore beyond reproach although the poor world is eaten alive by them. However much they pillage, steal, and commit adultery, they feel grievously wronged if they are put on a par with other men. Indeed, they are of the haughty opinion that they should be totally exempted from God's judgment, despite the fact that God has otherwise revealed Himself to them. True, the high and mighty often seem to escape punishment; but if we wait patiently, we will see God execute His sentence against them and we will know that He did not speak in vain. Rest assured that if they escape punishment in this world, God will execute a far more horrible sentence upon them on Judgment Day. Furthermore, if we fear and obey God, if we firmly believe that He cares for us and sustains us by His bounty, then we can rest assured that He will look after our offsprings and guide them not only in worldly matters but in order to make them participants in the Kingdom of Heaven, which He has promised to His own.

Following this holy teaching, we prostrate ourselves before the face of our good God, acknowledging our sinfulness. May He so reform us that we are no longer addicted to the pleasures and vanities of the world. May we be content with what He has given us. May we walk in all righteousness and justice among our neighbors. May we do good rather than evil. May we be blessed by fraternal charity, so that each of us ministers to the needs of the other. May we come to share in the Kingdom of Heaven. May He shed this grace not only on us but upon all the nations and peoples of the world, etc.

* * *

## (6) Tuesday, November 25, 1550

In this day, one shall take up a parable against you and lament with a sorrowful lamentation, saying, "We are broken. He has taken away some of my people. How can He strip away that which is mine so there is no restitution? For the enemy divides up our fields, etc." Micah 2

If we truly fear God's judgment, we will look beyond this world to eternal life. Although God may permit us to live comfortably, with all sorts of pleasures and good things, what would all this profit us if on Judgment Day we went to eternal damnation? Christ has asked, "What does it profit a man if he gains the whole world but looses his soul?" Do not fix your eyes upon earthly matters. We are created to live in the knowledge that each and every one of us faces an irrevocable judgment: Either we will be banished from the Kingdom of God and suffer the horrible condemnation shared by Satan and his people, or we will share in the immortal celestial glory God has reserved for His elect. But we are so hardened that we do not see a wink of all this. Worse yet, we turn our backs on the whole matter and are content not to think about it. For this reason, our Lord gives us some indication of His judgments, in this world. We really cannot imagine the Last Day; but we are warned of it sufficiently to know that it is foolish to seek our prosperity in any place other than in God's grace and blessing. Men will profit greatly from the goods God sends them, but not in any way

82

whatsoever from the things they themselves invent; for the Lord will curse their labor.

Nevertheless, we are so stubborn and hardened that we not only reject these warnings but we no longer have eyes that can behold them, as if Satan so bandaged our eyes that we see nothing of them. But God does not warn in vain. On Judgment Day, we will be rendered inexcusable; for our Lord worked very hard to teach us and yet we remained totally incorrigible.

So let us heed Micah's warning: Those who are so tormented by their lust to acquire great riches will be stripped of all their goods in the end. Let us realize that God's blessing alone is the gateway to all prosperity. Let us hear his threats and not expect Him to sustain our worldly wealth.

Micah says, "In this day, you will become a scornful example to all the world. You will cry out, 'God has given our inheritance to our enemies.' You will be shamed, having believed that all must be restored to you. Nothing will remain for you. No one will cast the cord to decide the lots of your divine inheritance." He is saying in effect, "You think that no harm can come to you, because you have great wealth. But God must have His authority. He will reveal in the end that all your riches, pleasures, and opulence are nothing; for He has the authority to strip from men whatsoever He has given them." Also they will be pillaged and sacked as they have so done unto others. This was not only the case for Babylon, but is a universal sentence, which means that God judges men as they have so judged others, and applies the same rules to them that they apply to others, as our Lord, Jesus Christ, reveals.

To better understand Micah's message, note that he speaks of a day when those who have committed violence against their neighbors must appear before the Judge to answer for their crimes. This will be at the Second Coming, when those given to fraud, cruelty, and violence will receive such payment as they have merited. True, for a time, our Lord will let them get away with devouring their neighbors. They will seem to have gained the upper hand and to have escaped God's judgment. All the world will tremble before them. True, our Lord will permit the wicked to enjoy prosperity; but He does have a special day reserved for their punishment. A criminal does not go to the executioner at once, for a date must be set for his trial. That is the procedure our Lord follows with us. True, in the beginning, He reproaches us for our faults, giving us the opportunity to return to Him and receive His pity. But when He sees all this is to no avail, He presses hard upon us. He no longer wishes to be our Father; He is our Judge, who institutes proceedings against us. God's threats alone are enough to convict us; for He made them quite clear to us, yet we pay no attention to them. Rest assured, then, that the Day of Judgment, which Micah speaks of as on the way, is not some future event, but already at hand.

Micah says that "they will be lamented by songs of mourning." By "they," he means men of power and wealth, whom he is mocking for being so enraptured with their high positions.

They think all the rest of the world exists for the sole purpose of pleasing and flattering them. On the contrary, Micah says, "You love praise and flattery. You will receive it, but in a new and strange way, one that you are not accustomed to. Because you can do what you please in the world, you think that you are above even God and that none can compare with you. But, behold, the day is coming when you will be mourned. Whereas now you are admired, on that day your fame will be gone with the wind, you will be brought to account, and you will pay for your arrogance. It seems that everyone sings your praises today, but they will change their tune and sing only laments for you. You have now your songs of joy, your delights, and your pleasures. But the time is coming when others will have to lament for you, for you yourselves will be unable to sing songs of mourning."

Micah says, "We are totally devastated, for God has stripped away our inheritance and given it to our enemies. We believed that all would be restored, but this proved a major disappointment." Micah here gives voice to the great suffering of those who refused to heed God's warnings and continued in their evil ways. In the end, they were stripped of everything, and nothing remained for them but total despair. True, God can chastise His people quite severely and harshly, as we often experience when God lays His hand on us. However, He always sweetens His scourges, so that there is always some degree of consolation and that we are not so confused that we cannot behold His great bounty and pity upon us. But when men stubbornly

85

refuse to give ear to warnings in God's name, He will so crush them down that there is no consolation whatsoever. That is what Micah means when he cries out, "We are finished, wiped out."

Such extreme measures, so we are often told, God has reserved specifically for the infidels, who will not come to fear Him, save by force. They mock all His warnings. As long as they do not feel the blows of His hand, His threats mean absolutely nothing to them and they continue to walk in ways contrary to the Lord. Should God's rod prod them in the least, they become so frightened that they completely go to pieces, losing all self-control and their capacities to reason. However, God's chastisements are intended to have a completely opposite effect upon the elect: They soften our hard hearts and return us to Him. Realizing He is our Judge, we come forth to Him in all humility to beg pardon for our sins. Although we may not immediately sense His bounty, we will never be without hope and consolation. We will never have to say, "We are finished, wiped out." Instead, we totally trust in God's promise to shed His bounty and mercy upon us. When we see daily these incorrigible, rebellious sinners who hold God's Word in contempt, we know to expect that God will deal with them as Micah reveals here. We will see the reprobate become vexed and gnash their teeth, as in the end they will become flustered and cry out, "Alas! All is lost!" Nevertheless, they will not become displeased with their vices nor ask God for pardon. They will resist all the more against

God and work themselves into a furious rage from which they will never be delivered.

Micah shows how God becomes such a source of frustration for the reprobate. They expect to have an easy time of it with God. But reckoners without their host must reckon twice, as the saying goes. Take, for example, the infidels. They think they have escaped the hand of God simply because they do not feel its blows upon them. If you warn them that God's evil is about to befall them, if you give them all sorts of examples of how God always punishes those who rebel against Him, they respond, "O, that's mere balderdash from the past." If you point to the fact that our Lord has punished many people in our day, they respond, "Such is Fortune. You have to be on guard constantly to have Luck in your way. I am so successful at my affairs that no one gets the upper hand on me if I have any say in the matter." How they rebel against God! It is precisely this foolish pride and arrogance that Micah addresses when he says that they believed everything stripped away from them would be restored. Let us not, then, become intoxicated by false hopes. Let us put all our hope in God and His promises, and we will never be deceived. But if we found our hopes in our own inventions, God will strip away everything. This is a very important teaching for us to bear in mind. Our natural arrogance puffs us up with pride. Although God may punish us harshly, still we think ourselves to be above Him, as if we are the most mighty. Seeing as we are subject to such a wicked vice as this, we must pay heed all the more to

Micah's teaching that we must not ground ourselves in the beliefs we invent. We must not make them the basis to hope that such-and-such will come to pass, for the hand of God will more than disappoint us. There is no remedy, save we return to Him and firmly ground ourselves in His promises. I emphasize that in the midst of the greatest misfortune that could ever befall us, we are never without this remedy.

Micah goes on to say that "the cord will no longer be stretched out to determine the portion of our divine heritage, in the assemble of the Lord." At that time, they measured lands by cords, as today one uses a pole to survey and measure land. Scripture, then, speaks of the cord, to signify how goods and inheritances were divided up into shares. Micah says the cord will no longer be cast, because they will be banished from the land God gave them. Our Lord will carry them off to Babylon, for they were not worthy of inhabiting their homeland. Whatever part of the world God lodges us in, always bear in mind that He alone has given us this place in which to live. So if we resort to violence against our neighbors, if we become insatiable gluttons and devour the goods and nourishment of others, God will banish us from our homeland and we will live in the world as if we really do not exist. Look at what is the case with men of great wealth: They own lands, serfs, vineyards, indeed all that there is. But they might as well be banished, for there is no certainty in their lives. What they grab up with one hand seems to slip right through the other. Look at how our Lord punishes their infidelity: Although they may lull themselves to sleep with false expectations, they will awake to find that they have wasted away all God's gifts and that there is nothing left for them in the world.

What should we do? Today, there is no land specially assigned to the Children of God, as there was to Abraham's children; for all the earth is blessed in order that the faithful may inhabit any part of it. Therefore, let us walk in fear of the Lord and be content with what He has given us. Let us rejoice in all the earth and in whatever part He wishes us to live. Then we can well say that we are His people and that we have received the good things He has prepared for us from the heavens above. On the contrary, we see how God strips the wicked of their goods, not that He fully executes His sentence against them, in this world, as I have said; for what, then, would remain for the Last Day? We should devote ourselves entirely to earthly matters, not worry over resurrection or Heaven. God need only give us some hint of His judgments, in order for us to know that the prophets do not speak in vain when they say that the rich and powerful think they can possess all the earth but that in point of fact nothing will remain for them. When Micah speaks of Canaan, it is not because it was the only inhabitable region of the earth, for there were other regions equally as fertile, but because it was set apart from the others in order that God be served and honored there. Unlike other lands, it was free of all pollution by idolatry. Jerusalem had the Temple, in which God

89

was worshipped in all purity. Indeed, God had set aside this land for Himself and His people. It was like Paradise, and its inhabitants were the happiest people on earth; but those who abuse God's grace must be banished from the Promised Land. Babylon, then, was Hell for the Jews, although it was a grassy, fertile land; for they had been cast out of a paradise and deprived of their God-given heritage.

SO let us come to appreciate what special grace God has shed upon us, not only that we are free to live anywhere in the world, but that where we now dwell is free of superstitions and worships God in all purity. This is a blessing of God that should be prized above all the riches and goods we could ever hope to have in this world. On the contrary, if we are driven from this place, we know that God is punishing us because we refused this blessing and so are unworthy of it. That is the key point of Micah's message.

In sum, first, let us not expect God to fully execute His sentence in this world. But whenever God threatens us, let us act as if this punishment is right before our very eyes, already befalling upon us, and so amend our ways immediately. Let us not allow the troubles and difficulties of the world to make us lose faith, for God does not speak in vain and will fulfill all His promises.

Secondly, let us not become discouraged when we see people bow and scrape to the rich and famous, applauding and honoring them as if they were little gods. Let us remember that our Lord can change all such honor into shame and embarrassment. He will show them what it really means to abuse the good things He has given them. He will make it clear that it would have been better for them to have been aborted by their mothers than to be ingrates who refuse to condescend to receive His gifts.

Above all, let us prize the great grace God has shed upon us that we live in a place where we have the freedom to serve Him in His Church. Let us prize this grace, I say, more that any goods we can receive in the world. When God is served in all purity, He dwells in the midst of us. Let us make good use of this precious gift God has given us, or we will be deprived of it by our ingratitude.

Let us not ground ourselves in our own foolish beliefs and opinions. Let us not be as the wicked who invent all sorts of foolish ideas about miraculous things, to deceive themselves into believing that they will always succeed. Let us humble ourselves in God's hand, let us fear His judgments; for the only assurance we can have in this world is that God has extended His hand to make us feel His favor and mercy. Our desires will never be frustrated; for when we trust fully in God we will receive more from His infinite bounty than we could have ever wished for.

We must realize that God does not execute His judgments so as to destroy the whole world. Far from it. However, the fact that chaos reigns everywhere should not lead you to think that God withholds His judgment. He will not tolerate for an instant the loansharking, raping, extortion, and other iniquitous acts that go on in the world. He cannot help but take some degree of vengeance already upon the wicked. Let us, then, wait patiently for Judgment Day, when all things will be completely destroyed. Let us walk in reverence, humility, and fear of the Lord. Although we are inclined to disregard God's threats, let us remember that they are made manifest to us through the preaching of the Word. We, then, are without excuse. The blame is squarely upon our shoulders if we have not been taught properly.

After Micah has thus warned the Jews for resisting God, he continues, "you who prophesy, prophesy not. Do not prophesy to them, that they be not shamed." This passage, by virtue of its brevity, is quite obscure. Translated literally, it reads: "Pour forth no more. They will say, 'They will not pour forth and they will not bring shame.'" Note that prophetic speech is likened to "rain" or a "downpour." Moses uses these metaphors in his canticle: "Let my teachings pour down as the rain. Let my words fall as the dew." Because God makes the Word of Life flow from the prophets' mouths, prophesy is likened to a downpour, and prophets are likened to rain and said to distill their teachings. Note that the passage first says, "Do not prophesy," and then right afterwards refers to the fact that they prophesy. Now, some think that he is speaking here the way our Lord did when he says in anger, "I will send my prophets and they will prophesy in spite of you." Nevertheless, when all is taken into consideration, it seems that Micah is attributing a kind of prophesying to the people, as the wicked wish to have the loudest voice and protest against God. When God opens the mouths of His prophets, the wicked preach loudly against them, as if it were a contest to see who could out shout the other. Micah is pointing to the diabolical arrogance of the wicked, who rise up against the prophets and defy God's threats. He says, "They prophesy from their side; and it seems to them that if no one talks back, God has shut up His prophets."

Next he says, "They will not prophesy, so that they will not be shamed." this statement suggests two conflicting interpretations. On one hand, Micah may be expressing the opinion of the wicked; for it seems to them as I have already said, that if God does not speak to them, they have escaped God's punishment. They assume that as long as the prophet does not speak to them, they can live as they please, giving free reign to their impulses. In brief, they think that God's judgment is encapsulated in the prophet's mouth. So if he cannot speak, they believe they will go unpunished. On the other hand, the statement may mean that God is saying in effect, "Well now, why is it you do not wish my prophets to speak to you? If their teaching troubles you, I will deprive you of it. Do I or my prophets really gain anything? Behold, they work so hard, yet their salary is nothing but insults and injuries! Behold what payment my servants receive: Because they work hard to serve me faithfully, they undergo more shame, injury, and other troubles than if they were the most wicked men in the world. Do you think that I want you to shame my prophets when they reveal my Word to

93

you? If you do not wish to receive it, I will take it away from you."

Now we come to the true meaning of Micah's statements. In the first place, he says that the wicked prophesy from their side. Why? To dam up the flow of God's Word. However, we cannot treat these matters in detail now. That will have to wait til tomorrow, at the pleasure of God. But at least we can begin, by noting that the wicked have no scruples whatsoever about opposing God, as we see daily. This is not true just for today, but for all time. Indeed, the Devil, who is the Father of Pride and Lies, has always prodded and incited his people to rise up against God and block the flow of His Word. It is very true that the wicked turn a deaf ear to all that is said against them and that they think to have triumphed when no one will speak out against them. They vomit forth horrible blasphemies; they conspire to do I don't know what all in their caverns in order to strip the Word of all its power. But they are totally unable to prevent the Word from stabbing them to the depths of their hearts, for it has the force to make them know that there is a virtuous power which torments them. This is why they reject the Word and oppose the prophets, for they wish to be flattered rather than to have God sound the depths of their evil hearts. If the Word had no real power, they would not mock it, taunting and laughing at it. Their laughter would not even have reached their throats, had not Satan taken total possession of them.

They feel God's judgment upon them and are wounded to the depths of their hearts, despite their light-hearted facade.

Punishment will befall all those who fight against God, His Servants, and His Word, though these rebels think to have escaped simply because no one reproaches them. Micah makes it very clear that their hope of escape is in vain. So let us heed Micah's warning and take care not to preach against God. When He speaks, let us keep our mouths shut and our ears open to hear all that He has to say. There is no use rebelling against God. There is no point in rejecting His Word, for that would be like turning rain into fire hot enough to consume us. Let us not resist against God, for it is a blessing that He is present among us: He leads, guides, and looks after us according to what is good and useful for our salvation. Let us realize that if we do not permit Him to lead us peacefully, if we will not walk in harmony with Him, then His presence will become our condemnation.

Micah says next, "They will no longer prophesy, so that they will not be shamed." He is referring here to the true prophets of God, and his point is that no greater evil can befall us than to be deprived of His Word. God here is saying in effect, "You refuse such a good thing? Fine, I will not quarrel with you. Since you wish to be quite of the Word, I will abandon you such as you are. You will be denied the pasture which is necessary to nourish your soul. Since you so hate it, get out of here. But remember that I will show you my Word can well stand without you and that it will come to strengthen and nourish others. Since you do not wish me to be your leader, I will depart from you and leave you to your chaos." Zachariah said the same thing, "I wished to be your shepherd, so I took up my staff called Beauty; that is to say, I brought about among you such law and order that one could see only God's grace and blessing among you. Next, wishing to show how deeply I cared for you, I took up another staff named Unity, to lead you into peace and amity among yourselves. But, in the end, you became quite disenchanted with me. What ingratitude! What baloney! All the thanks I get from you is a ten-buck tip, as if I were a porter or a bum. After all I have done for you, you treat me like some kind of scamp that leeched off you. I've broken my staffs and leave you to other shepherds who will eat you alive."

The greatest grace God can shed on us is when He governs us peacefully. The instant we abandon God, Satan will take possession of us and we will know how dangerous it is to renounce God. Furthermore, as I have already said, do not be seduced by this foolish opinion of the wicked that if the prophets keep silent, we have escaped the hand of God. Know that if we resist those who proclaim His Word, we will have to deal with Him. In the end, we will be destroyed, for He is the stronger party. More needs be said here, but that will have to wait until tomorrow.

Following this holy teaching, we prostrate ourselves before the face of our good God, acknowledging our sinfulness. May we trust completely in His bounty. May He open our eyes, so that we

96

no longer fixate upon things in this world. May we be more deeply grounded in His will. Blessed with the preaching of the Word in all purity, may we, wherever we may be and whatever may be the case, conform to His will. May we, in this way, be a shining example to lure others to Him, that His name be glorified by all in common accord. May He shed this grace not only on us but upon all the peoples and nations of the earth, etc.

All-powerful God, celestial Father, it pleases you to test our magnanimity by the quality of justice and charity that reigns among ourselves. Give us the grace that we do not become wolves who devour one another. Give us the grace that we may prove truthfully, without any sort of feigning, that we are your children, who diligently observe the righteousness and generosity among ourselves that you command. May we live our whole life in this spirit of equity, that finally we come to share in the felicity that awaits us in Heaven, through Jesus Christ, our Lord. Amen.

* * *

(7) Wednesday, November 26, 1550

You who prophesy, prophesy not! Do not prophesy to them, that they be not shamed. Do you think, O House of Jacob, that the Spirit of the Lord is soft? Does He take weak action? Is not my Word good to those who walk on the Path of Righteousness? Micah 2

Remember yesterday we were warned that we will be deprived of all salvific teaching if we rebel against God and refuse to accept His teachings. If God spoke to us according to our whims, we would be more than content with Him. We wish Him to please us, flatter us, and indulge us in all our vices. But all this is an utter impossibility. There are no two things more incompatible than the will of God and the lusts of men. They are like fire and water. Men are totally abandoned to evil and will not tolerate the least reproach. Our Lord, on the other hand, loving justice and righteousness, cannot tolerate men so abandoning themselves to evil, without reproaching and condemning them. That is why men hate God's word. That is what our Lord, Jesus Christ, meant when He said that those who do evil hate the Light.

It is no surprise, then, that the Gospel has always been as poorly received in the world as it is today. Before the time of the Gospels, the prophets encountered many stumbling blocks. People cried out and raged against them. Why? It all boils down to the fact that men, being totally perverse, wish to be left alone to wallow in their own shit. Our Lord, on the contrary, strives to awaken them, reveals His judgment to them. That deeply troubles them, so they rise up against Him. If we refuse God the authority to correct our ways, is it not more than fair and just that He no longer takes us for His people and abandons us to our own shit? Should He waste His time on us? He cares deeply for us and strives to return us to Himself in so many ways, yet all we do is rebel and defy Him out of our willful malice. Should not He abandon us and turn to those who will cooperate with Him and will not be so hard to subdue as are we? Is there any real reason why we should have the Doctrine Life, when we despise it so and would rather follow Satan and his alchemists than God? Should our Lord continue to shed His grace upon us when we are such disloyal traitors? When the rains come to nourish the earth, we recognize that God sheds His grace on us. Now, the life of the soul is much more precious than that of the body. Although we are careful to nourish properly our bodies, we are ingrates who refuse to accept what God gives us to nourish our souls. Our souls should be like the earth, which is always ready to receive the rain God sends. Then we will feel the Word penetrate us and give us nourishment. We will no longer be like dry rocks. But it seems to the wicked and the unbelievers that they have gained everything when God no longer speaks to them. Look at them living comfortably, having a good time, all the while thinking that God's judgment will not befall them simply because they have turned a deaf ear to His threats. They think God does not have a long-enough hand to reach them.

Micah shows what deceit this is: "Listen!" he says. "Do you think, O House of Israel and Jacob, that God's Spirit is soft? What audacity you have to shut up the prophets so they cannot proclaim God's Word! And what exactly are you trying to accomplish by all this? You are trying to dictate to the Spirit of God according to your appetites." He continues, "Whom do you blame evil on? If you have a famine, pestilence, or war, do you not say that God is the cause? Do these evils not befall you because of your sins? When the fire of God's wrath is lit, what is the wood it feeds on? Is it not your rebellion and ingratitude? Are your sins not the wood which consumes you? The evil that befalls you is all your fault because of your sins. You cannot truthfully say that God had any reason to do so, save that He is a fair and just Judge. What reason, then, do you have to complain if my words bring evil upon you?"

He continues, "My Word is good to those who walk on the Path of Righteousness. They find only sweetness and joy in what the prophets proclaim." The principal consolation of God's children is that He reveals His goodwill towards them when He speaks to them. Micah, then, says, "If my Word seems harsh to you, it is because of your ill-will. You are to blame, for you, my people, have become robbers. You plunder and pillage one another. I have chosen you for my children and wished you to live in my House. But you have become so wicked that there is nothing but cruelty, rapine, murder, perjury, and loansharking among you. Everything and everyone is preyed upon, yet you throw out my prophets when they reproach you." When Micah says that they are called the House of Jacob, he is reproaching their foolish pride, for the Jews always glorified themselves in the names of their fathers: "Are we not of the sacred line of Abraham?" They reproached Christ, saying, "Who do you think that you are talking to? Do you know who we are?" "Yes, yes," He responded, "I know well who you are. You say you are the children of Abraham, but you are really the children of Satan. What was Abraham like? Do you really resemble him in any way? He knew me and rejoiced in me before I came into the world. I am sent to you from God, my Father; yet you wish to put me to death as one of His enemies. Do you resemble Abraham in this? No! Do not say that Abraham is your father; for your true father is the Devil, who is the Father of Lies and Murder." That is precisely Micah's point, as if he were saying, "True, you bear the name of Israel; but you wrong its good name, to say that you are descended of its blood; for if you were truly children of Abraham, you would follow his faith and obedience of God."

Isaiah spoke even more harshly to them, "You say you are sons of Abraham? Be gone with you, sons of whores. Your father was an Amorite, your mother was a Hittite." These two peoples were the most heinous and detestable of all. That is why Isaiah says to the Jews, "You are descended from the wicked Chaldeans, Hittites, and Amorites, who are the most abominable people before God. Go now and glorify yourselves!" Of course, he is not speaking here according to the flesh. He does not mean that their mothers were literally whores; he means that they turned away from God to follow their superstitions. Physical parentage does not count before God, as Saint Paul says in Romans 10 and 11: "Those who claim to be children of Abraham are not true Israelites. Well may they be of the bloodline of Abraham, but they have been thrown out of the House of God because of their infidelity and rebellion. So do not boast of high-sounding titles, but serve God in all reverence and humility. That way, none can reproach us that we have pretended to be what we are not in truth."

Today, it is more honorable to be called Christians than it was to be called children of Jacob at that time, for we have the name of the Son of God. It is no longer a matter of claiming a privileged position because we are children of Abraham; for our Lord has shed this grace and honor upon us, so that we together share His name. Now, to be true Christians we must be reformed by the Spirit of God; we must be regenerated such that our carnal appetites no longer reign in us. We must not march under false banners, but bear a true sign that we are Christians, not only in body, not on the outside, but deep in our hearts. The Spirit of God must reign in us such that we witness to our adoption, by walking in fear of the Lord, taking Him to be our Father, and honoring Him as we should. If we erase this sign from our hearts, our name will be of no real benefit to us. On the contrary, this will lead to even greater condemnation; for it abuses the name of God if we take this precious and honorable title and yet do not have what it signifies.

Baptism is a sign of the remission of our sins; it represents the blood of Jesus Christ, by which we are washed. If we falsify this sign by our malice and ingratitude, so much the more inexcusable will we be, so much the more horribly will we be condemned by God for having abused our excellent name. Pay attention to Micah's statement, "You who are called the House of Jacob." True, they bear this name, but he tells them God does not accept them on that basis. Because God has so graciously given us the name of His only Son, let us not abuse it. When we orally confess to be Christians before men, may our faith be deeply rooted in our hearts. May our actions declare that it is not in vain we are called Christians.

Micah shows how outrageously arrogant men are to try and block God from chastising them when they have sinned. He says, "Is the Spirit of the Lord soft? Does he act timidly?" Men do not know the cause of their evil. Not only when God openly chastises them, but when He lays His hand upon them, still they do not recognize the source of [their torments]. But let us not make this same mistake; let us realize that all our afflictions are the scourges of God, by which he corrects us when we have failed, in order to make us pay attention to Him. We should freely submit to God's scourges, to better ourselves. But instead we gnash our teeth, grumble, and become vexed with God, each bitterly complaining, each deeply angered. We should not be surprised, then, that men try to strike back at God when His hand slaps them down, for they cannot bear the reproaches and threats made by His Word. This being the case, what are we to do when our Lord chastises us in all earnest? Should we not confess our sins, beg forgiveness, and humble ourselves under His mighty hand, as Saint Peter says? If we rebel against God, is it not reasonable that He treats us so harshly? Nevertheless, there is great mercy in all this; for when we have sadly failed, our Lord does not wish to punish without giving us the chance to return to Him. When we see such sweetness in our Lord, are we not so much the more wicked for continuing in our vices? Although He permits us to languish and to be afflicted head to foot, we must recognize His great bounty; for all the torments He inflicts upon us are signs that He wishes to sustain us. If we become docile and return to Him in true repentance, He will receive us in all mercy. What ingrates we are, that when our Lord exhibits more than paternal kindness towards us, we grumble, speak ill of His Word, and rebel against Him.

It is not without reason that Micah asks here, "Is the Spirit of God soft?" This warns us that when we resist against the Word of God, we are not fighting against mortal men, as many mistakenly assume, but we are attacking God. This saddens and provokes the Holy Spirit against them. Is this not more than diabolical audacity on the part of men? Satan himself trembles before the majesty of God, yet men who call themselves Christian wish to raise themselves above God and subject Him to their

foolish whims.  Is there no audacity more detestable than that?
Think hard on this teaching.  Today, we see that vice reigns as
much as it did in Micah's time, if not more.  Many are content
that the Gospel is preached, as long as they are not fingered and
reproached for their faults.  As soon as the preacher digs into
their shit to discover their faults, they become furious.  Well
may they applaud the Gospel; but the minute they see that God
wishes to reproach their faults, they abandon it.  Today, there
is so much grumbling and growling against God and His Word.
There was a time when such contempt of God was not expressed as
openly as it is today; for today nobody is brought to account for
belittling God and blaspheming Him.  Indeed, this goes on right
in public, right where such things should be forbidden.  Evil
seems to have free reign everywhere.  But do we really believe
that God will not destroy these robbers' dens, where they vomit
up all these blasphemies?  Let us take a long, hard look at
ourselves; let us scrutinize ourselves more carefully than we
ever have; for it is no trifling matter that Micah asks, "Do you
think God's Spirit is soft?"  Let us revere the Word, for God
reveals Himself through it.  The Word is not something human, and
ultimately our business is not with men.  We cannot tolerate
being reproached by others.  Indeed, we mock and reject them.  So
let us remember that it is not men but God whom we resist and
with whom we must ultimately deal.  Let us also remember that, in
the end, God will prove to be the stronger party.  Let us follow
Micah's example and identify the Spirit with the Word; for he

says that "the Spirit of God is not soft," to reveal that His Word bears the power of His Spirit and therefore should be revered by us. Let us bear these words very carefully in mind.

Next, Micah claims that men greatly wrong God when they blame Him for the evil they must endure. He asks, "Does God act in weakness?" as if to say, "What is God in His own nature? Is He not kind and full of all pity, although we have offended Him?" If men lived as they should, they would not attribute evil impulses to God; rather, they would say they find only kindness and gentleness in Him. It is not without reason that God says of Himself, "I am the living God, given to compassion and benevolence; I have been merciful to a thousand generations." When our Lord claims these virtues for Himself, there is no doubt that He wishes to demonstrate them to ourselves so we will know by experience that His claims are true. If bad times befall us, we, then, should not blame God; for no evil comes from Him, as Micah says. Instead, men should blame themselves and not fault God, although it is often said that God is the source of all evil. Scripture, however, does speak of God as the cause of our sufferings in this sense: If we reject God, if we continually provoke His wrath against us, He will be compelled to treat us quite harshly, whereas in truth He wishes only to be kind and generous toward us. So, on the contrary, if we receive God's grace, we will know Him to be the kind and merciful God He claims to be.

David says in Psalm 18 that God is kind to those who are kind, but quite wicked to those who are wicked. Pay close attention to what David is saying; it is very strange indeed, to say that God is wicked; for there is no real wickedness within Him, but only justice and kindness. No matter how mean He may seem, God is always fair in His judgments. David is saying that our evil changes God's temperament, forcing Him to be quite harsh and to act against His wishes.

Here we have a very beneficial teaching: All the evils and suffering we must endure in this world are all our fault, not God's; He takes no pleasure whatsoever in treating us harshly. We are the ones who bring the wood and light the fire. Although God torments us, He is always just. Evil does not befall people by chance, for everything is in the hands of God. He is the Judge of the world, so Light and Darkness, Life and Death are in His hands, as Isaiah says.

Jeremiah says in his Lamentations that there is neither good nor evil that does not come from the hand of God, but that this does not mean He is to blame for the ills of the world. As I have said, if we received God's blessing as we should, God's great bounty would flow perpetually to us. Think of God's bounty to be like a river. Now a river will incessantly flow on its course, unless, of course, it were to encounter obstacles. Now, we really cannot compare the power, virtue, and bounty of God to things down here; but when we see that God makes rivers flow incessantly, cannot as much be said for His bounty unless we were to block it? And since we do in fact block the flow of His bounty, He is compelled to be wicked towards us, as we cannot tolerate a revelation of His true nature. That is why God is named Perversity in Scripture. Know, then, that all evil comes directly from His hand; but know also, as I have said, that He takes no delight in tormenting us. Our wickedness compels Him to treat us wickedly, although He does not wish to do so. He wishes to be kind and gracious, to nourish and sustain us. But we turn our backs on Him, rebel against Him, thereby lighting the fire that will consume us.

We, then, can and do change God's will for the worst, as I have just said and as can be found in Scripture. The result of this is that we have absolutely no reason to complain to God when He sends us into poverty. We have no reason to say, "God is too hard on us." We are the cause of all evil, we bring it about. Evil is an unnatural action on God's part, for He is naturally inclined to do good. God wishes to be everlastingly gentle and kind towards us; but if we reject His grace by our ingratitude, we light the fire that will consume us. That is why all the evils and miseries of the world are the fruits of men.

Look at what the world was like in the very beginning. Our Lord did not create our father, Adam, to be subject to the many ills that we are. These come from sin. In the very beginning, was the condition of the human specie what it is now? No, for there was no sickness, poverty, wretchedness, not even death. Human sin is the abysm from which come all these misfortunes.

They are not God's doings; He is not responsible for evil. What Adam began, we continue. There is not a one of us who cannot experience something of God's great bounty: When we look at the natural order, whether we look high or low, there is not one place where the glory of God does not shine through. Yet, everything is corrupted. Know that this corruption is the fruit of our sins and that the pollution in us has spread throughout all the sky and earth. Although God created everything in all purity, there is nothing that is not polluted and cursed because of our sinning. When we see daily that fog arising from the earth obscures the sky, know that we have polluted everything-- earth, air, and sky. Thus, the misfortunes we must endure in this world are not God's doings, as Micah says. God, who is Judge of the entire world, will not fail to carry out His office and torment us; but the blame rests squarely upon our shoulders.

Micah now adds a third point, namely "my words are good to those who walk the Path of Righteousness"; that is to say, if you find my words harsh, that shows how truly wicked you are. Nothing more clearly reveals the evil nature of men than when they become enraged because someone screams about their vices. This is a sure sign that they are no longer men, but devils. Why? Because it is God who reproaches them, for He is their Judge. Go, complain to Him if you wish; but remember Micah reaches a conclusion here that should be obvious to all of us, namely the Word of God is good to those who walk the Path of Righteousness. This being the case, what happens to us when we

109

are deprived of the Word? We are banished from the Kingdom of Heaven and become the heirs of Hell. Where is the power of God to save all believers? Is it not in the preaching of the Gospel, as Saint Paul says? The instant men are deprived of God's Word, they are banished from salvation and from all good things. We, even we ourselves, are condemnable. What do we have by our nature? Only death, having been cursed by God through Adam. But God has called us to be His own, by His Word. He reveals that He wishes to receive us in all mercy and to our Father, even though we are wretched creatures not even worth the dirt under our feet. Nevertheless, He wishes to make us companions of His angels. Indeed, He wishes to so unite us to our Lord, Jesus Christ, His only Son, that we make up one body with Him. He opens the way for us, through the remission of our sins, which He does not wish to punish but to forgive out of His infinite mercy. That is why the Word of God is good to those who walk the Path of Righteousness.

However we may be poor, wretched sinners, let us not stray from the Path of Righteousness. Let us condemn the evil within us and desire only to return to God and serve Him as He wishes. God will encourage us along the Path: True, we will slip, stumble, and fall; but God will always pick us up and support us. By His infinite bounty, He will accept our desire for the perfection of actual fact. But, on the contrary, if we rebel and stray from the Path, if we give free reign to backsliding, we will feel the harshness of God's Word, as have all the unbelievers there ever were. But does this harshness truly come from the Word of God? No! But this is a very difficult point to explain. It is better grasped by individuals meditating upon it in private. True we have need of preaching, but it is also necessary for each of us to privately meditate upon what was said.

This passage makes three major points. First, the Word of God is good to those who walk the Path of Righteousness. God is not only just and righteous but also kind and gracious. The Word reveals to us that we are not cursed and far from God; for the nature of the Word is to come to us, lead us to God, and make us His children. It does not demand payment for our sins, but forgives them, through the righteousness and innocence of our Lord, Jesus Christ, His only Son. The Lord reveals His love and paternal affection for us; He reveals there is only immeasurable sweetness in His Word; the Word is the true source of all our joy. Such is the everlasting nature of the Word. But who can come to know such delight? Only those who walk in all righteousness; that is to say, they do not rebel, resist, or raise up against God, but graciously receive His chastisement and reproaches. Do we wish to share of the joys of the Word? Then, what we must do is simple enough: Keep on the Path of Righteousness. True, as I have said, we will trip and even fall; but all that is really necessary is that we have an everlasting desire to follow God, cling to Him, and conform to His Goodwill. If we have this strong and deep desire, God will receive us as if we had done all kinds of good deeds; He will accept us ne'er-do-wells, as the expression goes, and delight in us; for we have looked to Him alone; He will sustain us and treat us as kindly as a father would his own children. I emphasize that when we humble ourselves before our celestial Father, dedicate our entire life to Him, and no longer [rebel] against Him, we will find only sweetness and kindness in the Word of God.

Secondly, we gain absolutely nothing if we try to fight against God's threats, by shutting up His servants. Rest assured these evils will befall upon us. If we reject the good things that God offers us, we will find His Word harsh and bitter. Indeed, it will be like a sword that stabs us right through the heart, sending us to eternal death. Today, there are many who become quite resentful when preachers reproach their faults. They believe themselves to be greatly wronged. To avenge themselves against the Word of God, they think it sufficient only to absent themselves from the churches, saying, "Ah, what the hell! Let these preachers shout and scream as much as they want. I won't set one foot in that place." But if they are asked, "Do you really and truly believe, poor wretches, that you will be excused this way?" "No, certainly not," they will reply. True, they may turn a deaf ear to what is said here; but not one word leaves my mouth that God will not register against them simply because they thought they could so flee from Him. The Sword of the Word of God, as I have just said strikes in a way completely different from physical swords. When Saint Paul says that vengeance is upon all haters of God and His Word, he does not mean that those who did not wish to listen will be excused; he means all such rebels will suffer whatever condemnation they have merited by despising the grace God wished to shed upon them through His Word. For this reason, he says, "Behold how the vengeance of God is upon the unbelievers," as if he were saying, "My friends, our Lords does not wish to include you in His sentence against the unbelievers because they rejected the grace He shed upon them. The instant God threatens you, tremble in your boots and humble yourselves before Him. Then His threats will become sweet delights to you.

Thirdly, we must come to humble ourselves under the mighty hand of God, to hate our sins, and to appreciate being reproached for our vices; for those who are self-complacent and rest on their laurels are near eternal death, no matter how secure they may feel. Each of us must repent, come to despise his own sins and vices, and change his whole life to conform to God, if we wish to be His children and avoid the vengeance that befalls upon all rebels and unbelievers.

Following this holy teaching, we prostrate ourselves before the face of our good God, acknowledging our sinfulness. May He touch us to the quick, that we be no longer possessed by our evil impulses, as we have been. May we return to Him in all humility. May we seek only to obey Him everywhere and in all matters. May we, in the name of Jesus Christ, our Lord, His son, be pardoned for all our offenses. May He cleanse us of all sin, that we may

113

share in His celestial glory.    Thus we say together: "All-
powerful God, celestial Father, etc."

* * *

My people have risen up against the enemy coming towards them. They strip the shirts right off the backs of those who think to walk in safety, returning from battle, etc. Micah 2

Micah's message is that the Jews have strayed from the Path of Righteousness. Yesterday, he said that God's Word is found sweet and gracious by all who walk this Path. Now he says the Jews do not walk in righteousness and have become thieves rather than behaving as God's people.

Micah says, "My people," not to praise them, but to emphasize their ingratitude. God has to call out to them; for they turned their backs on God, abandoned themselves to all evil, and so are far away from Him. Since they are totally possessed by Satan and given to pillage and extortion, God is no longer feared by them. They corrupted God's grace into lies and therefore the severe punishment they receive is purely their own fault. When the prophets wished to admonish the whole of man's life, they customarily singled out specific sins to exemplify his fallen state, as we have already seen. They, then, do not speak of all vices and sins, but of particular ones that serve to symbolize the lack of justice and righteousness, as Micah here refers to the murders and robberies that were committed in Judah. "Behold," he says, "you should live in peace, as brothers. You should live in harmony, as one people. The fact that you share a common ancestry should lead you to love one another. However, all you do is devour one another; you eat each other alive. The vicious torment and pain you inflict upon widows, orphans, and small children is more than they can endure. You have no more charity and compassion than savage beasts." By pointing to these specific crimes, Micah is showing that in general the people do not walk in fear of the Lord. It is no surprise, then, that they no longer can taste the bounty of God's Word; for their evil impulses have made them ill, turning the Word into a gigantic stomach ache for them. Do we wish to taste the salvific power of the Word? Yesterday, we were told how: we must walk in all righteousness, treat each other fairly and honestly, and wrong no one. Then, God will be our Father; He will speak to us with such sweetness that we will rejoice every time He opens His mouth. So if we are full of cruelty, violence, and malice towards one another, this is a sure sign we no longer fear God. Then, we will forever be on the run from the Word; God's majesty will be a terror to us; whenever He speaks, we will quake in our boots, and not without good reason. If, on the other hand, we obey God, live in peace and friendship, God will show how deeply He loves us, and His voice will be of immeasurable consolation to us.

Micah says that the People of God, or at least those who are supposed to be, are called to live in peace and harmony among themselves. However, he says, the terrible truth of the matter is that they live in total rebellion against God. So in that the Lord chose us to be His people, we must live in such brotherly love and harmony that we constitute one body. True, the Jews had a physical sign of God's great love for them; but the covenant made with Abraham meant that they must live in peace and harmony with one another if they truly wished to be Chosen People. Indeed, Micah says later that Jesus Christ came into the world to eliminate all strife and war, and to turn the weapons of war into instruments that can aid the neighbor. When the Chosen People torment and pillage one another, each treating the other as his enemy, they make it painfully obvious that they do not wish to live in peace with God. There is but one reason God reveals Himself to us: that we come to live in this harmonious unity I have just described. If we fight among ourselves, we resist God's grace; we chase away the peace He wished to bring us.

Think hard on this point, when you hear Micah say, "My people raise up as my enemy." If we are going to be the People of God, we must be gentle, we must live in peace with everyone, as Saint Paul says. Satan devotes all his efforts to deprive us of peace; he provides countless opportunities for us to take vengeance upon others. Nevertheless, we must not cease striving for such peace as is possible. Even David sought after peace and would wish us to do likewise. However peace may seem to elude us, however men may be inclined to evil and spitefulness, we must not give up our quest for peace. Otherwise, we will become enemies to one another, warmongers who have forgotten what it means to obey God.

He continues, saying, "They steal the shirts right off the backs of those who think to walk in safety." If men trust us, we must not deceive them. If we are a people at peace, if we face

117

no imminent danger, do we not sin so much the more if we harm our neighbors? True, bandits will not be excused for their crimes, when they hide out in some forest, so travelers will warn one another, "Don't take that road; it's too dangerous." God will not fail to condemn these bandits for their crimes. But suppose you live in a peaceful city, in lodgings where you believe to be quite safe. Suppose now that you are robbed. There is no doubt that this is a more heinous crime than what men commit in the heat of battle. This is what Micah means when he says although a man may believe himself safe in Judah, it is a land full of robbers. Will God tolerate such cruelty?

The harder God works to make a place safe for us, the harder we must work to maintain peace. Men will receive double punishment for committing violent crimes there. Why? Whenever a city becomes noted for preaching the Word of God, so much the more must it maintain law and order. Now, if a city has no real law and order, if it is worse than if it had nothing of God's truth, what can be said of it, except that it is the most wicked city on earth? That is what people say of us, as we well know. "O," they say, "people in Geneva think that they are the wisest in the world"--these are the Papists speaking now--for they wish to reform the whole world. They think they are angels. Well, just take a good, hard look at how they govern themselves! When you visit their shops, you find just as much deceit and trickery as ever. They rob you, strip you to the bone. And it's not just in terms of merchandising, but in all matters, even the slightest, that you cannot do business without someone trying to con you. If you take a cart-load of merchandise to Mollard, the market place, you will run into more con artists and crooked deals than if the place had never heard of God's name. If you go to the authorities for help, you will soon find that the city most renown for having the Gospel has probably the most crooked and corrupt judicial system anywhere." Pay attention to Micah! He is speaking to us when he says those who think to walk in safety are robbed, have the shirts stripped right off their backs.

Because God calls us to be His people, we must be peaceful and amiable; we must not defile ourselves; all forms of extortion must be abolished from our midst. When, I emphasize, we profess to be the People of God, we are so much the more condemnable if we are unjust, if there is the slightest degree whatsoever of violence, deceit, or thievery to be found among us. It is certain that Micah passes sentence upon us when he says, "My people steal the shirt off the backs of those who think to walk in safety." Note that he is not speaking here of larcenists that can be punished, as today petty larcenists go to the gallows, that is, the ones stupid enough to get caught. Justice will reign over them. He is speaking of the most cunning crooks, indeed the cruelest of all, who are so clever that there is no defense against them. They cut the throats of their victims and strip them to the bone. It would be foolish to try and capture them. Our Lord knows that the long arm of the law cannot reach and bring to justice these criminals who secretly cut the throats of men, who devour everything around them; but He assures us that they will be brought to account before Him, however they may have escaped earthly justice.

How foolish to think that the Word of God extends no further than the arm of human law can reach! There are outrageous fools who will say, "Look! Isn't it enough that I tend to my business and apply all my energies to correcting my faults, without having to listen to all these sermons screaming out against injustice? They completely overlook that, as I have just said, it is necessary for the Word to push us beyond our human capacity for justice. Take the case that you have never committed a crime and that the magistrate devotes his life to maintaining God's honor as well as justice and righteousness among ourselves. Still there is disorder everywhere; for larceny, robbery, extortion, rapine, loan sharking, perjury, cruelty, extortion, and fraudulency occur daily in our shops. Those who commit these crimes are worse than those who commit their crimes in secret. Yet these crimes remain unpunished by us, although they are detestable to God and condemned by His Word.

Take a long, hard look at our leaders, who are supposed to administer justice. They are no less reprehensible than anyone else. They simply do not recognize the larceny in people. They see nothing wrong in stealing a bolt of damask cloth or silk. Their eyes are totally blind to the realities of crime. But this does not mean that God is blind, that He will not restore order

120

when He knows it to be expedient. Micah is not speaking here of highwaymen who hide out in forests nor of larcenists always on the lookout to finger I don't know what all; he is speaking of the thieves who are among the most honorable of men; he begins with those who have the responsibility to maintain law and order. So let us remember that our Lord does not judge according to the ways of men, but judges and punishes in a way totally incomprehensible to us.

Micah speaks of widows, infants, and orphans. Cruel as some men can be, still they will spare them. When they do not, it is a sure sign that they have not one drop of humanity and have become savage beasts. Widows, orphans, and children are vulnerable and unable to support themselves; therefore, take care, lest you injure them. If you do evil to a man who can take care of himself, that is one thing. It is, of course, an offense against God Himself. But it is a completely different matter if you harm some poor, feeble wretch. God will be doubly offended and personally avenge the poor soul. That is why God is called the protector of widows and the tutor of orphans. They are the ones that get run over first, for they are totally destitute of all human aid. That is why our Lord takes them into His safekeeping. If we do not stand up for their rights, we will have to deal with God in the end. Think long and hard on this point; for on Judgment Day, God will make it clear that if we have oppressed widows and orphans, it is the same thing as if we injured His own person.

Micah shows how cruel men can be. Widows are thrown out of their well-loved homes. Now, of course, a man is better able to take care of himself. But what will become of a poor woman who is thrown out of her home? This will scare her to death, frighten her more than it would a man. May we pity and be merciful to all homeless women. Micah adds that the children have been stripped of God's glory, as if he were saying, "When I put creatures into the world, I provide for all their needs. All that men have comes not from themselves but from me. When one steals from children, it is as if they have stripped me personally." When a small child is left something by his father, it is as if God Himself personally dresses the child and provides for its needs. If you steal a child's inheritance, you do not strip him of what was given by men, but by God Himself. The Jews were so cruel that they wished to torment not only men but God as well. It is no surprise, then, that, as I have just said, the Word was bitter and sour to them; for how could they possibly taste the sweetness of the Word when they rebelled against God and salvation? On Judgment Day, they will find God to be their Judge, for they did not wish Him to be their Father.

For this reason, Micah says at the end, "Go! Get out of here. This land is no longer your home, for your wickedness has soiled and corrupted it." He is speaking against the vain pride and confidence of the Jews, who think they can abuse the name of God and yet not be deprived of His grace. Although they had been warned for a long time that they would be banished from Canaan, they refused to listen to the prophets. "All is well," they say. "Has not the land been promised to us by God." They think that God is obliged to them: "Did not God promise Abraham that this land would be for his people forever?" True, but they paid no attention to the condition God had attached to this promise: "I will bring you into this land, that you serve me." Since the Lord made it clear to them that they had no right to the land unless they served and honored him, was it not just and fair that they were banished from the land because they had soiled it with their evil shit?

Whenever the prophets admonished the Jews that they abused God by being puffed up with foolish pride, they always referred to this condition, namely that they could occupy the land only insofar as it was not polluted by them. For this reason, the land is named Rest, as it is called in the Psalm where our Lord swore a mighty oath: "They will not enter into my Rest, that is, into the land assigned to them, there to rest." The Jews, as I have said, knew well God's promise, but paid absolutely no attention to its stipulations. They said, "This land is the Rest of the Lord. He wishes us to remain here and never be expulsed." True, but they ignored Micah's admonition: "Behold that God dedicated this land to His honor. He wishes to be worshipped and served in all purity. You have done completely the opposite; for your evil deeds are the shit that soils this land, inflicted by your abominations. How can you claim it as your heritage when you will be banished from it for disobeying God? But they paid absolutely no attention to his warnings, just as all hypocrites abuse God's promises. Indeed, you will find them to be the Pillars of the Church; yet they truly despise God, mock His Word, and reject all His teachings. They hide under the cover of God's promises, feigning to abide by them. "Has not God elected us to be His people, promising to sustain us?" they will say. They overlook the conditions God has set up. That is why Micah said, "This is no more your land. You have marched under false banners. You have smashed to pieces God's promises, taking up one piece and disregarding the others." The people said, "But how can this truly come to pass? Behold, God said that He will reign in the midst of us, that we will be His dwelling place." Micah replied, "God had declared that He will banish you from this land He gave you, and for a very good reason."

If we wish to live in peace in this world, the very first thing we must do is to insure that our Lord reigns among us. When His is our Sovereign Prince dwelling in the midst of us, then we will remain safe and secure in the face of all the assaults and injuries that the world can inflict upon us. His protection will safeguard us against all the harm that might come our way from the machinations of men, indeed even from Satan himself. But if we are so unfortunate as to turn our backs on God and reject Him so that He no longer dwells among us, how can we expect to have any peace? Will not each and every creature raise up against us because we have rebelled against our Creator? We refuse to honor God, yet we wish creatures to serve us! We wish to fight against God, yet we wish to have peace with men! Don't think for one instant that God is going to go along with these ideas. Remember Micah's words: "Get out of here! This is no longer your home." They mean that because God put us in the world to serve Him and yet we have so dishonored Him, we are no longer worthy of the land that sustains us. What a lesson there is in this for us.

Micah continues, "You have soiled the earth, so it must be rid of you." When God gives us a place to live, the least we can do is to thank Him. Then, He will dedicate the land to our service. Is it not necessary, then, to dedicate the land to His glory? What really is the life of man? Must it not be dedicated to His honor and glory, since He created man to this end? When the earth is polluted by us, when our evil deeds are the shit that soil and infect it, have we not dishonored God? Do we really think that we can resist God and yet survive, that He will continue to protect us? If we wish to be at peace among ourselves and with other men, we must first be at peace with God. When we are in harmony with God, he will see to it that each eats under his vine or fig tree, as it says in another passage. On the contrary, if we rebel against God, all creatures will declare war on us. Even if we are not preyed upon by man nor beast, we will have a terrible fear deep within us, so we will never be able to truly rest or feel secure. Indeed, there is no way we could ever rest; for if we are not in harmony with God, we cannot be at peace with His creatures.

Because the Jews were so hardened and obstinate, they would tolerate none of Micah's admonitions. He says, "Behold, if a man walks in the spirit, telling tales, saying 'I will preach to you about the joys of wine, beer, and other strong drinks,' truly that man is the prophet of my people." He is really saying in effect, "I know well that you do not wish to hear what I have to say. And why is that? You wish to be flattered; you wish the prophet to bring you the good news that you will be able to live well. You certainly do not wish to hear that God is angry with you and is going to deprive you of your goods. I can well prophesy to you good news. But why? I am a true prophet of God; I speak only the truth. Those false prophets who indulge you in your vices, promising you whatsoever you desire, will serve only to obtain yet greater condemnation for you."

Micah's statement "if a man walking in spirit" has two levels of meaning. The word "spirit" signifies wind; that is, the man is sailing with the wind, going with the times. The expression "telling tales" signifies the deceitfulness of the false prophets, so it denotes lying. Micah is saying, then, "The kind of prophet you want is one who is full of deceit, lying to you, telling you what you want to hear." Now, since he is speaking of false prophets and since the word "spirit" is addressed to them, the expression "if a man walks in spirit" can also be taken to mean "if a man boasts of having revelations." If a man is not esteemed to be a prophet, whatever he says will be of no value, no matter how important it is. Nobody will pay any attention to his teachings, no matter how worthwhile they may be. But if a man claims to speak on God's authority, if he proclaims that God has sent him with a message to be preached, people immediately honor and venerate him. Since the very beginning of the world, the Devil has used God's name to deceive poor souls, blinding them, nourishing them in their sins, and leading them to perdition. So much the more must we be on our guard to discern who truly speaks in God's name and who deceives us. Today, we see how Papists use the high-sounding label of Church and also God's name to whitewash all their abominations. They shout from their rooftops that they are Christians totally devoted to serving God. They do these things to disguise all the abomination invented and advocated by the Pope, for neither he nor his followers will admit openly that they wish only to resist and vex God.

This kind of deceit Micah is referring to when he says, "If a man lies to you, claiming to be a prophet, that is the man you will have as your preacher, for he will promise you wine and beer." The Hebrew word used here signifies all intoxicating beverages, as if he were saying, "You do not wish to hear of God's wrath or to be reproached for your sins; you wish only to be flattered and so look for a false prophet who will say to you 'All is well, my friends. You are as angels. God now and forevermore loves you. He has done good things for you in the past and will do even more in the future.' That is the kind of lying prophet you want."

127

Pay attention to Micah's words. Although he spoke to the Jews of his time, this same vice reigns among us now more than ever. Hear how men grumble when the minister warns them of God's threats. See how they gnash when he mounts the pulpit to reproach them. Why? They wish God would leave them alone to wallow in their own shit. When He stabs them to the quick, they become quite insolent towards Him, which grieves Him more than anything else they could do in the world. When we provoke His wrath against us, it is as if we pierced Him right through the heart. Indeed, God Himself uses this very metaphor when He complains through Zachariah that when we sadden His Spirit, it is as if we landed dagger blows upon Him.

Think hard on this passage, for the vice Micah reproached reigns now more than ever. We just cannot tolerate God to be our Master Physician. Why? We wish to hear only sermons on the subject of good hops and wine; we wish to be told we can live as we please. But wish as we may, God demands that we fear and obey Him. He patiently bears the injuries we inflict upon Him. Yet we, in turn, refuse to tolerate Him for an instant. That is why we are continually seduced and deceived. Men so provoke God that He gives Satan free reign to blind them so they will not know the difference between true and false prophets. God permits, as I just said, Satan to so bandage men's eyes that they cannot tell good from evil. Nevertheless, this does not render them excusable, for they can never be deceived unless they so wish to be. All those who search for God with a pure heart will not be

128

frustrated. Although He will permit them to go astray for a time, He will return them to the Path of Righteousness. But if we are deceived by false prophets, this is a sure sign that we do not wish to be taught by God, that we prefer lies to the truth. Men do not wish to believe in God, I say, simply because they do not wish to know truth. Since they wish to quaff down only falsehoods, God permits them to become intoxicated on lies. So do not blame God if men have perverted the truth, and false doctrines reign everywhere. Do not think for a moment that God takes pleasure in the corruption of men. But know that they got their heart's desire, for they wished to rebel against God and reject everything he had ordained for their salvation. I emphasize that men are never deceived unless they wish to be; and they wish to be so blinded by Satan precisely because this puts them at ease with their vices. God did not put us in this world simply to conform to our appetites. On the contrary, we must conform to His holy will. However repulsive we may find God's will, He shall fulfill it and condemn us for our stubbornness. So when we hear the Word, when it is preached to us in its purity, let us humble ourselves, repent of our sins, and obey God.

Following this holy teaching, we prostrate ourselves before the face of our good God, acknowledging our sinfulness. We pray that He be pleased to touch us deeper than ever before. May we, fully recognizing our depravity, wish only to conform totally to Him. May the Holy Spirit free us of our carnal appetites, that

129

we may look forward to the joy God has promised us. May we no longer soil and infect the earth by our shit. May we, by our shining example, lure the unbelievers to knowledge of the truth that all together we become one with our Chief and Captain, Jesus Christ, Our Lord, triumphantly sharing in His immortal glory. To this end, may God sustain true and faithful ministers of His Word, etc.

All-powerful God, celestial Father, we cannot honestly and truthfully profit from your Word, save that we sacrifice ourselves and totally subjugate all our opinions and desire to you. Give us the grace that we permit ourselves to be so pierced by the Sword of the Word that we are dead unto ourselves but alive to you. May we not allow flattery and sweet words to lead us to damnation. May we endure all your reproaches, however harsh and bitter they may be. May they serve as medicine which purges and heals our inner, secret vices. May we, reformed into new creatures, glorify your name by our holy life and may we, then, be received into the celestial glory which has been won for us by the blood of your only Son, our Lord, Jesus Christ. Amen.

* * *

(9) Friday, November 28, 1550

I will reassemble all of Jacob; I will gather up the remnants of Israel and bring them together as the sheep of Bozrah, as the flock in its fold, etc. Micah 2

Some think this passage is intended to console the faithful; for their faith in God's bounty is not in vain, as the Lord watches over them more carefully than He does the rest of the world. Now, it is true that God never threatened the Jews without adding some consolation to show the situation was not totally hopeless. God does not so destroy that He fails to preserve a remnant for Himself. He so moderates the rigor of His punishments that the faithful may hope for salvation and know that they are not totally abandoned by Him. Micah says that God will gather together the remnants of Israel, to signify that in its destruction God will preserve those who invoke His name and return in repentance to Him. Indeed, many passages can be found throughout all the prophets that make this same point. However, when all things are considered, it is readily apparent that Micah here continues the theme we addressed yesterday; so the faithful are not yet consoled. That is reserved for the next chapter. Micah's preaching follows a definite pattern. This is why the next passage begins with "I said." That statement does not introduce a new sermon, but is part of his overall pattern. First he reproaches the Jews for their iniquities. Then he pronounces God's sentence upon them, emphasizing how enormous and

131

detestable their sins are in the eyes of God.  He always follows this same pattern, which is found in today's passage.

Hypocrites always strive to justify their evil; they are full of subterfuges to try and excuse themselves before God.  So Micah has to call them to account anew, as if he were saying, "You were not touched by what I said, so listen up again.  I am going to begin with those who are supposed to bring order out of chaos.  That is you, you princes and governors of Judah; you are the pigs who eat my people; you devour them like they are meat from a cooking pot; you crush and break their bones like one chops up a piece of meat too big for the pot.  How, then, can you become so vexed when God, who has chosen you to be His people, raises His hand against you as a warning that His punishment is about to befall you?"  Micah's message, then, is hardly one of consolation.  Indeed, the terms he uses here, "reasonable" and "gather up," have two meanings in Scripture.  Sometimes, our Lord says, "I will gather up that which has been dispersed," as if to say, "I will put everything back into good order."  But sometimes He says, "I will assemble together all the kingdoms from the four corners of the earth."  Why?  To destroy all of them.  He also says, "I will lodge you there as in a nest and then I will drive you from the nest," as we read in Jeremiah 19.  Our Lord, then, sometimes assembles people together in order to take vengeance on those who think they can hide from Him.  Why do people find it so strange that God will punish them?  Each tries to duck His blows,

132

each tries to escape from His hand. But God takes great pains to punish the wicked; He will turn them into a heap of rubble.

This idea is perhaps better expressed when Micah says that God will visit among His people, just as Zephaniah says that God will search Jerusalem with a lantern. Micah means that nothing can be so hidden that God cannot find it. God searches so diligently that there is no dwelling place, land, or cavern that He will not visit. Micah, without a doubt, warns that God will search everywhere. Jeremiah makes similar threats, regarding corporal punishment. True, God always grants some ray of hope to good and faithful people; but this does not mean they will not be punished along with all the others, as it is said they too will be exiled to Babylon. Micah warns that all of his people will be destroyed, even the remnant, just as it is said that the grape-gatherer will return to pick what he has missed from each vine. Our Lord will leave nothing standing among His people. But, as I have said, this does not mean that the Church is damned, lost forever; for our Lord does not leave His own without some hope of His mercy, which they will come to know at the proper time and place.

When Micah says next that the king will march before his people, it seems this is to their advantage; for when a king marches at the head of his people, it is a sign that all is well. But Micah means that the hopes the Jews have in their king will be frustrated; for he will lead the parade when they are led into captivity. As we saw in Jeremiah, the king was not treated in the customary manner. He stood trial in Riblah, where he had to watch as they cut the throats of his children. Then his eyes were poked out, he was chained up like a savage beast, and he had to endure every conceivable kind of insult and injury. That is what Micah is alluding to when he says, "You think this kingdom is indestructible, but your king will be the first to be shamed when God exercises His vengeance upon you." He also says, "The Lord will be on your head." This expression, a favorite one in Hebrew, meaning "He will be at your head" or "on your head," has both a positive and a negative connotation. We read in Joshua, "Whosoever departs from this house, his blood will be on his head." Also we read, "Whosoever enters this town, his blood will be on his head, and we will be guiltless." On the contrary, the men also say, "If we deceive her, the blood will be on our head, for we are liars." When Micah puts God at the head of his people, he does not mean that God will lead them, but that He will break and smash their heads in with great blows of His ax.

Now we have the main points of Micah's teaching. There is no doubt that he wishes to expose things to the core, reveal all that was heretofore hidden. This way, he can attack the vain glory of the hypocrites. They abuse God's grace by making it their shield; they hold to God's promises, but forget all the conditions he laid down. In brief, they wish to hold God obligated to themselves, yet they wish to do whatsoever they please. They wish God to be gentle and gracious to them, yet they incessantly provoke His wrath. Micah, then, wishes to

134

reverse matters, as if he were saying, "God's promise has been and still is that He will deliver His people. Having delivered you from the other nations of the earth, he promised to sustain you. But what conditions did he lay down for this?" In Deuteronomy 28, God says, "After you have been dispersed throughout the world, I will reassemble you into one nation. But that will happen only after I have punished you, carried out all my threats against you for all your sinning. When you come to fully acknowledge your sinfulness and become thoroughly displeased with yourselves, I, your God, will pardon you. Whereas you were dispersed to the four corners of the earth, you will now be gathered together as one people." Now the hypocrites see only one side of this promise, saying "Since God has chosen us above all the other peoples, will He not sustain us?" They overlook the conditions, which are that they fear, serve, and honor God. They do none of these things. Thus Micah says, "God will reassemble you in a novel fashion; it will be to light a fire in the midst of you." Pay attention to what our Lord has to say: "It seems that God will preserve a remnant from among you, but those left for the final picking shall be plucked from the vine." Also He says in Jeremiah, "Your remnant will be destroyed as well." The people, of course, were not all exiled at once; but eventually those left behind were also led into exile. See how Micah reproaches those who abuse God's promises, by hiding behind them, without true faith or repentance.

The same fate awaited the king, as we have already seen. His kingdom was intended to symbolize the Kingdom of our Lord, Jesus Christ, which contains all our happiness and salvation. Specific mention is made of the Kingdom, when the redemption and restoration of the people is spoken of: "God will raise up again a king from the House of David." But the following conditions are always attached to this promise: "Fear the Lord and confess your sins in the spirit of true repentance. Then God will take pity on you. In revealing Himself to be your God, He will send a Savior from the House of David. You will live under his rule." All the prophets make this claim. But now Micah, seeing the stubbornness of his people, says, "Your king will march before you, but it will be in shame. Do not look to the House of David until you have truly returned to your God."

Now that we have heard Micah's message, let us see what it teaches us about ourselves. We learn that God can gather us together in two radically diverse ways. One way is that we are brought together to be His flock. For this reason, He is often called our Shepherd. How deeply He loves us! How very much He cares for our salvation! Can He do any more for us than to stoop and humble Himself to be our Shepherd? Mankind is hardly an honorable state; yet God wishes nothing but to reveal His love and affection towards us. He cares for us in a way that transcends all human capacity for caring. That is why He is called our Shepherd. When He is gracious enough to lead us, we must subjugate ourselves totally to Him. Because we are all too

136

prone to go astray, we now have the most vigilant eye watching over us through our Lord, Jesus Christ. Paul says that He was sent from the Father to renew and put all things back in order in heaven and earth. If we are not united to the person of our Lord Jesus Christ, we have abandoned God, as we will find to our dismay. Know that it is Christ's office to unite us to God, His Father, so that we constitute one body, a true and perfect harmony with our God. That is how we come to share in all His bounty.

God, I emphasize, governs us such that the responsibility is solely on our shoulders if we are not consoled or do not profit from His bounty and teaching. God does not teach us just for a week or a month; He teaches us everyday, to more and more deepen our unity until we are in perfect harmony with Him. Yet we recoil at His very approach. We do not respond to His voice; we are not like sheep who go to the fold when the shepherd blows his whistle; we are like vicious, savage beasts; we do everything contrary to God. Christ's reproach to Jerusalem is also addressed to us: "Jerusalem, how often have I wished to gather you together as a hen gathers her brood under her wings, but you would not allow me!" When our Lord compares Himself to a hen and when we see that a hen takes such excellent care of her brood that she could do no more without bursting into pieces, can we ask anything more of God? We are savage beasts, as I have said. Despite all God's efforts to return us to Himself, we cannot be subdued, as we know from experience. Do we persevere in the teachings of our God? If we have had one or two years of teaching, all is forgotten in an instant. We see this ingratitude even in people who have tasted God's bounty for very long periods of time, only to turn their backs on Him in the end. When our Lord sees our ingratitude, when He cannot rejoice in us, when He cannot take us under His wings, is it not reasonable that He abandons us? What will it profit us if we are no longer under the protection of our God? It seems that we have escaped from God like children who run away from home. One grows up to become a robber, another a plunderer, another a murderer, and still another an adulterer. In the end, they all go to the executioner. Whenever the Devil so blinds men and gets them under his thumb, God forsakes them, gives them over to him to be their master. That is how men acquire such free reign to do evil.

For this reason, the other way God gathers us together is to totally destroy us. We are all too prone to stray from the fold; we seek after the pleasures and vanities of the world, which will lead us only to perdition. God warns that He will forcibly expel us from His flock, that His punishment will be so terrible that He will gather up and destroy each and every remnant of ourselves. So let us take care that He does not raise His hand to take such vengeance against us; let us take care that we are truly His sheep, truly his flock, that we docilely submit to His voice and come to Him as soon as He calls. Let there be only one flock and one Shepherd. God has guaranteed us that we will be

138

protected in His name. He specifically designated Christ as our Shepherd. Let the Lord lead us! If we truly obey Christ as our Shepherd, not a one of us will perish; God has given us all to Christ for our safekeeping. When He calls us, jump, come running to Him; for He so protects us that none will perish. When we obey the voice of Jesus Christ, His Son, we will have ample proof that God has elected us from the beginning of the world; we will also have total assurance that none of us will perish, as I have just said. Our salvation is completely guaranteed because He has promised it to us through His Gospels. Indeed, God will save the Church in a miraculous way that none can comprehend. Nevertheless, He will gather up and destroy all the wicked of the world. I emphasize this in order that we do not become deceived by our hypocrisy; men are always searching for subterfuges, thinking that they can fool God.

God has revealed that His Church will always be in the world. Even when earth and sky turn themselves upside down, He will sustain His people, as it is written "Whosoever invokes the name of the Lord will be saved." But do not think for an instant that this applies to you, unless you walk with a clean conscience, or unless, having gravely offended God, you return to Him, truly displeased with your sins, condemning your evil nature, asking only that it please God to receive you in all mercy. Remember what Saint Paul says, "Whosoever invokes the name of the Lord must segregate himself from all filth." If we wish to pray to God as we should, we must purge ourselves of all our hypocrisy, acknowledge our faults, and, trembling before God, beg pardon for our sins. Let us trust fully in His great bounty and mercy. Although all the world must be destroyed, He will preserve us. But if we are stubborn and persist in our evil ways, He will destroy us, obliterate us from the face of the earth. Whatsoever we thought to be eternal will be abolished. What, then, will become of the Church? It will continue to exist; but God will make it clear to us that we are not of His flock, being only savage beasts. Think long and hard on Micah's words. The people of Israel were God's flock; He had separated them from the other peoples to make them His eternal heirs. But Micah says that now they will become the flock of Bozrah. True, Bozrah, which was in Idumea, was a bestial place. However, Micah means to say that God will no longer govern them as His flock but as He so governs the pagan flocks; that is to say, they will be brought to their ruin.

Next, he says that the enemy, the breaker, will come to smash them, that he will enter and leave by the gate. This means that Jerusalem will be without protection, when God takes vengeance upon it. Isaiah and Jeremiah say that God will be the wall and the rampart of Jerusalem, that he will be its moat, munitions, and fortification. Perhaps more to the point is Isaiah 55, where it says that Jerusalem will be so well protected by God that His might and power will cover it top to bottom. The Lord reveals Himself to be the Protector of Jerusalem; He serves as its moat, rampart, wall, munitions, indeed as everything necessary for its defense. Isaiah also speaks of how the gates were left open even at night, for there was no danger, and incessantly oblations were brought to the Temple. But now Micah says that the enemy will enter from all directions, even though the gates are closed. Why? God ceased being the Protector of Jerusalem. As it says in one of the Psalms, if God does not protect the city, you will have to be on your toes night and day; for all its defenses and munitions are nothing, save that God dwells there as its King and Prince, saying, "This is the city I wish to sustain." So we would have no security, even if we had all the munitions in the world. Our safety rests solely in the fact that God dwells in our midst. So let us be of one heart and mind with God. May we never turn our backs upon Him.

The Bible tells us that the people were destroyed because they made golden calves. Why? Because to make an idol is to destroy the glory of God. Whereas God had been their Prince and King, now they are exposed to the Devil and all the dangers of the world. Do we wish God to be our Protector? Then, He must dwell in the midst of us in all His majesty. And He will dwell in the midst of us only if we are holy; for He is holy and so will not dwell in the midst of our shit. So let us be purified. Then, God will dwell among us and serve us well as our rampart, wall, and fortifications. On the contrary, if we are ungrateful, we will drive Him from our midst, and all the fortifications in the world would be of no avail to us. Nothing will stop the enemy from entering our city. What a sharp contrast that would

141

be to what Christ says in the tenth chapter of Saint John. There, he says that if we accept Him as our Protector Shepherd, we will live in peace, without any threat of danger. But Micah says that the breaker will enter and leave by the gate, as if to say that there will not be one entrance or exit where evil will not be found. Why? The people could not tolerate being governed by God. Let us not make that unfortunate mistake, for otherwise our salvation is completely assured. I emphasize that we must look upon the Lord as our true defense, munitions, and fortification. Lord Jesus Christ, our Shepherd, stands guard over each and every one of our doors. So let us never stray from His fold, no matter how hard the Devil tries to turn us from Him.

Remember, the reason why Micah says that the king will pass before the people and that God will be upon their heads is because their kingdom was intended to symbolize the Kingdom of our Lord, as I said earlier. But the Jews were unable to connect up the symbol with the reality. They thought of their kingdom's power purely in a physical sense. "Why do we need a Savior?" they asked. "We have God's promise to sustain the Kingdom of David." That is how they mocked Micah; for it seemed to them that God cannot contradict Himself, which in fact He never does. They refused to accept the fact that God's promises are to no avail except to those who accept Jesus Christ.

Today, we no longer have such symbols, as did the Patriarchs, who lived under the Law. Jesus Christ is revealed to us. Behold the King God has appointed over us. He sits in judgment upon the entire world; He takes possession of His Kingdom, through the Gospels. What must we do? Recognize the true nature of the Kingdom, namely that Christ governs by His teachings in order to bring us into harmony with God, His Father. When our Lord, Jesus Christ, has such authority over us that our carnal appetites no longer rage against Him, when we accept the Word of Life as our governor to subdue our impulses, when, I say, the Son of God is truly our Head, then we can claim to be subjects of His Kingdom and also boast He so well protected us that Satan cannot destroy us. But, on the contrary, if we make Christ into something inert, mute, as many do by glorifying themselves in His name and yet allowing him no real authority, do not think for an instant that we can call Him our King in this cheap, easy way. If He is truly our King, He always has dominion over us and must be obeyed. It is not enough to banter about the name Christian; we must demonstrate the truth of our claim that we are the People of God and that we wish to be governed by Him through the person of His only Son. If we do that, we will have a King to rule us. But, on the contrary, if we deny Him the authority to order our lives according to His will and teaching, we will be stripped of everything.

If we are truly Christians, we will tremble at these words that God will be on the head of those who were supposed to have Him as their Savior. Our Lord promised the Jews: "God will be your leader. He will continually govern you as a flock of sheep, indeed as small lambs." But now the Lord says that He will be at

143

the head of His people in order to crush their skulls. However, He does not wish to cruelly exploit us; He does not wish to rule us as a sadistic and fierce tyrant. When we conform to Him, His hand will sustain us. May the Lord be our Shepherd and we be His sheep; He will reveal Himself to be our Father if we are willing to be His children. Because He cares so deeply for us, He is not content merely to be named Father but also wishes to be called Mother, for there is no limit to His caring love for us. It is certain, then, that we cannot escape Micah's threat, if we turn our backs on God's paternal love.

Micah's reproach is not only directed against the Jews but against ourselves as well, for we have these same vices rooted deep in our nature. We will not confess our faults unless forced to do so. We, like all men, are basically arrogant; we take great pride in ourselves and refuse to believe that we will ever have to appear before God to answer our sins. When God calls us to repentance, we search for all sorts of foolish excuses to exempt ourselves from His judgment. Pay close attention, then, to the situation Micah is addressing here; above all, note carefully what he has to say to those in charge of the people: "You, princes of Israel, and you, governors of the House of Jacob, is it not your responsibility to know right from wrong?" Here Micah is repeating himself, for he has already reproached their exploitation of the people. Once should have proved sufficient. Could God govern us any better than by sending His prophets to reveal His will? Are we so hardened that we cannot

144

be moved by one admonition alone?  Earlier, we heard him reproach the wicked conduct of the leaders.  That is why he now adds, "I have said," as if to say, "Men are so evil and hardened that the very instant God reproaches them for their own benefit, they rise up against Him and wish to contest matters, as if they wished to enter into a suit against Him."  When we enter into a litigation against a mortal man, it causes us great pain and anxiety when we stop to realize that it is men such as ourselves who are responsible for administering justice, though we have a good case.  Yet, when God summons us to plead His cases against us, we all seem to have ice water in our veins, as the expression goes. We know well that we are so insolent and audacious that it seems we are ready to overthrow His Throne.  Now, as I have said, this gains us absolutely nothing.  When those whom God has put in positions of great power and authority rebel against Him, they are so much the more condemnable because they have abused their high calling.  That is why Micah reminds the leaders that it is their responsibility to know right from wrong and warns them that God will slap them down hard if they do not carry out their office faithfully.

Following this holy teaching, we prostrate ourselves before the face of our good God, acknowledging our sinfulness.  May He be pleased to so touch us that we come to Him to confess our sins, with a truly repentant heart, indeed without any feigning on our part.  May we be so displeased with ourselves, that this repentance serve to unite us to Him throughout the whole of our

145

lives.  May He so subdue our carnal appetites that nothing will block us from becoming one with our Lord, Jesus Christ, His Son. May we share in the eternal kingdom which He has prepared for us. May we so dedicate ourselves to God, His Father, that we may rejoice in all the glory to which He has called us.  May He not only shed this grace on us but upon all the peoples and nations of the earth, etc.

* * *

(10) Saturday, November 29, 1550

I said, "Hear me, you princes of Jacob, and you governors of
the House of Israel. Is it not your responsibility to know right
from wrong, you who hate goodness and love evil?" etc. Micah 3

Yesterday, we heard Micah's reproach against the leaders of
the people. Their high calling had blinded them with pride.
They refused to punish the wicked; for they believed themselves
to be above all laws and rules, since they were in positions of
such high authority. We see this happen every day. But if there
is an illness, then there is also a remedy. Men of great power
and position would willingly put themselves on a plane above God
if they could; they have no idea what it means to be subjugated
to Him; they have no desire whatsoever to conform to God's will.
So much the more harshly, then, must God chastise their pride and
arrogance. Micah speaks to them to try and get them to correct
this fault. When leaders fail to correct their own faults, evil
is doubled in the world. Why? People look to them as examples.
When a lowly man lives a wicked and dissolute life, ah well, so
what? Nobody cares, nobody finds him particularly inspirational
anyway. But when the leaders are wicked, many will emulate them
and sincerely believe that living in sin is truly the way to
live. In brief, the way leaders live changes the whole life of
the community, either for the better or for the worse. A
community may have all sorts of laws; but if the leaders are
wicked, these laws are all in vain, absolutely useless, just so
much waste paper. On the other hand, there are leaders who rule

147

in all righteousness. Although they have no laws, ordinances, or statutes, their lives serve their community well. Each member will wish to emulate and pay heed to their leaders, who have so ordered their lives in obedience to God's will. At the very least, there will be some semblance of decency in this community. Should no examples such as this be very carefully weighed in the minds of all who aspire to be leaders? Leaders need to study and go to school, just like everyone else. Micah's teaching is addressed to all the people; he reproaches vices in general, without making exceptions for persons. Nevertheless, it is necessary that the leaders be singled out and specially reproached by the Word of God, since their scandalous lives have a far more drastic effect upon the people. Thus Micah first reproaches the people, then focuses specifically upon the leaders.

Micah does not mince words with the leaders: "It is your responsibility to know right from wrong. Yet you hate good and love evil." He could not have said worse of the leaders of Israel; for it is the height of all iniquity when a man loves evil and hates goodness. He spared them nothing; his words were well chosen, very relevant to his times. As we have seen, he preached during the reign of Hezekiah, who was as good a king as had ever reigned in Judah; he was like an angel of God; he took great pains to insure that God was served in all purity; he purged the land of all the idolatry and superstition that heretofore reigned there; he was the rock upon which the

148

salvation of his people was grounded; he was a place of refuge in a time of storm; when the winds, rain, and thunder came, the faithful could find shelter under his protection; fear of God reigned everywhere because of him. Nevertheless, Micah says to his counsellors, "You who are supposed to show the way to others, you are the damnation and destruction of the people. You hate goodness and love evil." He had to repeat himself again and again, for things were not going well. But that was not the king's fault; he was helpless to stem the rising tide of evil, even though he did all that he could. Evil men are like a violent torrent of water or a large river whose current is so powerful that no one can stop it. If you try to dam it up, so much the greater becomes its fury to destroy all that is in its way; it will uproot trees, houses, everything. This fast-flowing river is content merely to follow its course, evil men continue to grow in power. There is absolutely no stopping them. Nothing in all the world can compare with man's capacity for violence.

So, then, we see how necessary it is for each and every one of us to obey and fear God; for otherwise, all the laws and statutes in the world would not serve to maintain order among us. Our princes and magistrates should be very diligent in their high calling. This is not to say they have been neglectful of their duties but that they must work far harder than they have been. It is no surprise that chaos reigns among us, indeed throughout all the world; for where is the zeal and care of the princes,

149

magistrates, and other public officials to see to it that God is served? How can we expect them to maintain any real degree of law and order, when God's honor is the very last thing on their list of priorities? Men are prone to do evil, so there is no reason for us to become shocked and upset when we see things go badly. Let us cry out to God and pray He deliver us from our chaos.

As I have said, it is the height of all iniquity when men love and hate goodness. These things are one and the same: If you love evil, it is necessary that you hate goodness. When the Devil gains control over us, we lose our capacity to distinguish good from evil; he confuses us, making us desire what God has condemned and quite happy to provoke His wrath. Whenever men abandon themselves to evil, it is inevitable that they become prey to such confused thinking. True, the symptoms may not appear at once; but in the end, they will all lose their minds, as we know from experience. Some men are content to let others walk in righteousness while they themselves give free rein to their evil impulses. True, for a time, these men will at least give the appearance of knowing right from wrong; but in the end, they too will fall prey to such confused thinking.

Micah says that the root of all such confusion and iniquity is the fact that those in power are such greedy guts. He says that they strip the people to the bone and eat their flesh, that they crush and chop up their bones to make them ready for the cooking pot. Although he accuses them of having committed the most horrible atrocities, he does not mean they actually carried out such acts. He speaks the way he does, because men always seek to excuse their iniquities and justify their evil actions by hiding them behind a facade of righteousness. Micah forewarns them how wicked they could really become, in order to cut through their facade of innocence and to confuse, embarrass, and shame them right on the spot. Note that he speaks in terms of figures, as they are called, also in order to forewarn us of our sins and to remove the bandages from our eyes so we no long measure ourselves according to our own standards, as we are prone to do.

Here is a passage worthy of careful consideration. Men consider their sins a trifling matter, whereas they are an abomination before God. Avarice is as prized as it should be condemned; it always provides men such a convenient facade behind which to hide their wickedness. Take the case of a man obsessed with greed, one who is in truth a loan shark, a bandit who pillages from one end of the land to the other. Many will say of him, "What a righteous man he is! He is an excellent worker who knows his business and really pushes himself; he is an excellent provider and takes very good care of his family." In brief, all the virtues will be attributed to avarice, all possible praise will be heaped upon it, in order to make appear as righteous this vice God finds so detestable. Saint Paul says, "Avarice is the root of all evil." Examine avarice carefully and you will find that there is not one evil it does not bring with itself. When a man is possessed by avarice, there is neither loyalty nor honor

151

in him; all he cares about is getting what he wants; how does not matter; he will stoop to all sorts of cruel and inhumane behavior; he will resort to perjury, treason, loan sharking, rapine, and even murder, if he believes these methods will satisfy his lust. True, not every avaricious soul resorts to such ruthless methods, but the vast majority are willing to. That is why Saint Paul says that the root of all evil is avarice.

It is no surprise, then, that our Lord speaks harshly against the leaders of the people: "Who are you who devour my people, oppress them by pillage and extortion? You strip them to the bone and eat their flesh. You smash and chop up their bones like one prepares meat for the cooking pot." Our Lord speaks this way in order that men no longer use their hypocrisy as a shield to hide behind, as they are wont to do. Our Lord says as much in His Law: "You will not bear false witness." He also forbids lying, emphasizing that it amounts to the same thing as bearing false witness, as if to say, "It may seem to you that lying is a small matter, but I say you are perjurers when you do so." Is not lewdness condemned by God? Yes, but men are so given to evil that they think it is merely a minor vice and more or less pardonable. But the Lord says, "Guard against lewdness as you would against adultery, as you would against an abomination that horrifies you." He says the same of all other vices.

Remember, if we oppress our neighbors, if we steal their sustenance, if we wrong or injure anyone in any way, it amounts

152

to the same thing as if we were to have broken up God Himself, chopped up His own bones, and eaten them. That is the sentence God has pronounced against us. So we must guard against flattering ourselves; we must stick to what God has revealed and stop relying upon our own judgments, saying, "O, such-and-such seems like a very good idea to me"; we must not deceive ourselves into thinking that God will be the least impressed with our false facades and excuses; we must not abuse God's patience by assuming His reluctance to punish us means He will not take vengeance upon our hypocrisy; we will all be brought to account in the end; there is no way of escaping God's judgment. In Micah's time, people put on all sorts of airs, just as we do today. The king's counsellors were considered to be very righteous men who governed justly. But Micah sharply reproached them because they were committing all sorts of atrocities in the name of justice. If we do not wish the Lord to pass sentence likewise against us today, we must learn to discern good from evil and stop trying to excuse our sins by saying that we are merely doing what everyone else does. We must live by the principle of natural equity; that is, we must treat others as we would have them treat us. This rule holds for everyone, without exception. Micah, however, focuses specifically upon the king's counsellors because nothing is more detestable to God than when the administration of justice becomes the excuse to oppress the poor by devouring their flesh to the bone and then crushing up their bones for the cooking pot.

153

Micah adds yet another warning, saying, "They will cry out to God, but He will not hear them. He will hide His face from them, for they have not ceased to do evil." What a horrible threat! What refuge do men have in their time of great need, save to pray that God sheds His mercy upon them? When the greatest possible misfortunes befall us, our sole consolation is that we can go to God and invoke His name. That, I emphasize, is the only remedy for all our ills. Micah's threat is the worst that could ever befall us: God rejects us, no longer hears our prayers. Even if we had everything we wanted, still we would feel quite unhappy and lost if we could not go to God because He has turned His back upon us.

Remember, Micah's main point is that we must not fashion God according to our whims and rest content with what seems good according to our standards. As I have said, it never fails that we will take to be a virtue what is in point of fact an abomination in the eyes of God. However men may honor and prize all forms of extortion, God will turn a deaf ear to the prayers of those who harm their neighbors. I emphasize that our Lord finds extremely detestable all crimes committed against the poor. Solomon said much the same thing as Micah: "Those who have turned a deaf ear to the poor and cry out to God in their time of need will find God will turn an equally deaf ear to them." Saint James says, "Judgment without mercy to those who have not been merciful." We will be treated as we have so treated our neighbors. True, God will never be cruel with us. Nevertheless, the cruelties we have inflicted upon others will not equal even a hundredth part of the punishment God will land on us. He will submit us to torments far more horrible than we could ever inflict upon our neighbors.

If we wish God to be merciful to us in our time of affliction; then we must help our neighbors in their time of troubles. Those who refuse to aid their neighbors are already condemned. Those who treat their neighbors cruelly will receive double punishment. Though we may well view ourselves as men of iron or steel, just stop and think how deeply crushed and let down we will feel when God refuses to condescend to hear our cries, because we refused to aid our neighbors. What, then, must we do? Each must attend to the needs of his neighbors, so that mutual charity and tender love reigns among us. Remember, we are called human, from which the word humanity comes. So let us not treat each other cruelly, like savage beasts; let us live up to our good name!

It may seem strange that Micah says God will not hear those who cry out to him. How is it possible God can ignore men when they speak to Him? The Bible says that each time a sinner cries out, God will forgive him. It also says that God never rejects the prayers of men. How is it possible, then, that He turns a deaf ear to those who invoke His name? This seems to flatly contradict the promise I just mentioned that wherever and whenever a sinner cries out, God will hear him. But note carefully that men do not always invoke God in truth. That is why it says in one of the Psalms that God is with those who invoke His name in truth. But what exactly is meant here by the word "truth"? Many men cry out to God out of their own despair and impatience rather than out of faith and repentance. Those are the ones whom God rejects, for they cry out and yet know not to whom. Take the case of Esau. He cried out bitterly, ranted and railed when he realized he had been stripped of his inheritance. But what good did that do him? His tears were in vain, as Micah says that God turns a deaf ear to those who cry out as such, because they have no real faith in His great bounty, are unwilling to be His children, indeed refuse to do anything of the like. God will not hear them no matter how hard they cry out for His help; for they are motivated solely by their own pain and torment, nothing else. That, I emphasize, is the key point to grasp here.

Note, then, that God does not always give us the grace to invoke His name as is fitting, though unbearable agony and suffering befall us. God gives only His elect the special gift that they may call Him Father when their mouths are open and their hearts are ready to pray. However they may have failed, however many sins they may have committed against Him, His mercy will never fail them. But there is such great stubbornness and hardness in some men that they refuse to return to God, no matter how hard He works on them through His Spirit. So let us take care, lest we become so incorrigible that God cannot succeed with us; for then He will give us over to Satan and turn a deaf ear to our prayers, no matter how loud we scream. Think long and hard about God's vengeance upon the downtrodden whom He refuses to console, because they refused to come to Him in true faith and repentance, as we must do. God gives men the power to do good in order that they aid one another. All those who are compassionate and charitable towards their brothers will find God to be likewise. But if we are cruel and inhumane to one another, we will feel the wrath of God upon us; He will make it very clear that we are not worthy to be His children.

After Micah had spoken to the magistrates, he turned to the prophets, for they are like the two eyes of the body. When either a magistrate, who is charged with governing the people and administering justice, or a prophet, who is responsible for their education, fails, the body is one-eyed. When both fail, the body is totally blind. If the magistrates are perverse and if the prophets are like muzzled watchdogs who refuse to attack the unrighteous, if they cunningly disguise all vices as virtues, perverting God's teaching to make it pleasing to men, then the whole body is blind; all the people will go to Hell. Why? They, I have just said, are the two eyes that guide the body. That is why Micah focuses upon these two groups, turning to the prophets after the magistrates: "You who are supposed to maintain law and order, and you who are supposed to uphold the true religion, reproach vices, and be a shining example to others, both of you have taken to flattering the wicked and have consented to all their iniquities. I will not spare you on the Day of Wrath; I will make you objects of scorn and contempt before all men on earth."

Look at what great grace God has shed upon us, that we be taught faithfully, that we have His Word to lead us and keep us on the Path of Righteousness. This is indeed a blessing that surmounts all others. If we refuse to profit from it, so much the greater will our condemnation be. But if we graciously receive our Lord's remonstrances to correct our faults, He will continue to instruct us. Then, the magistrates will no longer be obsessed by greed, acting purely on their own self-interest, gnawing on this man here, nibbling on that man there. They will faithfully carry out their calling, maintaining law and order among us. When things run this smoothly, I say, we will know well that God truly cares for us. Indeed, it is as if He gave each of us two strong bodyguards to ward off all evil. But, as I have said, if the magistrates default, the body is one-eyed. If the prophets, who are supposed to bear the Word of God, pervert His teaching, the body is totally blind.

Micah says of the false prophets, "They bite men with their teeth." These men were quite cruel. Then he adds, "They promise peace." But what peace? By flattering the wicked, they deaden them to their iniquities, so they no longer hear God's threats. They say, "Look! Don't get so hot under the collar! Everything is going to be all right. Sure, you have heard someone prophesy that you will be destroyed. But don't believe that rubbish. Everything is going to be just fine, better than you ever hoped."

Now that is only if they are given something to eat or drink. If you do not, says Micah, then they threaten you. He is saying in effect, "They are nothing but mercenaries who sponge off others to fill their own bellies. As long as you feed them enough, they will sell you the most beautiful fortunes you could ask for. A man may be a larcenist, murderer, pirate, robber; it does not matter to them; they will tell him, "You are the most righteous man in the world! Why, you are almost an angel!" It does not matter a bit to them that all the world is numbed to its iniquities. But if a man refused to pay up, then they declared what translates as a "holy war" against him.

Indeed, these false prophets said it was a "holy war" whenever they persecuted God's servants, or the infidels, for that matter. Their pretext for war was that they had to maintain their sanctity, which in point of fact denoted a tyranny far crueller than could be found among the pagans. Today, the Papists do the exact same thing. If the Pope declares war against the Turks, then it is a holy war, even though it is a defense of a tyranny far worse than that of the Turks. What the false prophets did when someone refused to pay up is exactly what the Pope does today. Contradict him, and the Papists will warn you, "Be on your Guard! He has declared a holy war against you." His major weapons are excommunications, major and minor, He will fume against poor souls, threatening to send them to the deepest part of Hell, which he truly believes he can do. But we know what deceit all this is, how his threats are merely children's

159

horror stories.    Let us examine more specifically Micah's reproach to the seducers of his day.

His main objection is that they promote peace, whereas God's wrath is everywhere kindled.  We saw in Jeremiah how the true prophets always had to struggle against the vain expectation the false ones created in the people by saying, "True, you have been seriously threatened by Isaiah, Jeremiah, and others.  But don't let that bother you.  Their threats amount to nothing.  Have we not God's promise to dwell among us?  Do you think that He will allow the pagans, infidels, these uncircumcised dogs to vanquish us?  Does it make any sense to assume God will not keep His promises?"  That is how the wicked use God's promise to their own advantage.  If there were no false prophets, men are so vain and desirous of flattery that they would still deceive themselves. False prophets, then, are a major problem because they serve to worsen this situation by helping men to become more deeply corrupt and to deceive themselves.  It is very difficult to hold men to the purity of God's teaching.  After they have been shown the path to salvation, the slightest occasion may lead them to stray from this path, as our nature is far more inclined to evil than to good.  When seducers are present to lead others into temptation, evil continues to multiply.  False prophets are like adding thirst to drunkenness.  Moses said, "Take care that you tremble at God's threats.  Watch out for the iniquitous ones who will try to deceive you, saying that it is nothing to worry about when God rages against us.  Don't be seduced by them.

160

Throw them out, for they are instruments of the Devil. If you listen to them, it will be to add thirst to drunkenness"; that is to say, God's wrath will be so much the more inflamed. His metaphor is well chosen. Those who drink heavily will down wine until they vomit. Then, when it seems they can hold no more, they will come up with some novel way to down even more. They will do the meanest things that are too shameful to mention. The wine entices them to swallow more, although they are far beyond their limit, as if they are truly sorry they could not drink until they burst themselves. Moses uses this metaphor to show that those who promise peace when the wrath of God is at hand serve only to kindle it so much the more.

Micah makes two accusations against the false prophets. On one hand, he says, "You promise peace. But to whom? To those who bring you something. They could be dangerous men who think nothing of cutting the throats of helpless passers-by in the woods, provided they get their share of the booty. Yet you will lie and say to them, 'You are righteous men.' That is, of course, only if they grease your palm with enough gold." On the other, he says that they become so enraged with those who will not pay that they actually declare war on them and try to kill them. True, the Word of God brings peace, but it is not at all like that promised by the false prophets. In coming into the world, our Lord, Jesus Christ, brought us to peace to be reconciled with God, His Father. He promised the faithful that He will never turn His back on them, that they will have unlimited access to Him. Saint Paul says that if we are not rebellious and stubborn, we will have peace with God. If we subjugate ourselves to God, we will be reconciled to God. Then, all our anxieties will be alleviated by virtue of our total and complete trust in Him.

On the contrary, what is the peace Micah chastises? It is when men enjoy only a false sense of security because they deceive themselves into believing that they are tucked safely away far beyond the reach of God; it is when they numb themselves to their vices; it is when they believe all will go well for them, as if they had a pact with the dead to intervene on their behalf with God. This is a very dangerous peace.

Therefore, if we wish to feel truly secure, we must open ourselves and embrace the peace borne by the Word of God. If we reject this peace, we will be overwhelmed by deep-seated anxiety. Even if we had all we could ever desire in this world, still we would have not peace of mind. If a man has all that he could ever hope for but is cursed by God, all the good things he has will be turned into evil. What once was good will now serves only to torment and destroy him.

So then, what should we do? We must overcome our needs for others to flatter us. Men gain absolutely nothing by deceiving themselves into believing they are like angels in order to numb themselves to the reality of their own evil. Nothing will get us into more trouble than this. All it serves to do is kindle God's wrath so much the more against us and make Him land on our heads all the more quickly. If we wish to know true peace, we must return to God at once. If we are truly penitent and displeased with our sins, we will be pardoned in the name of our Lord, Jesus Christ, and we will share and rejoice in the peace He promises us in the Kingdom of Heaven.

Following this holy teaching, we prostrate ourselves before the face of our good God, acknowledging our sinfulness. May it please Him to so open our eyes that we no longer wish to be flattered by vain promises that numb us to our vices. May we come to tremble at all His threats. May they displease us in ourselves and serve to correct our vices. May our Lord, Jesus Christ, pardon us and take mercy on us to cleanse us of all the evils we are subjected to in our present life. May He shed this grace not only on us but upon all the peoples and nations of the earth, etc.

All-powerful God, celestial Father, since you wish your justice to shine through magistrates and princes, may you now so bless those empowered over us that they rule in your name. May, in this way, we have a sign to witness that not only do you favor us and watch over us but that you have taken our salvation to heart. May your Word shine so brilliantly upon us that it will never be eclipsed by avarice and chaos. May its pure light guide us along the path you have ordained for our salvation, until, having reached the Kingdom of Heaven, we share in our eternal heritage, won for us by the blood of your only Son, our Lord, Jesus Christ. Amen.

* * *

The Lord God says, concerning the prophets who seduce my people, bite with their teeth, cry peace, and declare war against those who put nothing in their mouths, "Night will befall you so you will have no visions, darkness will befall you so you will not divine. The sun will go down on the prophets; the day will be very dark for them, etc." Micah 3

We have seen that Micah reproached the false prophets because they did not call the people to repentance but instead flattered them, numbing them to their own sinfulness. That is how they were able to promise peace and prosperity. True, it was concluded that we are charged by God to proclaim peace, but this peace means that we return to God and live in the spirit of mutual charity. Why then, are there false prophets who promise peace to those who war against God? Micah's answer is that it is avarice which leads the false prophets to deceive men into believing that everything will be just fine, that they are like angels, whereas the truth is these men are attempting to sanctify their own filthy shit. Money and the belly: What other reasons could there possibly be for perverting God's teaching to please others? Saint Paul compares those who pervert the Word to con artists who falsely advertise their wares to deceive customers. But the Word of God, I emphasize, is not to be treated as a commodity to be bought and sold. That is why Micah chastises the false prophets because they promised peace, or anything else one

164

might want, as long as they were well paid but declared war instantly against those who refused to pay through the nose.

When God punishes the false prophets, night will befall them, the sun will no longer shine on them, and they will be as blind men. Micah says they will "cover their lips"; that is, they will hide their faces in shame. Why? No longer will they be able to prophesy in the name of God. What a horrible thing it is to falsify God's Word. It is a treasure so precious that it can be handled only with the greatest reverence. When men pervert the truth into lies, that is a sacrilegious act God will not tolerate. Furthermore, if we consider to what end God ordained His Word and how He intends it to be used, it is not at all strange that He will land such terrible punishment upon those who falsify it; it is a matter of God reigning over us and saving our souls. The two things we must prize above all else are the glory of God and then our own salvation. That is the central message of the teaching God sends down to us. When, then, His teaching is falsified, this amounts to destroying God's glory and to sending poor souls straight to Hell. Do not be surprised, then, that our Lord is so deeply angered when we do not follow His Word as He commands. True, Scripture oftentimes uses the words night and darkness to signify any kind of calamity; but Micah is being more specific here: He is warning that God will so blind the false prophets, who have abused their office, that they will be stripped of all their special powers. Men will see only ignorance and brutality in them. He focuses in detail upon their punishment, by contrasting opposite things: night versus vision, darkness versus divination. "Their eyes," he says, "will be confused." The reason is that prophets are called seers in Scripture, and their prophesies are called visions. Micah, on the contrary, says that their eyes will no longer see a wink, that they will no longer have visions, that God will so bandage their eyes that they can no longer exercise their office.

This punishment, as I have said, makes it perfectly clear that our Lord will not tolerate His Word to be falsified; for He resorts to extremely harsh and severe punishment when He blinds men and assigns them to the ranks of the reprobate. Our Lord does not play favorites with those who He has called to bear His Word. If they do not diligently attend to their calling, He will throw them away and severely punish them to serve as an example to all preachers that they must uphold the pure truth of His teaching. The Devil, from time immemorial, has used false prophesy to seduce poor wretches. Today, the Pope is a prime example of this. His success in maintaining his tyranny, abominations, and the unquestioning obedience of his subjects is due to the fact that he has seduced the poor world by his claims that he is the true Head of the Church, that his bishops are prelates ordained by God, and that this holy order is not founded upon men but constitutes the true Apostolic line. Men are easily led astray by very righteous-sounding titles. So let us carefully bear in mind that when Micah says God will blind the false prophets, he is not threatening the pagans or those without any calling but those who enjoy positions of great power and authority in the Church.

It is not enough that a man hold high office; he must diligently carry out all the responsibilities that go with it. In brief, there are two requisites for those who wish to be heard by others: The first is that they are called by God; the second is that they faithfully discharge their duties, serving God in all purity and earnestness. If a man meddles in the affairs of others without any calling, he shows his recklessness. Saint Paul, when he wished others to accept his teachings, stated he was ordained an Apostle on God's authority. A man must be totally grounded in God's teaching, in order to have the authority to speak. Furthermore, it is not enough to have this calling, for God has called many who do exactly the opposite of what their office requires. So that we are not seduced willingly by these men, Micah says that God will blind those who were heretofore prophets. Do not think that this is an uncommon problem that we need not be on the lookout for; false prophets always attack the true ones. Jeremiah had great difficulty with the false prophets of his time. They said, "Come, we can easily gain the upper hand over Jeremiah. He is just one man. Are we not the Church and the clergy that God ordained? Are we not the prelates that God ordained to preside over His cult?" The Pope uses the same strategy against us today. But did Jeremiah shut up? No! Will we? No! For we are confident that God will blind all false prophets so the world will no longer heed them.

167

In sum, the second verse of today's passage teaches us two important lessons. The first is that we must guard against all superstitions, out of fear that God will assign us to the ranks of the reprobate for having falsified His teaching. Bearing this firmly in mind, we will not be so easily seduced.

The second is that our faith will be so much the more strengthened to the extent we can be sure the minister preaches the pure Word of God, what he has received from the Master, and not what he has invented out of his own imagination.

Micah says that "they will be shamed, for there will be no answer from God" to emphasize that all teaching must be sanctioned by God; that is, preachers must be thoroughly grounded in the Word. Otherwise, we must throw them out, turn a deaf ear to them. This verse is just as important as the preceding; it makes quite clear that our Lord does not wish our faith to be shaken, that He does not wish us to be as a flower blown about by the wind; rather, He wants us to be like a rock that holds out against all winds and storms; He wants our faith to stand strong and firm against all Satan's temptations. When all the forces of Hell press upon us, our faith must remain invincible. But how is that possible, save it be founded on God's truth? If our faith is founded upon men, it will be only lies and vanity; we will be in constant doubt. So heed Micah's warning that "they will be shamed when they receive no answer from God," as if he were saying, "There is no reason why we should hold with a teaching, save that God has so spoken and therefore sanctioned what men

bring us. If that is not the case, their teaching is rubbish."
All teachings conceived of by men must be thrown out; God did not
give men the authority to speak for themselves. Preachers must
be guided by God alone; they must be able to profess truthfully,
"It is God who speaks through my mouth." Anything less than that
is, as I have said, rubbish.

Many glorify themselves by claiming to speak in God's name,
but that is not what they are really up to. Today, the Pope
refuses to admit that his teachings are founded on men; quite the
contrary, he will claim that everything he says comes from the
Holy Spirit. Well, just let him try and prove it! He says
flatly that all his rulings are celestial revelations; but if you
ask for proof of this, he can give none. On our end of it, we
must continually examine ourselves to make sure that our
teachings come from God, that we hold strictly to His Word. God
has given us sufficient proof of Himself in His Law, in prophetic
teachings, and in the Gospels. All we have to do is open our
eyes and we will see it is God who speaks here.

So how exactly do we test teachings to make sure they are
from God and not men? We carefully examine them to see if they
conform to Scripture. For what are sermons and doctrinal
teachings, save expositions of Scripture? If we add anything of
our own making, however small and insignificant it may seem, this
falsifies and corrupts the Word. Our Lord has given us perfect
and complete instruction, in the Law, the prophets, and the
Gospels. The preacher, then, should add nothing of his own; his

task is to provide a more ample exposition of Scripture in order to ground us deeper in God's teaching. The goal of all sermons and lectures, I say, is that we be better instructed in the will of God. When anything is put forth to us, we must always inquire as to whether God is speaking or not. All preachers must bear in mind above all that it is not permissible for them to add anything of their own making. They must take great pains to insure that what they profess comes not from themselves but from the infallible truth of God.

Now the question arises: How is it possible Micah can threaten the seducers they that they will be confused when God no longer responds to them, when we see the contrary happening today? What about the audacious claims of the Pope and his troop? How he fumes against those who refuse to listen to him! How he perverts God's teaching to justify his traditions! How the world trembles the instant he twitches the tip of his tongue! Do he and his troop seem confused, shamed? Far from it! It is true, however, that God no longer speaks to them, that they have no teachings of God; the Pope's Prelature is more brutal, more bestial than the cattle and asses. They glorify themselves out of their own ignorance; they view it as beneath their dignity to take the pains to prove anything they might say. Despite all this, they are not shamed; if anything, they seem to become more puffed up with their own pride and arrogance every day, as I have just said. Why, then, does Micah say they will be shamed because they have no response from God? Be patient! Know that God will in time reveal their turpitude so they will become objects of shame to all men. As Saint Paul says, the evil ones will cease to advance once God blocks their way.

For a time, our Lord permits the false prophets to reign and to usurp the authority to preach; but in the end, He will take pity on His people. Then He will put to shame all these men, throw them out of their high office. The prophet Zachariah says that those who were heretofore prophets will put on the shepherd's cloak and say, "I no longer know what it means to prophesy; I must go tend the beasts in the fields." Listen to how Zachariah says God will redeem and reform His Church. "Behold," he says, "God will close the door to all seducers, who have deceived the ignorant, led souls straight to Hell. He will throw them out of office; they will be compelled to say, 'I must go tend the beasts; I am no longer a preacher or doctor.'" Micah makes the same point when he says that God will confuse and shame the false prophets, expose their wickedness and turpitude to all the world, that everyone will come to know them to be the seducers and deceivers they really are and how they have perverted God's teaching. Thus we pray it pleases the Lord to so put before the world the truth and purity of His teaching, that the seducers, who lead poor souls to Hell, be so confused and shamed that each will know how horrible these deceivers have abused the holy name of God and His Church.

Micah adds, "But I, I am full of power by the Spirit of the Lord, of judgment, of might, to declare to Jacob his sin and to

Israel its offense," as if to say, "You would rather believe in the false prophets that deceive you than in God's truth. You wish to be deceived, and God permits you to be so. The false prophets glory in themselves when they see what a multitude they have won over. You have rejected me, but I will resist you and all of their assaults, through the truth of my God. The world is so armed against me that it seems I must perish at first blow, but the multitude will not scare me into reneging on my God-given commission. Do not think you can discourage me, for it is God who sustains me. I am not carrying out a man-made charge or commission; it is God who calls me and works through me. Just as you cannot overcome the living God, so you will never succeed in dissuading me from the mission I have undertaken in the name of God."

Note carefully that Micah claims he will carry out His God-given mission and resist all adversaries of the truth, by virtue of God's power. He would have been unable to withstand his adversaries' attacks as one man alone, so God had to sustain him. He says as much, and we will see the results by and by. When one man stands alone against the multitude in Jerusalem, he is subject to no small temptation. He hears the priests cry out, "Are we not the ones God has chosen and elected? Does not the Law of Moses expressly require our office?" The High Priest says, "Did not Moses clearly state that if one has difficulties with the Law, he should come to me as sovereign judge and I will decide the matter?" Next they say to him, "Are we not also prophets as well as you?" When all this is thrown against Micah and yet he firmly stands his ground, does not this clearly indicate that he draws upon a power far beyond the human realm? Certainly he would be unable to resist so strongly were not God fortifying him, as if to say, "Behold the man I have sent you. I guide and lead him; he is my servant."

If we wish to be servants of God, we must have this same inner strength. If not, we can at least aspire to be that strong. True, God does not give everybody an equal measure of His Spirit; but we cannot fulfill our God-given charge unless the Spirit sustains us, giving us the kind of strength Micah speaks of. Men in themselves are worse than useless; it would be very difficult, if not impossible, to find even one who on his own would serve God faithfully and stand up against the whole world. What must be done? God Himself must take matters in hand and work through us. That is why I have said that it is a rule without exceptions that all ministers of the Word must seek guidance from the Holy Spirit. This will become clearer as we proceed.

To better understand matters, note carefully the prophet's own words: "I, I am full of the power of the Spirit of God." He stands in opposition to the people, as if to say, "True, you are a great multitude; true, you pay no heed to my warnings; true, I am merely one man standing alone; but it is also true that I walk in the power of the Spirit of God." Now this word "power" signifies the strength God gives His own. Where in the world do we find men who are capable of doing anything of lasting value on their own?  Not only are men worse than hopeless at such a task, but Saint Paul brings up another point: "Who is truly capable of carrying out a charge as important as bearing the message of salvation?  All our sufficiency comes from God."  The word "power" which Micah uses means sufficiency, signifying that he is adequate to the task of proclaiming God's Word.  He says that He is filled with this power, as if to say that God did not give him some small taste of it but so strengthened him that he would not be vanquished, were he to encounter the greatest opposition possible.

Next he adds "in the Spirit of God," to show that their opposition will be in vain, that however strongly they may resist him, they will get nowhere.  After power, he speaks of judgment and might, which are the two principal things we must have to proclaim God's Word.  We must have the skill to teach people how what we have learned from Scripture can be applied to their own benefit.  That, I say, is the gift the prophet is most especially blessed with.  But that alone is not enough; we must also have an invincible inner strength, so that however we are assailed from all directions, however it may seem that every minute we are about to be destroyed, we persist at our task and do as God has so commanded us, despite the fact the world stands over and against us.  Micah says that he "declares to Jacob his sin and to Israel its offense," as if to say, "It is very difficult for me to cry out against you, to expose your iniquities, and to condemn and accuse you in the name of God. This is a very painful task for me and very strange to you. But it must be done in spite of you. God wishes it to be so, and I will do it. Well you may resist me, but you will never conquer me."

God teaches us in a similar fashion for our own profit and salvation. He sends us preachers capable of exercising their office because they are adorned by the Spirit. Their power must come from above; as I have just said, it cannot be found among men. We are far from adequate to perform any of our necessary duties. That is why Saint Paul says that we could not even move our tongue to say that Jesus Christ is our Lord, save that the Holy Spirit empowered us to do so. Well does he combat all human pride when he says we are so worthless that we could do nothing to the glory of God, save that the Holy Spirit works within us. When Micah says, "But I, I am strengthened by the power of God's Spirit," he is confessing that he does not possess a keener intellect than other men. He claims no prize; for all that he says, God has put in him.

If we wish to be strengthened by the Lord's power, we must begin with the realization that in ourselves we are nothing, totally empty of all goodness. Above all, those charged to preach the Word should realize that they are merely mortal men. Even the combined forces of those who believe themselves to be especially talented and to have high intelligence and very good sense will not suffice, save that God sends His Spirit among them. They should know from the very start that a man's own power and capabilities are not sufficient to serve God; he must be strengthened by a higher power that can come from none other than God Himself. Micah also speaks of judgment and might: "These two virtues are requisite in a good and faithful minister of the Word of God." True, he could have compiled a long list of requisites for ministers, but he did not intend to preach a long sermon on this subject; he felt it sufficient to mention the two basic requirements, which are judgment and perseverance.

He speaks of judgment, because the preacher must be certain of God's will in order to teach others how to apply it to their benefit. If he cannot do that, all his teaching is just so much babbling, hot air; no doctrine will take roots in the hearts of men and serve to their benefit. True, there are some golden-tongued, highly intelligent preachers whom God lets ramble on and on, their words evaporating like mist in the air. But good preachers have the two qualities I have just mentioned: Knowing the will of God, they must teach it to others, making them certain of what the Master has revealed. This capacity does not come from men in themselves; it comes from God's Spirit, whose office it is to show us how we must teach the people and sustain them in the knowledge of God's truth. This power, I say, can come only from On High.

Perseverance is a rare quality in men; it takes very little to frighten them off; those who boast of being the boldest are the first to default when the going gets tough; they refuse to trust completely in God, do not recognize that only He can sustain us. But when a man is sustained by God, he can rest assured of being victorious, no matter what battles he faces; our Lord will never fail us when we ground ourselves in Him; His power will give us the strength to persevere. Saint Paul says, "We have not a spirit of fear and faint-heartedness, but of power," when he writes to Timothy. The Church at that time lived in terrible fear, for it was undergoing horrible persecutions. Thus Saint Paul exhorts Timothy not to lose courage. Here is Timothy, a young man; here is Saint Paul, who is upon his deathbed. "Take care," says Saint Paul, "that after my death, you do not weaken but are strengthened. How? Through the Spirit." Saint Paul does not say, "You must prove yourself a brave man," but "Look to Him who has called you." Let us, then, pray to God that we be not timid, but be blessed with such strength that we remain invincible against all Satan's assaults, whatever machinations he may cook up against us. Let us trust in the power of God's Spirit. May it so strengthen us that we triumph over all the assaults levied against us by the haters of the truth.

Pay attention to Micah's words that he is filled with the Spirit of God, that this is what empowers him to execute his mission, that this is what enables him to surmount all the temptations of the Devil and the world. When he speaks this way, he is warning us to take a long hard look at ourselves in order to come to know our infirmity and to realize that God alone is the remedy. He is telling us that if we lack this inner strength

177

to persevere in our calling, our only resource is to pray that God sustains us by the power of His Spirit. Let each take care that he has renounced the world and all its voluptuous delights, for otherwise God cannot be served. That is a general rule for all ministers. If they refuse to abide by it, then they will suffer the shame Jesus Christ warns of in Saint John: "When the Holy Spirit comes, it will prove that the world is wrong about sin, righteousness, and justice."

When He speaks of the Holy Spirit as our adjudicator, He is referring to the preaching of the Gospel. When the Gospel is preached, God sits in judgment upon the world and condemns all of it. No one is spared. We, even we who are the Church where the Word is preached, are condemned. The Lord wounds us to the depths of our hearts to humble ourselves before Him. However our condemnation may vex us, we must not take out our anger on those who bear the Word. Though we may believe we are fighting against only mortal men, we are in fact attacking the living God. We will not remain unpunished, and our punishment was brought about by our ingratitude, which surmounts all others. But we cannot go into details now. This topic will have to wait until tomorrow.

Following this holy teaching, we prostrate ourselves before the face of our good God, acknowledging our sinfulness. We pray that it please Him to touch us more deeply to the quick than ever before. May, in this way, our hearts be readied to receive the grace He sheds upon us. May we come to Our Lord, Jesus Christ, and be strengthened by His power; for in Him alone is the courage

178

to withstand all the assaults from the world, Satan, and ourselves. May He be Captain and Sovereign Prince, that we may share in the power of His Spirit. May He shed this grace not only on us but upon all the peoples and nations of the earth, etc.

* * *

(12) Tuesday, December 9, 1550

Hear me, I beg you, you princes of the House of Jacob, and you judges of the House of Israel. You abhor justice, pervert all righteous things. You build Zion by blood, and Jerusalem by iniquities, etc. Micah 3

Yesterday, we learned that everyone must be reproached. The true office of God's Word is to reveal to men their sins, in the hopes this will so humble them and displease them in themselves that they will beg God's pardon. Some wish only to submit to God peacefully and accept His condemnation. Indeed, they expect to be condemned; they are greatly displeased with their sins; their only wish is that God will change their lives; they wish to offer themselves up as a sacrifice; that is, they wish God to put to death their perverse nature, to renew them in all righteousness, equity, and justice. Others, however, refuse to accept God's condemnation: they become quite angered against Him and remain hardened in their sins. They will be persecuted by the Lord. But those who willingly submit to God enjoy great happiness. It is a sweet and easy death, more than profitable, when the Sword of the Word stabs us to the depths of our hearts, cutting out all our evil impulses. What a blessed death this is! Those who try to escape will only increase their condemnation; they will be destroyed, despite themselves. So let us come to God in true repentance. May His Word be more to us than mere fables and pleasant stories. May it so pierce us as to destroy all that is within us.

Micah continues to reproach those in public office, saying, "Listen to me, heads of the House of Jacob, and you, governors of the House of Israel." Then he turns to the priests and prophets. As I have said, they are like the two eyes of the body, the one eye being the princes and magistrates, the other being those charged with teaching the people the Word. If both eyes go blind, everything goes to rack and ruin. That is why Micah focuses upon the leaders. Previously, he said he was sent to reproach the House of Jacob for its sins, and Israel for its iniquities. Now, however, he focuses exclusively upon the princes and prophets. Here it would seem he is overlooking the vast majority of the people and therefore not carrying out his office; he was commissioned to reproach sin in general, yet he focuses upon a very tiny portion of the population. No, he was not failed in his calling; he is going to the source of all evil. He is not exempting the rest of the people; he is not claiming that the merchants, artisans, and other tradesman are just and innocent and therefore beyond all reproach; he is claiming, however, that the leaders are responsible for all the evil. That is why his attack is primarily aimed at them. Sin, whenever and wherever it is found, must be thoroughly condemned; but those who are the cause of all sinning must receive the greatest condemnation. That is why Micah reproaches the magistrates as much as he does the priests and prophets.

Now, regarding the magistrates, he says that they "abhor justice, pervert all righteous things," as if to say, "You do not

181

sin out of ignorance, but out of deliberate and willful malice and rebellion. That is why you so hate your office, which is to maintain law and order. You were supposed to have taken the reigns in hand to keep everything in order. But, on the contrary, you have perverted everything." Now we see why the leaders were admonished separately. As I have already said, those in charge are responsible to correct any wrongdoings among the people. But when they themselves become corrupt and encourage iniquity, what else can the outcome possibly be, save that the people become worse and worse to the extent there is neither honesty nor any fear of God among them? Sin must be reproached without exception of persons. However, it is necessary to focus upon those who lead the parade and corrupt the rest of the people. They must be reproached the strongest, for they are like wolves who have entered the fold to devour the sheep. No one is immune to corruption. Today, we see that many suddenly get out of line, although they had been good soldiers. All it takes is one bad actor to lead a whole troop astray. If we truly want to remedy this situation, it is of no benefit to spare those who have strayed; but we must focus our energies primarily upon the main instigators who are responsible for leading souls straight to Hell.

It should come as no surprise, then, that we cry out so often against these seducers, who are as wicked as they can be. Since we lived under the dark shadow of Papism, there has never been a time of such terrible wantonness as there is today.

Although there was honesty and fear of God among us at that time, today evil has free run of the place. The fumes of Hell blow everywhere, destroying all order. Today, the pure light of God's truth shines upon us, but I say that we have not changed our evil lives one single bit. If anything, we have gotten worse. Today, when the Devil's henchmen are everywhere, do not be reluctant to throw them out. If they are tolerated, they will succeed in turning everything upside down, which is what they set out to do. Our first order of business is to get after these henchmen. A good physician does not merely cool down the fever in the hands and feet; he applies his talents to get to the root of the illness. Likewise, when we see that contempt for God and His Word runs rampant today, we must get to the source of this evil if we are to remedy it. Now, as I have said, there are some very bad actors who desire only to be Captains of Satan, wish only to throw all into chaos, want only to send souls straight to Hell. We cannot close our eyes on such a tragic situation; we cannot betray our God-given mission. Let us, then, follow Micah's example.

Those in public office should diligently attend to the tasks of their high calling and be very circumspect in their actions; for if there is the slightest disorder or scandal, the blame will fall squarely on their shoulders. They, of course, come up with all sorts of feeble excuses for not doing their duty: "O, we cannot come up with a remedy for such-and-such an evil; our hands are tied by so many strings." But nothing really blocks them, save their own lack of courage. They have no real stomach for their work, so they have no more strength and vigor to fight against evil than would a fencepost. That is why God, through Micah, passes an irrevocable sentence against them. Indeed, public officials should look long and hard at their responsibilities. If evils are covered up or ignored, the entire body will be punished. Nevertheless, our Lord begins with the leaders: "You, heads of the House of Jacob, and governors of the House of Israel." As I have already said, Micah is attacking those who pervert justice, who abhor righteousness, who are happiest when things go badly. What horrible vengeance God will take upon those who delight in their sins! This will be made plain soon enough. Although Micah is speaking specifically to the magistrates in this passage, there is a lesson in it for us: We are so much the more condemnable because we can distinguish right from wrong. If we willingly pervert justice and abhor what God sanctions, our punishment will be so much the more grievous.

Micah continues, saying, "They build Jerusalem out of blood, and Zion out of iniquity," as if to say, "pillage and plunder are the ways they make themselves big, important. They build; but instead of mortar, they use the blood and sustenance of men." Here he is attacking the avarice of the governors, as it is a pernicious vice in all public officials. Avarice always leads to cruelty. This is a rule that admits of no exceptions whatsoever. Whenever and wherever a man becomes obsessed with amassing wealth, he becomes as cruel and inhumane as a savage beast.  On the contrary, if we are moved by pity and compassion for our neighbors, it is certain avarice will no longer reign in us.  Charity, then, is the true remedy for avarice.  Just as fire is extinguished when it is put in water, so it is impossible for the charitable soul to burn with envy.  Micah has good reason, then, to attribute such great cruelty to those he condemns as murderers, saying, "They have built Jerusalem in blood, and Zion in iniquity."  By the word "blood," he signifies that they are so cruel they suck the blood and juices right out of a man, as I have just said.  By the word "iniquity," he signifies that we cannot so desire to enrich ourselves that we do not come to amass wealth through loan sharking, rapine, fraud, and all sorts of other ways of wronging and injuring our neighbors.  Iniquity and the spilling of blood are inevitably bound to avarice.  That is why greedy men are cruel.  Furthermore, these men honor neither equity nor righteousness; their burning desire is to amass goods through ruthless, reckless, violent means.  The word "blood" has deep meaning; for it signifies that if we do not have compassion for the poor, treating them in the worst possible ways, God will condemn us as murderers.  True, blood itself cannot witness against others, but God can see more clearly than men.

However we may deny that any blood has been spilt when we eat our neighbors alive, God will cry out that we are murderers and that we have spilled the blood of the innocent.  We are without excuse before God.  If we do not wish to be condemned as murderers, we must take pity and compassion upon those in need;

185

we must take great pains to aid them rather than piling evil on top of evil. The rich are always on the prowl. When they see a man in poverty, they say, "This is the place to set our habit. He has a field or some inheritance which will please us. Let us trap him!" That is how the great fortunes of the world are made. If we resort to these tactics, God will charge us with our crimes; for it is up to Him to judge our sins and denounce them. Such cruelty will be condemned as murder before Him. Habakkuk makes the same point. He says that the walls of the great palaces and buildings will cry out from all sides as if they were cantors. The one will lament, "Woe is me, for I am built of the blood of the poor." The other will lament, "Woe is me, for I was erected by murder, rape, loan sharking, and pillage." There is not nearly as much water in their mortar as there is blood of the poor. As I have said, avarice brings with it all other evils, for it is the root of all evil. The magnificent palaces and beautiful buildings erected by greedy men, all were built by fraud, rapine, loan sharking, extortion, violence, and other like crimes. So if we wish to be blessed and to be truly heirs to the place our Lord has provided for our lodging, we must not build in blood. May our homes not witness against us to demand vengeance before God. May the blood of the poor not cry out against our cruelty.

The princes try to excuse themselves, as they are prone to do, by saying, "We don't see any blood. Do you? Where exactly is all this spilt blood?" Micah, then, says how specifically

they have build in blood: "You judges take bribes, you priests
and prophets will not perform your duties unless you are paid."
In brief, he says everything has been ruined by the corruption
among themselves. As I have said, he is reproaching the two
institutions which serve as the two eyes of the body and which
are the sole sources of all enlightenment. How is a city, land,
people to be sustained? The magistrates must uphold the honor of
God; they must use their power to insure that God is everywhere
honored and served as He should be; they must maintain such
honesty and equity among men that each may receive his due
without having to wrong or injure anyone; they must abolish all
wantonness and scandalous behavior. The preachers and ministers
of the Word of God, on their side of it, must insure that the
glory of God is maintained at all costs; they must see to it that
Christ reigns everywhere and that all obey Him; they must not
turn a blind eye to evil, but must harshly reproach all vices;
they must stand against everything evil. That, I say, is how a
people should be properly governed. But when the eyes are blind,
what happens to the body? In walking, it will stumble, breaking
an arm and a leg. In the end, it will go to rack and ruin. That
is what will happen.

Thus, Micah lumps together the priests and prophets with the
magistrates, saying they are all totally perverse and corrupt.
That is why I have said there is no more pernicious vice among
public officials than avarice; for once they become greedy, there
will be neither righteousness nor justice. When ministers of the

187

Word become obsessed with greed, they become con artists who falsify the Word of God and His salvific teachings. Yesterday, we mentioned the passage in Saint Paul where he says, "We are not like those who falsify the Word of God, who falsely advertise their wares to deceive customers; we walk in all simplicity and righteousness." But that is impossible to do once avarice gets a hold on us. The ministers will lack the courage to reproach sin, and the judges will be without justice, unless they serve God in all sincerity and purity, faithfully exercising their charge. That is why Micah focuses upon these two offices, declaring that if either one becomes possessed by greed, everything will be corrupted. Whatsoever God had ordained for the good of the people will go to rack and ruin. If, for example, the princes and the magistrates take bribes, what happens? The first thing is that the poor have no recourse to justice. The magistrates will say, "If they have nothing to bring us, let them not disturb our ears!" Their doors will be open only to those who can grease their palms. Furthermore, there will be no charity. You can expect no aid from a greedy man who will say, "What will you give me in return for what I will do for you?"

Well we see that although God dwells in our midst, the Devil reigns more than ever among us. However we have been enlightened by the Gospels, however much God has revealed hidden things to us, we are as blind men; we do not see the good things God brings us; we are not touched by His bounty. There can be no justice, I say, when those in public office are so possessed by greed. The poor are thrown out, despised, although they are the very ones the magistrates must protect, as they are destitute of all aid. But whom do they really defend:  Whosoever can bribe them sufficiently.  Who wins his case in court?  Whoever can bribe the judge.  What if a man causes a great scandal?  The magistrates will say, "Well, provided we are paid off, the matter is all water over the dam; it is nothing.  Let him cheat!  Let him deceive customers!  He is a good friend of mine.  He has done me some favors, so I owe him.  I'll get him out of this jam."  The magistrates are all blind.  You can cook up the worst scandals in the world and go unpunished.  You have absolutely nothing to fear, that is, if you have enough money.  Why can a man commit all sorts of violent acts upon the poor and innocent, yet go free?  The magistrates were paid off.  In brief, once a magistrate becomes obsessed with money, he no longer has any regard for righteousness or justice.  That is what Scripture means when it speaks of bribes corrupting the most wise and perverting the hearts of the most just.  Pay heed to this warning; for there are magistrates who will say, "Sure, I accept gifts from various people, but that doesn't mean I fail to carry out my office."  Are they wiser than God?  For the Lord says that it is impossible for a man not to be corrupted by the gifts and presents he receives, though he may be among the wisest and most just.  Boast as some will that they can take from all hands and not be corrupted, the Lord's words are true.  Any magistrate who wishes to exercise his office faithfully and honestly must have a heart purged of all avarice, as I have just said.

The same thing holds for ministers of the Word. Just as a magistrate obsessed by greed will not punish sins committed against God and man, so also the minister will lose his courage to speak out against sin, when he becomes obsessed with his own personal gain. He will be like a muzzled watchdog who refuses to attack those who deeply offend God. Because he is totally obsessed with his own greed, he is oblivious to all else. When he preaches, his words have no real feelings behind them. Indeed, they cannot. He will pervert God's teachings, as I have just said. He will become quite cruel and flatter the wicked. Provided they pay him substantially, his tongue will always be ready to praise them and tell them whatsoever they wish to hear. He will declare war on the innocent and righteous. We see, then, how there is no greater pestilence than avarice among ministers.

Saint Paul makes the following recommendations for the elected officials of the Church of God. He says, "They must not be of an avaricious spirit, given to villainous and infamous gain," for if they are greedy, God's teaching cannot be maintained in purity. That is why Micah cries out so against the greed of the magistrates and preachers; God intends them to lead the people and correct all vices. Otherwise, things will go from bad to worse.

When magistrates turn a blind eye towards evil, when they are supposed to keep a tight rein on bad actors but in point of fact egg them on, these scum become more and more audacious. When one offense goes unpunished, they will commit another, and yet still another, until their wickedness has grown beyond all measure.

Not only does Micah admonish the people for allowing their leaders to get away with all their crimes, as if one dare not say a harsh word to them, but he also reproaches the magistrates for accepting gifts, and the prophets for teaching on a salary basis. So the question now arises whether or not Micah is really being fair in his accusations. If God does not wish magistrates and judges to receive gifts, why did He ordain that they be on a salary in the first place? Why is it wrong for them to receive gifts, when God gives them the authority to collect taxes from their subjects to finance projects for the good of the public? If the prophets are forbidden from accepting any salary, why has God ordained from all time that the Church support its priests, which still holds for the Christian Church? Saint Paul strongly argued this point, saying, "If the cattle must be nourished to perform their work, is there not far greater reason for you to sustain us? Since we have nourished your spiritual needs, is it too much that we ask you to nourish our bodily needs?" It seems there has always been some repugnance to the idea of supporting ministers and public officials.

However, if a magistrate truly believes that he is ultimately accountable to God, if he diligently fulfills his duties without making exceptions for persons, he should not be accused of accepting bribes or judging for gifts or anything of the like, when he receives his duly ordained salary. When a man feels called to preach the Word, he must so swear, "It has pleased God to call me to this office. I fully understand the charge to which I have been commissioned. I will fight against all decadence in the church, to the best of my abilities. I will reproach all vices." When, I say, a minister is loyal to this oath, fully carrying out his Master's commands, he can receive with a clean conscience all that God has ordained for him. What support he receives from the church, he accepts graciously, as if from the hand of God Himself. He does not, I emphasize, preach for profit, or praise for presents; he applies all his energies to serving God and diligently carrying out his office. Micah, then, is not reproaching what God has ordained; it is licit for a minister to receive money from the Church, provided that he is true to his God-given calling. He can receive his salary with a clean conscience because he can honestly say to himself, "I fulfill my calling, which is to serve God." Micah is crying out against something altogether different: He is saying that all sins begin there. If a man is given to avarice, then cruelty, treason, perjury, and disloyalty follow by and by. So first Micah attacks avarice, then he turns to the fraudulency, violence, treason, and perjury that will come to possess a man once avarice gets a hold on him, as we have already seen.

Having shown that the princes, governors, priests, and prophets were all possessed by greed, he says, "Nevertheless, you lean upon the Lord and say, 'Is not the Lord among us? He will well protect us.' But I say to you that Jerusalem will be plowed as a field, that Mt. Zion will become a wasteland. There will be desolation everywhere. Think hard on this, for you are puffed up by false confidence." He seems to do them a great wrong by saying, "They lean on the Lord, but they will be destitute." What does he expect them to do? Is there truly something more beneficial for men than to lean upon the Lord? What good things would we have, save that we put all our trust in the Lord? Does not Scripture expressly command us to trust in God alone? Are we not taught in our very first lesson to trust fully in God? Micah seems to condemn as a vice what God otherwise praises as a virtue in man. What could he possibly mean here?

Now, consider very carefully whether or not men truly trust in God, for the trust we have in God is hardly too excessive or very great. Let us not feign trusting in God, for that would abuse His name. Saint Paul says that the infidels glorify themselves in God, but that this glory serves only for their condemnation. Jeremiah says that whosoever glorifies in himself must glorify himself in God. Saint Paul, by the way, makes this same point in another passage. When Jeremiah says that we should glorify ourselves in God, he does not mean that the wise should glory in their wisdom or that the rich should glory in their power and wealth; he means that men should humble themselves before the majesty of God. Micah's point is that we find all our power, wisdom, and glory in God alone. However, there are many who glorify themselves in God and yet offend and mock His Word, as do the hypocrites. They trust in God's promises, but completely disregard the conditions He has established; they think that God is obligated to them and will let them get away with anything they want; they wish to hold God on their laps; they make Him into a small child so His anger may be easily appeased by presents and He must obey their every command. That is how hypocrites hold to God's promises and yet mock His great majesty, totally disregarding His Word.

We see, then, whom Micah had to fight against and for a very long time. Indeed, all the prophets had to fight this same battle. Today, those who wish to faithfully bear the Word must still fight against them. I mean, of course, the hypocrites, who feign being the most faithful, the Pillars of Christendom; yet, in truth, they abhor God and His Word.

So much the more, then, must we draw upon his words: "You lean on the God and say, 'The Lord! The Lord!'" True, God had revealed that He would dwell in the midst of them. The Temple was built in Jerusalem, in which one could worship Him and experience His great bounty and grace firsthand. The prophets and princes trusted in this promise but in the wrong way. Our Lord has said, "Be holy, for I am holy; otherwise, I cannot remain with you." Our Lord declared He would dwell in the midst of them, provided they were cleansed of all the world's filth. But what did they do? To them, the promise was all that mattered; they overlooked God's demand and abandoned themselves to all evil. The ones were idolaters; the others were loan sharks, robbers, bandits, and full of all iniquity. They abused God's promise as if God could be broken into pieces. But can God be broken? No! We cannot receive only half of God's promise; we must meet His conditions; then we can lean on Him. God must be served in faith and repentance, and this we can do only if we accept and honor the conditions attached to His promise. If we can do that, if through the Holy Spirit we can come to live in perfect harmony with Him, then He will not fail to sustain us. So when God calls us to Himself, as He has done through the preaching of the Gospel, let us go to Him purged of all hypocrisy.

Following this holy teaching, we prostrate ourselves before the face of our good God, acknowledging our sinfulness. May He so open our eyes that we no longer trust in ourselves, as we are wont to do. May the sight of our own poverty and weakness humble us before Him. May we accept and so profit from the chastisement of the Word that He will fulfil His promise, given through the Spirit and the Gospel, to be our refuge. May His name be glorified everywhere and in all things. May we grown in faith and repentance. May we renounce the world and all its delights, to glorify better His name. May He shed this grace not only on us but upon all the peoples and nations of the earth, etc.

All-powerful God, celestial Father, it pleases you to govern us by the preaching of your holy Word. Give us the grace that our leaders are so fortified and strengthened by your celestial power that they act not out of their own self-interests but apply all their energies to serving both you and ourselves. May they so edify us that we become your dwelling place all the days of our lives. May we, in the end, reach the Celestial Sanctuary, to which you call us daily; for its gate has been opened to us by the blood of your only Son, Jesus Christ, our Lord. Amen.

* * *

## (13) Wednesday, December 10, 1550

They lean on the Lord, saying, "Is the Lord not among us? No evil will befall us." Therefore, because of you, Zion will be plowed as a field, Jerusalem will be a rock pile, and the mountains where the Temple stands will be a wasteland, etc. Micah 3.

Yesterday, we saw how hypocrites abuse God's promises; they interpret them solely from the standpoint of their own self-interest; they completely ignore the reason why God makes us promises in the first place, namely that He wishes to be our Saviour. If we wish God to be our Shepherd, if we truly wish to be His flock, then we must obey Him. If we wish God to be our Father, then we must act as His children. But the hypocrites abuse and falsely glorify God's name by perverting all His teachings. They wallow in their own shit, give free rein to their evil impulses; they believe God obligated to obey their every wish, as if He were their child. It is no wonder, then, that Micah here mocks their confidence; for it is not true faith but the boasting of the flesh that lead men to believe that God is obligated to them and that they do not have to obey Him.

"Do you think," he says, "that God will dwell among you and that no evil will befall you? Then listen up! He has declared that Mt. Zion will be plowed like a field, that there will no longer be any Temple, that the land will be totally desolate." This means God will fulfill His promises to us, provided that we are truly displeased in our offenses and that such bounty as we

197

have tasted moves us to go to Him as our sole refuge. Our Lord will dwell among us only when we are truly His temples, when we are consecrated to His honor, and when we wish only to serve Him with a clean conscience and in all sanctity. Our Lord will not dwell among us when he sees we are profane and totally polluted. In that case, there will be a great distance, indeed a war, between ourselves and God. True, if God dwells among us, no evil can befall us; He has more than enough strength in His hand to defend and sustain us. But it is also true that God will maintain us only if we obey the Word, in which He reveals Himself and through which He is to be served and honored.

We have an excellent example here of the great inner strength Micah stressed earlier when he spoke of being fortified by a great power to announce to the House of Jacob its iniquities. "Behold," he said, "God has given me wisdom, judgment, and invincible strength." It was good he had such strength and courage, seeing how the people of Judah were so puffed up with pride. Even as he spoke the words of today's passage, he was in mortal danger. Indeed, a tribunal had been convened against him, as we saw in Jeremiah 26. He stood accused of being the enemy of God, of wishing to abolish all His promises, as he had spoken out against the Temple. If King Hezekiah had not intervened, he would have lost his life; for, as we read in this passage, the entire tribunal was resolved to put him to death, and the people cried out against him. It was a unanimous decision that he be put to death for mocking the

Temple. Only Hezekiah was in his corner and spoke up for him, saying, "My friends, see if you have not offended God in some way. Look closely at yourselves and you will find that you are all worthy of blame. Don't be shocked when God condemns us through Micah and his other prophets. He wants us to feel His wrath upon us so we will be motivated to correct our faults. Take care that you do not rise up against God and so provoke His wrath that He destroys everything. We will gain absolutely nothing by rebelling against God. Since we have so grievously offended Him, what else can He do, save condemn us all? Do not harm this man, for that would be to declare war on God and only worsen our situation." That is how Hezekiah saved Micah's life. His example also served to save the life of Jeremiah. When the prophet was on trail, facing the death sentence, certain elders stood up and said, "During the reign of Hezekiah, the prophet Micah was sentenced to death. But the king came to his rescue, saying that we must receive in all humility God's chastisement. Because of this, God's great anger was appeased for a time. But what has happened since? What have the kings gained by resisting the prophets? That serves only to kindle God's wrath so much the more." That is how Jeremiah escaped with his life.

These events are of particular relevance to our situation today. It was difficult for the people to accept that the Temple would be destroyed, for God had ordained it to be built. It was the only one of its kind in the world at that time; it was the forerunner of our Lord, Jesus Christ; it was not only the place

199

God Himself had chosen for His worship, it was also the center point from which God's power would radiate outward to redeem the entire world. Certainly it would seem, then, that Micah wished to crush all their high hopes. God had pronounced a very harsh and difficult sentence upon them. However, they had to be taught to humble themselves before Him; for His mercy and great bounty can be tasted only through humility. When our Lord threatens us with punishments, let us not become vexed with God. Let us acknowledge our faults, confess them, come to a true displeasure in ourselves. That, I say, is how we must respond to God's threats when He thunders against us. Rebelling against Him will gain us nothing, as I have just said. If anything, it will serve only to augment evil and make our condemnation so much the more grievous. Does it not make us look just awful when even a mighty king like Hezekiah will humble himself and bow his head before God's threats? There will always be wicked men who will curse God; but what will they truly gain by this, when even a mighty king can be humbled by Him?

Remember, God's threats are for our own benefit; there is no other way we will come to acknowledge and confess our sins, save that God forces us. Although God's threats seem outrageously cruel by our standards, that does not mean they are in point of fact excessive; for our sins always merit a punishment greater than what God lands on us.

Bear in mind that Micah, as well as all other prophets, never threatened the Jews without leaving the faithful some ray of hope that God would deliver them from their afflictions. That is why he says, "In the last days, the Mountain of the House of the Lord will be exalted. People will gather there, saying, 'Come on! Let's go to the House of the Lord so we can learn His ways and walk in his paths.'" At first glance, this seems like an awful place to go, since Micah says that Mt. Zion will be a wasteland. But he says next that God will exalt it above all the other mountains. Although it was only a small, little hill, it will be so exalted and glorified that not one of the other, larger mountains will be able to compare with it.

But what does Micah really mean, that there will be a terrible desolation followed by such a marvelous restoration that never was the House of God so magnificent? However severely God may punish the people, He will never forget the covenant He made with the Patriarchs. Now, this covenant is not grounded in men but in the infinite bounty of God. Therefore it must transcend the enormity of human sinfulness. Micah, then, as I have said, is consoling the faithful so they do not lose all hope and courage. He is assuring them that God will not punish them without some hope for salvation. He is saying in effect, "True, you will be taken into captivity, the Temple will be destroyed, and the land of Judah made desolate; but don't forget that God will restore the Church in His own good time."

Micah's reasoning makes good sense! If it is said that God is merciful to a thousand generations, it is also said that he will punish the children for the iniquities of their fathers. If

201

our Lord can receive men in mercy, that should not prevent Him from punishing those who have offended Him. If God, as Judge, can severely punish all rebels, He can also pity those who trust in Him and will deliver them from the horror of death. When the world is given to evil and therefore subjected to universal punishment, still He will find a way to maintain His Church. When the Church is about to collapse, He will bring it back to life, making it yet more magnificent than ever.

But you will not understand these things unless you know what he means by "the last days." He is warning us of the end of the world. There will be a period of great chaos and horrible desolation. Then God will send His Son to redeem us and pour out His Spirit on all flesh. All the prophets testify to this truth, Peter in Acts 2, Paul in Galatians 4 and I Corinthians 10. We know now where our hope lies: in Jesus Christ, who will restore and bring to perfection all that was lost and broken.

Now we can understand why he says, "The Mountain of the House of God will be exalted." Certainly it would not be the most cherished place on earth because of its great physical beauty. Nothing could ever be physically more magnificent than Solomon's Temple. When the elderly, who remembered Solomon's Temple, saw the one Zerubabble built, they cried and lamented, for it was like a little hut, compared to Solomon's. But Micah is speaking of purely spiritual beauty when he says peoples and nations will come to the Mountain. What a great day it will be when the Lord comes to set His House in motion! All men will be of one mind, one faith, and totally obedient to God.  "Come!" they will say.  "Let us go up to the Mountain of the Lord, that we may learn from Him and come to walk in His ways."  The whole world will then be ruled by God from Zion and Jerusalem.  No longer will His Law be confined to Judah; it will be publicized throughout the world, to the very ends of the earth; our Lord will lead all the world to salvation.  Mt. Zion will be exalted because all truth and salvation will emanate from there.  Ezekiel compares Zion to a fountain whose waters will flow throughout all the earth, nourishing everything.

Let us sum up.  Our Lord promises to restore the Church. Because nothing could be more important than this restoration, our Lord sent not one but two prophets, Isaiah and Micah, to proclaim this promise.  Although they were contemporaries, Micah was the elder of the two; he began his preaching much earlier than Isaiah and was the first to pass away.  Isaiah continued on, preaching up through the reign of Manasseh.  They spoke as of one mouth, so that Isaiah gives word for word what Micah says in today's passage:  The Mountain of the House of the Lord will be exalted.  Many peoples and nations will congregate there, saying, "Come!  Let us go up to the Mountain of the Lord.  The Law will come forth from Zion, and the Word of God from Jerusalem."

Micah, threatening the Jews, says, "The Mountain of the House of the Lord will be a wasteland."  But he adds shortly thereafter, "The Mountain of the House of God will be exalted." Why does he make such contradictory statements?  The hypocrites

203

abuse God's name by using the Temple as their shield to ward off His punishments, as their cloak to hide their iniquities. "Do not speak of God's Temple," says Jeremiah, "for you have made it into a robbers' den." Reproaching their foolish pride, he goes on to say, "Although Mt. Zion is called the House of God and although it is the place where God's Temple is built, it will be totally demolished." But now Micah says that the Mountain of God will be so exalted above all other places that its glory will be known throughout the world and that God will be worshipped there in all purity. It will be a temple truly dedicated to God, and there He will dwell among the faithful. No longer will the rebels and hypocrites have a material temple to use as a cover-up for their iniquities; no longer will they be able to boast of being God's people, when in fact they are not.

Although men have provoked His wrath from the very beginning, He never fails to be merciful. Despite all the great troubles and upheavals in the world, He will see to it His Church remains even when the world is about to end. His infinite mercy always overcomes His wrath and will surmount the iniquities of a people who deserve to be exterminated right down to the last man. He will always preserve some remnant who will worship and trust in Him. He had good reason to spare Hezekiah, Micah, Isaiah, and a small throng of faithful men. But after their deaths, He would have been totally justified in exterminating the entire Jewish race. Yet He did not do so. That is an excellent example of how His infinite mercy surmounts the iniquities of men.

God sustains and restores His Church solely through our Lord, Jesus Christ. First Micah speaks of horrible desolation. Then, in the next instant, he says Mt. Zion will be exalted. So two things must be borne in mind. One is that men merit God's great vengeance upon them. The other is that the power and office of Christ is resurrection and life, as He is so called. He comes to put back up what has been knocked down, breathe life back into men who are in the grips of death, and restore all that has been lost. Whenever men merit severe punishment, the Church will be in the dilapidated condition it is today. That is the way it has always been and that is the way it will always be. But it is also true that Christ will always restore all that has gone to rack and ruin. The Church will be renewed! That's what Micah means when he says the Mountain of God will be exalted above all the others.

The honor and reputation of the Church are more important to God than anything else on earth. We must not confuse the Kingdom of our Lord with worldly kingdoms. Their glory consists of garish displays of sumptuous living, wealth, power, and the like. But we must not confuse the glory of His Church with these things; they mean nothing to God. What counts with Him is that He is feared and obeyed. The Church enjoys the position of highest honor, because God so loved it He adopted it as His dwelling place. That is what Micah means when He says Mt. Zion will be exalted above all others. Are we not humbled by the great honor God bestows upon us by inviting us into His own home?

When He adopts us to be His children, is that not an honor that surpasses all the other honors in the world? Few men realize what a great blessing it is to be numbered among the children of God. Most men prize more I don't know what all worldly vanities than they do the immeasurable blessing that God invites us into His home and adopts us to be His children. But Micah is not talking through his hat. So when we hear him speak of the Church being exalted among all the mountains of the world, let us recognize that it is of such grandeur that being counted among the Children of God is a far greater honor than anything the world could ever confer upon us.

In the day when the Church will be exalted, many peoples will say, "Let's go to the Mountain of God, so that we can learn His ways and walk in His paths." When Micah speaks of the many peoples, he is drawing a hard-and-fast distinction between the Church as it had been under the Law and the Church as it will be at the coming of the Lord. The Church under the Law consisted of only one people, the children of Abraham, who were elected to hear salvific teachings. God was speaking to this people in particular when he said, "I am your God, who has delivered you from Egypt." From then on, He was named the God of Abraham, Isaac, and Jacob. But now Micah says that God will sound His trumpet to the farthest ends of the earth, just as it says in Psalm 2 that God the Father will give the Son dominion over all the earth, from where the sun rises to where it sets. See what

206

great honor is conferred upon us when he says all the peoples will assemble at Mt. Zion, the House of the Lord.

Our faith is so much the more strengthened when we realize that it was not a sudden, capricious decision on God's part to call us to the Gospel. Our fathers were poor Pagans, who had no covenant with God; they were far from His Church; the promise of salvation was not extended to them, as Saint Paul reminds the Gentiles in Ephesians 2. But now we are joined to Abraham and his lineage; we have been grafted into this root which was the People of God. This was all accomplished through the Gospels. We cannot say, "We are saved purely by Chance; God's prophecy has nothing to do with it." We know that this is not the case, for Scripture tells us otherwise: Although God did set aside a special people to receive His Law, He always intended salvific knowledge to be revealed throughout the entire world; He eternally desires that all peoples of the world come to share in one faith and live in harmony with one another; where peoples have lived separately and far from one another, they will be brought together into one people; where great barriers have existed between peoples, these will be knocked down and they will come to live in harmonious unity. That was the promise given to Abraham, Moses, and all the prophets. So much the more, then, is our faith strengthened; for we realize our salvation is not by chance, but by the eternal decree of God.

True, Micah seems to put all the faithful in Jerusalem; but he, like all the other prophets, was speaking in the language of

207

his times. When Isaiah said altars will be built in Egypt, Assyria, and other places, he did not mean it will be necessary to have sacrificial altars in the time of Christ; he was speaking according to the customs of his time. For this same reason, Micah says God will bring all the peoples from the four corners of the earth to Jerusalem to worship Him, as if to say, "In that day, all the peoples of the world will be of one faith, whereas now they are of many opposing faiths." But shortly thereafter, he says the Law will come forth from Zion, and the Word of God from Jerusalem. He means that God will fill the whole world with knowledge of His saving truth. Psalm 110 says the subjects of Jesus Christ will come to Him willingly, without having to be forced, in that day. Furthermore, Christ will rule over all the world from Zion. In other words, the Word of God will be no longer confined to Jerusalem, but will be publicized throughout all the world. Micah, then, does not mean that everyone will have to come to Jerusalem to worship God; he is speaking in terms familiar to those whom he addresses.

A distinction must be made between how God was to be served under the Law and how He is to be served at the coming of our Lord. True, there was and is only one true faith; true, the Patriarchs worshipped God to the same end as we. But they as well as the prophets knew only a foreshadowing of Christ. Today, however, we no longer live in the world of shadows, for the Veil of the Temple has been ripped down. We worship a God who is fully revealed to us through the Gospels. The true meaning of

Micah's claim that all the peoples will come to the Mountain is that God will be known throughout the world because His Gospel will be preached everywhere.

Micah emphasizes how ardent our desire must be to go to God when He calls us, for He wants us to come to Him willingly, without having to be forced. Psalm 110, as I have just mentioned, says that we must come to God out of our heart's desire to obey Him, without being forced or constrained. Micah says we pay God proper homage when we come to Him willingly, out of an ardent desire to serve Him. In short, each must come to God of his own volition. But remember, if we choose to ignore God's call, if we cringe and shout back when Christ takes us by the hand to lead us to salvation, we are, I emphasize, more than deserving of being handed over to Satan to be blinded and perverted. Also remember that each and every one of us must encourage his neighbor. Micah's text does not say that each man should go alone; it says, "Come! Let us go!" Each man should take his neighbor by the hand, as it says in another passage. But do not sit around and wait for others to take you by the hand; you must take the initiative; you must be the leader. Remember, Isaiah says that men will grab Jews by their coat sleeves, crying out, "We wish to worship your God!" Now, if you cannot encourage others or they will not encourage you, then it is right for you to go alone to God. But remember, it is the duty of every Christian to try and lead his neighbors to salvation.

Have we put Micah's teaching into practice? Alas! Far from it! We are so asleep that our Lord does not know how to awaken us. Although our ears are ringing with His exhortations and reproaches, still we are so lazy that we will not take one step towards Him. Those who make any effort to progress take two steps backward for every step forward. Why are we in such sad shape? We do not taste the great grace God shed on us when He adopted us as His children; we are too busy seeking after the vanities of the world to take the time to look Godward. Not only do we fail to encourage our neighbors to come to God, but, worse yet, we actually block their way and manage to stifle any ardent desire they may have had to come to the Lord. We will not condescend to come when God calls us; we slam the door in the face of the ignorant; we shove and trip them up along the Path of Righteousness. Our malice merits horrible punishment. Yet there is still hope. God speaks to us in our depraved conditions to assure us our Lord will restore all that has gone to rack and ruin. But, I emphasize, we can be renewed only if we willingly go to God to be united in one faith and to invoke the name of our Father by one heart and one mouth.

Where is it that we find God? Only on Mt. Zion. But that means in His Church, not on some far-away mountaintop. There is no longer a special, material temple set aside for God's dwelling, because He wishes to be served spiritually, that is, throughout all the world, without any exceptions. Nevertheless, there must be a Church; we cannot be children of God unless we are raised in His home, and the Church is our Mother. Saint Paul says that since the Word has gone forth from Zion, the Mountain has been our Mother. But the Temple is truly everywhere, as Zachariah says. If we wish to go to God, we must go to the Mountain together; that is, we must be of one mind resolved to be the true Church here and now and to be numbered among God's children.

Micah says that "the Lord will show us His ways and we will walk in His paths." There is much to say here, but that will have to wait until tomorrow. But at present we can at least note that He gives us excellent advice here; he shows us the true purpose of going to the House of God: We go there to learn His ways, to follow Him; we most emphatically do not go there to invent doctrines according to our whims. True, God teaches through the mouths of men; they are His instruments. But we must take care not to pass off our idle fantasies as doctrines that must be accepted. God alone is the Master and Doctor of the Church; He alone governs us through His Son. If we want to be the People of God, we must learn to walk in His ways and we must reject all proclamations other than those received from the holy mouth of the Word of God. It is impossible for us to profit in the School of God unless, as I have said, we listen only to the voice of God and follow it wherever it may lead us. That is the only way we can come to learn His ways. Micah also says that "we will walk in His paths." But that will have to wait until tomorrow.

211

Following this holy teaching, we prostate ourselves before the face of our good God, acknowledging our sinfulness. We pray that it please Him to so change us that we are prepared to renounce ourselves to follow Him wherever He may lead us. May our only wish be to enlist under our Master and Captain, Jesus Christ. May we be renewed by His grace and strengthened by His power. May He so lead us that we are no longer what we have been. May we so submit to His care and may He so reign in us that we are always governed by His Holy Spirit. Thus we say together:

All-powerful God, celestial Father, you condescended to establish the Throne of your Son among us. Give us the grace that we, who are under the safekeeping of our King, entrust ourselves so completely to Him that we never wax or wane from His commands. May we so obey and subjugate ourselves to the King you have given us that He takes us to be His own people. May we so glorify your name that we no longer slander it by our wicked wantonness. May we witness by our works that we are truly your subjects. May you have such total and complete control over us that your name is sanctified and your Holy Spirit governs us. May your Son, who delivered us from horrible desolation in which we were as dead, receive us in His celestial kingdom, acquired for us by His own blood. Amen.

* * *

(14) Thursday, December 11, 1550

Peoples and nations will assemble themselves at the Mountain, saying, "Come! Let's go up to the Mountain of the Lord, to the House of the God of Jacob. He will teach us His ways and we will walk in His paths, etc." Micah 4

Let us pick up where we left off yesterday. Micah proclaims that all the world will be brought to God through the coming of the Lord. This reconciliation has already begun, is taking place among us right now, and will continue up to the end of the world. In virtue of the prophesy, our Lord daily unites men in faith and obedience. Yesterday we were warned that men have no authority whatsoever to teach according to their whims; they must stick to God's teaching and encourage each other to listen only to His Word. God alone is the Master of the Church; He alone has the authority to teach us. Our duty is to hear and obey His Word. Whenever men are governed by resolutions they have forged out of their own imaginations, there can be no order acceptable to God; indeed, there can be only chaos. In Papism, when it is a question of passing a certain resolution, no one pays the least attention to the Word of God. Papists take the attitude: "What? Scripture? Word of God? Poppycock. It's manmade laws that hold sway." Well may the Pope glory in his hierarchy, as he calls it, but this ruling body is totally contrary to the perpetual order God has ordained for His people. If we truly accept Christ as our King, only He alone has the authority to teach and govern us.

Micah stresses that we have the responsibility to lead our neighbors to God. "Come," we should say to our neighbors, "let's go to God to learn His ways." We have the responsibility to lead the way, saying, "Follow me!" We are negligent in our duty if we let others stray from the path. We must value our neighbor's salvation just as much as our own. That is what Micah means when he says, "Let's go to the Mountain of God to learn His ways."

Micah adds that "we will walk in His paths." He means that the Gospel is the teaching of life; it has the power to put us on the right path to God; it is not some foolish opinion we have dreamed up on one hand, only to turn around on the other and admit that we really don't know what we are talking about. Pay attention! Most of us abuse the Word of God; as long as we can boast of having it, that is enough for us. But God really means business when He shows us the way to salvation; He expects to see results in our lives. So let us really get on the ball! Let us prove we are truly members of Christ's flock by being prompt in encouraging our neighbors and quick to discern the voice of our Shepherd from those of others. That, I emphasize, is the kind of responsiveness God expects from His church.

Next, Micah says, "the Law will come forth from Zion, and the Word of God from Jerusalem." Up to this point in time, only one people had been chosen by God. Now, however, God will shed His grace upon all the world; His Law will no longer be hidden among one particular people; the Word will go out to all peoples and nations without exceptions. The Jews, then, will no longer enjoy their privileged position. By the word Law, Micah does not mean the institutionalized Mosaic codes; he means the whole of God's salvific teaching. Indeed, the word "law" means to teach. He refers to the Law, only to speak in accord with the customs of his time, as we saw several examples earlier. When he says that "the Law will come forth from Zion," he means that living according to God will no longer be the exclusive right of Abraham's line but will be a privilege extended to all the world. This has come to pass, for the Gospel has been made available to all creatures. What a great miracle it is that all nations have been taught the Gospel. Even the Apostles themselves were overwhelmed by the universality of God's salvific teaching. They found it difficult to believe that the Gentiles could be saved. When Peter went to Cornelius, he was fearful he would dishonor the Gospel by sharing it with a Gentile. Nothing was more sacred than the teachings of Christ, and so he had grave doubts whether Gentiles should be permitted to share in them. True, when Christ sent out His Apostles, He did not say at first, "Preach to all creatures"; He expressly forbid them to leave Judah. "Go," He said, "gather us the lost sheep of the House of Israel." The restoration and perfecting of all things, which we spoke of yesterday, could not happen until after the resurrection. Thus, before the resurrection Christ forbid His Apostles to preach outside Judah; after the resurrection, He said, "Go, preach to all creatures." This commandment baffled many men. Let us see why.

At Micah's time, it seemed all God's teaching would be lost when the people were led into captivity. The Temple was destroyed; there were no longer any sacrifices; all their religious rituals and observances were brought to an end; there was no longer a High Priest or any kind of ecclesiastical order. It seemed that the Jews would be bastardized by Chaldean ways, that God's Law would be corrupted and perverted. But, on the contrary, Micah said that not only will God sustain His truth in the time of greatest troubles but that He will make it flourish more than ever, proclaiming it to the ends of the earth. "Up to now," Micah says, "Jerusalem has been the school in which you were taught God's truth. Now this school is closed because you people have been taken into captivity. But our Lord is going to radically change all this! In the past, we Jews had the exclusive privilege of knowing God. Now, however, all the world will rejoice in Him; His Law will be proclaimed to all creatures."

God had to step in and take matters in hand to sustain and advance His Word. How could a people in captivity maintain the Word? What else could they think, save that all of God's teaching would be lost? Furthermore, things went from bad to worse. Antiochus, a cruel tyrant, profaned the Temple and burnt all the holy books of the Law and the Prophets. He forbid on pain of death that one single world of Scripture be preserved. It seemed certain, then, that all God's teaching would be lost.

What has happened since those days? Great troubles and conflicts have cropped up all over the place because God's teaching has been perverted. At the time of Christ, all men were led astray and corrupted by false doctrines. Indeed, the Scribes had so drowned the people in false superstitions that no one could rescue them. Christ shouted out against the hypocrites, "You have forsaken and perverted God's commandments to give way to your traditions." Today, the Papists are just as perverse. Instead of God's teachings spreading throughout the world, they seem to be losing ground, about to disappear completely. But let us not despair. God always fulfills our hopes beyond our wildest dreams. The infinite power and bounty of God has preserved the Bible down through the ages. His saving truth has in fact been extended to all the nations. God has in fact fulfilled Micah's promises, which were more than necessary to sustain the faithful at the time when they faced total destruction.

But, on the other hand, does it not make us quake in our boots when we see the terrible vengeance God visited upon Jerusalem, the city He loved so much, the cradle of His teaching? What is Jerusalem like today? God has sown the land with salt. There is no more desolate, marred place on the face of the earth. Yet, at one time, it was His Throne, the place where His Temple was built and His name was invoked. Today it looks like the pit of Hell, although it once was a paradise. What brought about such horrible desolation? The sinful ingratitude of the people. God first revealed His salvific teachings there. Christ preached there, followed by His Apostles. The Gospel was preached there before it went to any other part of the world. Countless miracles were performed there in proof of God's teaching. Despite all this, the people remained incredulous. They so bitterly rebelled against God that they persecuted the Gospel and purged from their midst all that God's grace had given them. That is why such terrible vengeance befell Jerusalem.

Let us take care, lest such horrible punishment befall us. If we rebel against God, the Lord will stand over and against us as our Judge. He will shame us before all the world. He will sentence us to the most severe punishment possible, for He has shed so much grace upon us. Let us be aware that Christ is not in any way obligated to us. If we become perverse ingrates, He can well rescind His grace at any time, as the example of Jerusalem proves all too well. If God out of His infinite bounty chooses to reveal Himself to us, let us listen to Him in true faith and obedience.

What a madman, then, is the Pope to loudly boast that he is empowered by the Holy Apostolic See. When we cry out against the Papists for their abominations beyond imagination, idolatries, false doctrines, and diabolical inventions, they respond, "What? It is possible for the Holy Apostolic See to err?" Beware how the Pope and his henchmen use this fancy title to cover up their iniquities.

Did anyone ever claim for Rome what Micah claimed for Jerusalem: "The Law will go forth from Zion, and the Word from

218

Jerusalem!" Where was this ever said of Rome? Despite God's great love for Jerusalem, He punished it with a vengeance that makes your hair stand on end when we hear of it. Is Rome more privileged than Jerusalem? To whom should Rome be given, save to Satan to be its master?

Micah says that "He will judge many peoples and rebuke mighty nations." There is no doubt he is referring to Christ as Judge, for God wishes to govern the world through His Son. Micah says God will judge among peoples, because heretofore He governed only one people. But now God wishes to govern the entire world. In Hebrew to judge means to govern, so Micah is saying that Christ will govern not just the Jews or some small corner of the world but all the nations. This does not mean that all nations will submit to Him, for many will resist His call. It does mean, however, that there will no longer be a certain people designated as the People of God. Since God's grace is shed upon all nations, it is up to us to decide whether Christ will be our Governor as God has so empowered Him to be.

How exactly will Christ govern us? Through the Gospels. The Kingdom of our Lord does not consist of force or mundane glory but of teaching. Micah speaks of Christ rebuking nations, to emphasize that the world must be reformed. Men must be reprimanded to change their ways. If the world stays the same, there can be no Kingdom of Jesus Christ; men are by nature enemies of God, full of malice and iniquity. Christ cannot govern as long as men remain in their natural state. Men must change their ways; otherwise the Throne of Christ cannot be among us.

Micah makes it clear that the true Church is where Christ reigns, where He alone is recognized as Sovereign Prince, where each subjugates himself to Him. In short, the true Church is where "He will judge." This means that men must not have the audacity to govern themselves; they must surrender all authority to Christ. Each must so abase themselves before Him that only He alone is exalted. "But how can this be?" one might ask. Is it not necessary for there to be various levels of rank within the Church?" Yes, but these must not be allowed to detract from the authority of the Master. When Christ ordains pastors, ministers, doctors, evangelists, and apostles, He does not give them the special prerogatives that belong to Him alone. Men are not His fellow colleagues. They are to serve Him in order that He may teach through their mouths. All teaching must come from Him and Him alone. The purpose of the Church is not for us to become very attractive and popular among people; the Church exists for the express purpose of leading everyone to our Master. The Church will never be properly managed unless Christ alone is served there and all totally subjugate themselves to Him.

Micah also reveals to us the condition and nature of the Kingdom. Jesus Christ will not reign in the manner of earthly princes, but by teaching alone. For this reason, he says Christ will rebuke. Do we wish to have Christ as our King? Then, we must not imagine Him as it would seem good to us. Papists claim to worship Christ; but in point of fact they spit in His face, holding all His teachings in abomination. Satan is their master. Do we wish Christ to take us as His people and be our King? Then, we must accept His teachings, permit Him to guide and conduct us. Then we can boast of ourselves, saying Christ is our Savior and King. Remember, the purpose of His teaching is to rebuke us, so that we come to change our ways. If we cannot tolerate His reproaches, we will not profit from the School of Jesus Christ. Whoever wishes to remain in his natural state, whoever refuses to renounce his whims and foolish fantasies should seek out a master other than the Son of God.

Those who trust in themselves are too proud to humble themselves and make room for Christ in their lives. Those who demand to be heard seriously threaten the authority and pre-eminence of the King. Those who refuse to submit to Him have nothing to look forward to but their own sudden destruction, which will come sooner than they think. How ungrateful can men be! Let us pray that the Holy Spirit, which is the Spirit of Compliance, so tame our fierce pride that we cooperate fully with God. However harsh and severe His reproaches, may we never refuse these good things. May we overcome our natural resentment of criticism, so that our only desire is for God to correct our faults as a loving father would his child's. In short, if we wish to come to Christ, the first step is that we humble ourselves, realizing that in ourselves we are but pieces of shit. The next step is that we pray Christ so cleanses us that we may present ourselves to God with our heads held high.

Micah says that the powerful mighty peoples, who live like savage beasts, will become like gentle lambs and sheep to be numbered Christ's flock. If men are to be governed by Christ, they must not boast of their wisdom, power, strength, virtue, or anything else. Men must renounce all pride, for it is the major stumbling block along the path to Christ. Men who have absolutely nothing to boast of will act so proud and fierce that you are half afraid to be around them. Men who have something to boast of let their pride go to their heads. They are overly ambitious and extremely egotistical; they are filled with nothing but spite and contempt for others; their tongues spit lethal venom on God and their neighbors. But Micah says that when God's power radiates forth from Mt. Zion, all peoples, even the most proud and fierce, will humble themselves before Him. Isaiah 11 says that God will so tame the ferocity and cruelty of savage beasts, such as bears, lions, and wolves, that a small child could lead them. That is the kind of meekness we will have if we benefit at all from the Gospel. If we want to prove to God and men that we are star pupils in the School of Jesus Christ, we must do two things. The first is that we show we fully accept Christ as our Judge and Governor. The second is that we show we came to this decision of our own free will without being coerced in any way whatsoever.

Having shown how Christ wishes to govern, Micah turns to the fruits of such governing. "Their swords and spears," he says, "will be turned into pruning hooks and plowshares." By this, he means Christ will bring peace and tranquility to the world. Men will be transformed. They will no longer be inclined to evil, but will take great pains to aid one another.

Now, there are three important points to note here. First, it is our nature to quarrel with one another. If men do not accept Christ, they will fight like cats and dogs. There will be only cruelty and hatred in them. They will wish only to destroy one another.

Although we may not realize it, human nature is totally depraved through and through. There is not one evil that cannot be found in man. Each of us is an abysm of all iniquity. We cannot deny the fact that men think only of themselves. Out of this self-love, men come to hate each other and to seek continually their profits at the expense of their neighbors. Men are by nature ill-tempered and intolerant. They refuse to take what they have dished out on others. If they are made to suffer the slightest injury or inconvenience, they are ready for a major war. They will remain in such iniquity until Christ totally reforms them.

Secondly, since Christ is our Reformer, He will so govern us that each aids rather than harms the neighbor. No man will ever profit from the Gospel until he is stripped of all self-love and all his evil impulses to harm his neighbors.

Thirdly, we must do more than merely abstaining from harming our neighbors; we must do everything possible to aid them. Micah does not say, "The swords will be smashed and broken"; he says they will be turned into pruning hooks and plowshares, as if to say, "Not only will men who raged against their neighbors be tamed but they will aid all those in need." Plowshares and pruning hooks are instruments to work the land, from which we derive our nourishment. So Micah is prophesying that God's children will have an abundance of goods at the coming of the Lord. In that day, they will devote themselves to helping others, rendering whatever service they can, as our Lord commands. God wants all His children to rejoice in His blessings at the coming of the Lord.

Note carefully Micah does not mean that God's children will enjoy an abundance of worldly goods. More often than not, God's children are among the poorest when it comes to worldly possessions. Christ's Kingdom is purely spiritual, so we are sadly mistaken if we think it is our ticket to material prosperity. In fact, that is precisely the reason why many refuse to accept Christ as King. He commands that we serve the neighbor, whereas each and every one of us is selfishly preoccupied with his own physical well-being. True, we like to brag that Christ is our King and we love flaunting all over the place what good Christians we are. But in the end Christ will make us rue the day we so abused His name. So let us not boast of being Christians until Christ reforms our nature! When we are no longer given to hatred and quarrelling, when our only goal is to do everything possible to help the neighbor, then we can call ourselves true Christians.

We will never be at peace among ourselves unless we are at peace with God. How will we come to live in brotherly love? When we are reconciled to God. How can we be reconciled to God? When we accept Jesus Christ in our hearts. God and man have been mortal enemies locked in eternal combat. Although God has rained down terrible wrath and horrible vengeance upon His enemy, He has also sent His Son to be the Peacemaker between Himself and man. If we accept the peace Christ brings through His Gospel, then we will be at peace with God. We will know we are at peace with God, when we live in harmony and brotherly love. So if we truly wish to have peace with God, we must first of all make peace with our neighbors. How can we boast that we live in God's House if we cannot get our neighbors. How can we boast that we live in God's House if we cannot get along with His children? That is absolutely impossible! If we wish Lord Jesus Christ to reconcile us to God the Father, we must be joined together into one harmonious unity. And how are we to go about that? First, we must stop harming and hurting one another. Secondly, we must apply all our energies to helping our neighbors. It is the sworn duty of all Christians to devote themselves fully to tasks that serve the good of the community. For example, Micah speaks here of working the land. True, there are many other necessary tasks, but it is a matter here of what serves the neighbor. If we apply

225

all our energies to work for the common good and not for our own advantage or profit, others will no longer resent the fruits of our labors, so speaks the prophet Micah.

True, we will never attain such perfection in this world until the very end. Our Lord's Kingdom has only just begun. Yet right in the midst of us there are fanatical madmen who wish to abolish all civil authority. "Behold," they shout, "Micah and Isaiah say that the swords will be turned into plowshares. The Lord is among us. Down with all magistrates and governors!" Indeed! We would certainly be in a fine mess then. Since Christ's Kingdom has just begun, it has to be nurtured along until it reaches its final perfection. Since we are far from the peace of which Micah speaks, Christ has ordained that we be governed by civil and ecclesiastical authorities to insure that we understand our calling and diligently attend to the needs of our neighbors, physically as well as spiritually.

Following this holy teaching, we prostrate ourselves before the face of our good God, acknowledging our sinfulness. May it please God to open our eyes to know His son, who is His living image. May we render Him due honor. May we so trust in Him that our lives are a living testimony that our only desire is to serve Him and be His people. May we profit from the teaching of the Gospel, so that we come before God, confessing our sins and begging His pardon, truly confident He will forgive us in the name of Jesus Christ, His Son. May Christ's death and passion truly be to our benefit and serve as the anchor which keeps us from going astray. May God multiply His grace upon us according to our needs. May He shed this grace not only on us but on all the peoples and nations of the world, etc.

* * *

(15) Friday, December 12, 1550

Each will sit under his vine and under his fig tree. No one will be afraid, for the Lord of multitudes has so spoken. Each people will walk according to its own god; but we will walk in the name of the Lord, our God, for ever and ever, etc. Micah 4

Yesterday, we saw how the Gospel serves to our benefit: It is the vehicle by which Christ reconciles us to Himself in order that we be at peace with God. This reconciliation requires that we live in brotherly love. We must no longer live according to our perverted nature, by which we are inclined to all evil; we must live not only in peace and tranquility with our neighbors but also apply all our energies to serving the needs of our brothers. Then we will truly be the Church of God.

Also we recognized our own powerlessness to bring about such a dramatic change in ourselves. It is necessary for God to work within us. According to Micah, the mission of the Son of God is to so reform the hearts of men that they will live in brotherly love. In that day, each will sit under his vine and under his fig tree without being afraid. Now, when he speaks of the vine and the fig tree, he means that God will afraid, he means that we will not fear being savaged by our enemies. What great blessings God sheds upon His children when Christ dwells among them! There is nothing we prize more than peace, but we have not searched for it as we should. Peace comes only when Christ reigns among us. If we seek peace apart from Christ, it is as if we have broken up God into separate, conflicting pieces. But, of course, that is means that we will enjoy our goods in peaceful tranquility, that we will not be sacked and pillaged by our enemies. What great blessings God sheds upon His children when Christ dwells among them! There is nothing we prize more than peace, but we have not searched for it as we should. Peace comes only when Christ reigns among us. If we seek peace apart from Christ, it is as if we have broken up God into separate, conflicting pieces. But, of course, that is impossible. If we truly wish to have peace, we must be totally subjugated to Christ, then we will enjoy the peace and abundance of goods He promises here through his prophet.

But remember, all these promises of the Kingdom will never be fulfilled completely in this world. Christ's Kingdom is just beginning, so it will grow day by day. As its growth advances, God will shed yet more grace upon us. But the final perfection will come only when we are stripped of the flesh and have departed from this world. Because Christ's Kingdom is purely spiritual, we must not expect the world to ever be Paradise. If life on earth were in fact perfect, we would be misled into confusing His Kingdom with the vanities of the world. True, Saint Paul has said that if we serve God with a clean and pure conscience, we will be aided and nourished in this life by the infinite bounty and grace of God. But we must look beyond this life! We must realize that our present life is only a passage-way we must hasten through. We will never enjoy the peace of which Micah speaks. We live in mortal fear of our enemies, we suffer, and there is great poverty among us. The Kingdom has hardly come to perfection among us. If we stop and think for a minute, we will thank God that this is so. It is a very necessary and good thing that God sends all sorts of afflictions upon us, in order that we look away from this world and focus upon the promise of the celestial life to come.

This promise is contained in the Law. It is said, "You will enjoy your goods in peace and tranquility. If you plant a vine, you will receive its fruit. If you purchase something, it will serve you well. You will sleep soundly, undisturbed by worries." But there is always a condition attached: These things will come to pass only if you do such-and-such, as God has so commanded. If you do not keep your part of the bargain, you will be without excuse before God and He will curse you according to the Law. So has the Lord warned all those who would break His commandments.

Micah's point, however, is that this situation has radically changed. There is no longer the condition "you must do such-and-such"; there is now a remedy against the curses of the Law. God sent His Son because He wished to abolish the merit system and receive us in all mercy. The curses of the Law have been converted into blessings. Our promise is grounded in the infinite mercy of God, not in contractual stipulations. Thus our promise is not like those of the Law, which were contingent upon the works of men. God does not send His blessings upon us according to our merits; nor does He wish to punish us according to our demerits; He wishes to be merciful and forgive us; He wishes to reveal to us that His love for us is far deeper than any paternal love we might ever know or imagine.

Nevertheless, as I have said, God's grace is not going to create a totally perfect world. The reason is our refusal to accept Christ as our King. It is no surprise that we will never enjoy goods in such abundance as Micah promises here. The reason is simple: We refuse to accept Christ as Lord and Master of the entire world. Saint Paul says in Hebrews that God made Christ Heir of the entire world in order that we might share in His inheritance. If we do not accept Christ as Heir, we will be deprived of the many services rendered us by creatures. Furthermore, if we turn our backs on Christ, we can enjoy no peace; He contains within Himself the peace that must exist between God and man. Why is there so much trouble in the world today? Why do the good things of life slip right through our fingers? Why do we not have the leisure to enjoy them in peace and tranquility? What brings about all these wars and pestilences? Why are the poor so afflicted? Men refuse Christ as their King, just as we deny God any authority over us. On the one hand, there are the Papists, the sworn enemies of the Gospel. They furiously rage against it, taking great pains to abolish it by the sword, fire, and all sorts of horrible torments. On the other, there are ourselves. How much have we really profited from the Gospel? If all it took to be a Christian were to mouth a few good words, we would all be Christians on the tips of our tongues. Truth is, there is not one square foot of our land

231

where Christ has any authority. So it should come as no surprise that God deprives us of His blessings and that we know no inner peace. Since we have rejected Christ, is it not fair He refuses to share with us the good things He bears?

Granted, one might argue, "Micah is contradicting himself. He says that the promise of the Kingdom is founded solely upon the infinite bounty of God. How, then, can he blame men if the promise is not fulfilled?" True, we had absolutely nothing to do with God making this promise; but we are to blame, because we reject God's grace. He reveals His Gospel to all the world, but men everywhere refuse it out of their ingratitude. Nevertheless, God will never be without His children; there will always be a small throng of faithful men. However scattered they may be and however hidden and invisible they may seem, they constitute the true Church and share in all things promised by Jesus Christ. Trust in the Lord! If we do not have a vine or fig tree, if we are menaced by enemies, if the land will not support us, if we have only a crust of bread left to eat, believe and the Lord will sustain us: If we are persecuted, fear not. Trust in the Lord and He will protect us. If we are troubled by bodily afflictions, poverty, illness, let us make peace with the Lord and He will lighten our burdens. Look at how the faithful enjoy God's promise: If they are totally destitute, if they do not own one square foot of earth, if they have neither vine nor fig tree to bear them fruit, they are consoled because they can say with true conviction, "Our Father will sustain us." That is why the faithful can rejoice in all the world, even though they have nothing. If their lives are hanging on only by a thread, they say, "God has the whole world in His hands. Although we are attached from all sides, we feel secure, for we are all in His safekeeping." The faithful are at peace in the midst of the world's worst turmoil, because they trust in God. If we are anxious and deeply troubled, it is because we lack true faith. If we wish to be at peace, we must accept Christ as Heir of the world. Then we can rest assured that He will so sustain and nurture us that we will lack nothing. If we are in the midst of our worst enemies, who are coming at us with all their might, let us believe in the Lord and He will give us strength and courage. If we are dying, fear not! For the Lord calls us to eternal life. God ordained death, that we might go to a greater life beyond. In the meantime, however, we must bear great hardship and suffering.

God exterminates our exterior man, as Saint Paul calls him. He purges us of all worldly things. Remember, as I have said, we will never come to God unless He brings down our pride by submitting us to countless afflictions. If we have to suffer great poverty and deprivation, it is because God so wishes to mortify our flesh that our lust after worldly goods will no longer be the major stumbling block to our coming to Him. Our Lord permits there to be great wars and conflicts, so that we may come to cherish more deeply His spiritual peace. That, I say, is what Micah means when he says each will rest under his vine and under his fig tree.

Micah continues, "For the mouth of the Lord has so spoken, the mouth of the Lord of multitudes." He means that God holds the whole world in His hands, that He alone decides the course of all events. This is an important point, for God's promises seemed null and void among the Jews. First Micah harshly rebuked them. Then Jerusalem was besieged. After the Jews had languished for a time, they were taken into captivity. The Temple was destroyed. The people were in terrible desolation. It seemed that all was lost and that God's promises were annulled. The people were in terrible trouble and subject to great temptation. They asked, "How can Micah say that the Law will go forth from Zion, and the Word from Jerusalem when in fact these places have been totally destroyed? There is no longer the Temple, in which God was served and worshipped. What has become of God's promises?" Even the most faithful among the Jews were subject to such temptation, so God had to strengthen their faith in His promises. That is why Micah says that "the mouth of the Lord has spoken," as if to say, "My friends, I know you are in terrible trouble; I know you will think me a madman for what I am going to say, since you see no signs that the Lord will restore His Church. But do not believe according to your senses. Look to the power and the strength of Him in whose name I speak and I will lead you through these difficult times; for He has the power to fulfill all His promises, although that may now seem difficult for you to believe." Micah, then, is not adding any new promises; he is trying to remedy the seemingly glaring deficiencies in those God had already made.

Here is a rule of thumb that all of us should follow: Whenever our Lord makes us a promise, do not measure His power according to our standards. Know that He has the power to fulfill promises beyond your wildest dreams and in ways totally incomprehensible to us. Do we wish to have sure and certain faith? Then we must believe and confess with all our hearts: "God is faithful, He does not lie, His power will never diminish, He will triumph over all." Men think that they are great sages; they wish to argue and decide matters according to their own fantasies. That is why they have no certainty. If we wish to have certitude, we must hold fast to God's promises.

Above all, let us trust in the Lord to restore the Church! That is Micah's message for us today. He says it is in the very mouth of God Himself who has so spoken, to strengthen the faith of the Jews by assuring them that God Himself has personally put His official seal of approval on this promise of world peace through Jesus Christ. Today, when the world is in such turmoil that it seems about to collapse, let us hold fast to this promise. However great the discrepancy between the actual conditions of the world and God's promise, let us remember that He has personally guaranteed the Kingdom will be perpetual and the faithful will live in everlasting peace.

Micah continues, "The peoples will walk, each in the name of its own god. But we, we will walk in the name of the Lord, our God," as if to say, "True, all the world follows false gods. Men are prone to superstitions; they will have their idols and walk according to their own fantasies. Let them do whatever they want. They cannot block us from following the Word of God; nor can they tempt us to stray from the Path of Righteousness and abandon our calling. We will hold fast to God's truth!"

Micah, however, seems to contradict himself here. Earlier, he said that all the peoples and nations would humble themselves before Christ, that the world would be of one common faith. Now he says each people will follow its own idols. The contradiction is only apparent. Micah does not promise that the world will be of one faith in point of actual fact. He fully realizes that has never been the case and never will be. His point is that God's grace is available to all the world because one people, the line of Abraham, truly served God. There are no longer any distinctions between Greek and Jew, Gentile and Barbarian, as Saint Paul says; for every people, every nation has the opportunity to share in God's promise if it so desires.

But how many men truly desire to come to God? How many true Christians are there here in Geneva, where the Gospel is preached. The Gospel is available to everybody, but it is far from the case that everyone accepts it. God renews us through His Holy Spirit, so the Gospel is not a manmade word and does not govern us in the ways in which men are accustomed to governing themselves. Many will profess that they are Christians and true friends of Christ, yet they wish to be governed according to their natural impulses. There is no more of an alliance between them and Christ than there is between Christ and Satan's demons. That is the way it has always been with the vast majority of men and that is the way it will always be. Micah did not promise the world would be so renewed that not one single man would disobey God; he wished only to say that God has made available the opportunity for significant renewal to all the world.

Micah says that the fact others turn their backs on God should not give us occasion to stray from Him. This is a very important point. Our faith is not founded in men, so we must not allow ourselves to be tempted when we see them stumble and falter and run here and there after their idols. When all the world is going straight to Hell, when Satan destroys everything, we must stand firm in our faith; for true faith is not founded upon the world. When we see men reel about in all directions like a windblown sea, we must remain steady on course. We walk in the name of God, not in the name of men. If our faith is grounded in God, we will have the invincible strength to withstand all the temptations and troubles Satan throws in our faces. That, I emphasize, is the basic point of Micah's teaching.

How we sadly lack such faith! Our faith is so weak that it takes hardly anything at all to veer us off the Path of Right-eousness. The smallest whisper of temptation is easily confused with the Word of God, so that we backslide when we think to advance. The reason is simple: Our faith is not grounded in Jesus Christ. We have not profited from the School of God; for Micah has taught us that the major stipulation of God's promise is that we remain steadfastly grounded in the Word. Although all the world is going to Hell, we should remain unshakable in our faith. How shameful it is that those who call themselves Christians do not have near the strength of conviction in their beliefs as have the infidels and pagans in their foolish fantasies. Remember Jeremiah's reproach to the Jews: "The Pagans and Infidels are loyal to their gods, but you, you will not hold to my Word!"

Look at the Papists. They are demons who follow I don't know what all superstitions. They are not founded upon one single word of Scripture. Yet they are absolutely unshakable in their abominations. You cannot gain an inch of ground with them, no matter how hard you try. Look at the Turks. They are filled with a diabolical rage and ferocity. Although they are grounded only in Mohammed, they would have no difficulty dying for their law. Now take a good look at ourselves. The slightest temptation would suffice to sway the vast majority of us to renounce our God-given calling. Few, if any, of us would be loyal enough to risk their lives for the Gospel. There are even devils among us who, without any provocation whatsoever, relish trampling down the Gospels. Many among us who profess to be true Christians hold no more to the Gospels than does Satan himself.

May, then, Micah's words "the peoples will walk according to their gods, but we will walk in the name of the Lord" be firmly engraved in our memories. They mean we must not allow ourselves to be corrupted by the fact that the vast majority of the world was, is, and always will be given to superstitions. Today, we see many foolish wretches who try and excuse themselves by saying, "I just don't know what to do. I'm so overwhelmed by so many conflicting opinions that I just don't know what to believe." In order to make us more certain of His truth, our Lord warns us through Micah that the world will always be full of false religions, that there will always be poor wretches blinded by their own idolatries and superstitions, each going about his own special devotions. Must all this lead us astray from our calling in the name of our God? Now, by "our God," Micah means the God who has revealed Himself to us. We have the true God, not a god forged out of thin air, as have the Papists. When you ask them about their god, you will find they really do not know when they worship. If you ask the Turks, they will say they believe in a god who created heaven and earth; but they sharply contradict themselves by their refusal to accept Christ, without whom God cannot be known. Regarding the Jews, they still live in the world of shadows with the veil over their eyes. But we know whom we worship, as Christ said of the Jews when they kept to the Law and worshipped as He so ordained. We know, I say, that it is our God we serve and that everything we have comes from Him alone. In brief, Micah is saying we must understand our faith to

239

be fully guaranteed because God has revealed His will to us. We are then, obliged to stand firm against all the other religions of the world, for we are fortified in the name of our God. We must persevere wholeheartedly in our calling and follow the Lord wherever He may lead us, not just for a month or a year but until the end of our days. When we are assailed from all directions, our faith must be like the root of a tree, which remains unshaken when the branches are blown in the wind. We will see great struggle and turmoil in the world, but we must never allow these assaults of Satan to shake us from the certitude we have in the Word and in the Gospel.

Today the world is blinder than ever. The Papists, pagans, and infidels rage more than ever against God's teachings. Of course, this is nothing new. Micah prophesied that people would walk according to their own gods, as if to say, "You should not be shocked that men wander off on idle ventures. That is what must come to pass." So Micah's message for us today is: Do not complain; just thank God that He gave you the grace to know Him so you are not left in the lurch with mere opinions formed out of thin air, as is the poor Papist, who can say only, "I think I know who God is; I'm really not sure, however." We have been given ample assurance that the Word is the infallible truth of God, that He will never default upon His promise, and that we will never be vanquished by all the temptations Satan will throw at us.

Micah continues, saying, "God will assemble she who is lame and she whom He rejected. She who is lame will be made strong and powerful. She whom was rejected will be made mighty." He means that although the Lord may afflict His own, He will not fail to take pity on them. He compares the Church to a woman, which was common practice among the prophets. He stresses what sad shape she is in, saying that she is so powerless, so lame, crippled, and deformed that it seems the hand of God is about to crush the life out of her. Note that he says not only is the Church afflicted by the world but also by God's own hand. He intends this passage to strengthen our faith and patience. No matter how sad of shape we may be in, we must not give up hope that God will deliver us. The Lord has promised not only to deliver us from all the assaults of the world but from all Satan's evil machinations to destroy our faith. Trust in God, I say, to be our refuge amidst the great troubles of the world!

Today, we are like a man lost in a storm at sea, pounded on all sides by wind and fury. We must not lose courage, as men often do in such danger. We must remember that the Lord has stretched out His hand to rescue us. The Lord will permit us all to be afflicted for a time. Indeed, it may even seem that He is against us. Nevertheless, in the end, He will deliver us from all our adversaries. God has promised to so strengthen us by His grace that we will surmount all Satan's machinations and crush him under our feet, as Saint Paul says in Romans 16.

241

Following this holy teaching, we prostrate ourselves before the face of our good God, acknowledging our sinfulness. We pray that He so opens our eyes that we see Jesus Christ clearer than ever before. May we come to recognize that He alone is the source of all our happiness. May we apply all our heart and all our might to building the Kingdom. May the Holy Spirit so strengthen us that nothing will deter us from this task. May we hold firm to the course Christ has set for us and not be blown astray by all the turmoil and wickedness of the world with its overwhelming multitude of false religions. May our eyes be fixed on Christ alone. May we never be separated from Him. May we approach closer and closer to Him until He is revealed to us in all His plentitude and perfection. May God shed this grace not only on us but on all the peoples and nations of the earth, etc.

All-powerful God, celestial Father, with the coming of Jesus Christ, Your Son, You fulfilled what all the prophets have promised for so long. Each day you strive to unite us in one faith, that we serve and worship you of one mind and one heart. Give us the grace that we no longer remain scattered and separated from one another, each walking according to his own chaotic, perverse appetites. May Christ gather us together and deliver us to you. May we not merely say with our lips that we obey you but may we prove our obedience by living in true piety and fear of Your name. May we be united into one brotherhood, so that each will lovingly minister to the needs of his neighbors, as so you wish your name to be served. May our adoption meet with your ever deepening approval, so that we may invoke boldly and confidently our Father through Jesus Christ, our Lord.   Amen.

* * *

(16) Saturday, December 13, 1550

And you, daughter of Zion, fold of the flock and sanctuary, it will come to you. The first power will come, the kingdom to the daughter of Jerusalem! Why are you crying now? Is the king not in you, or is your counselor dead? Why do you cry out as a woman in labor? Micah 4

Yesterday, we heard Micah's promise that God will perpetually aid the Church. The Lord, he says, will so strengthen the Church that it will never perish. There will always be some remnant. When the Church undergoes its greatest afflictions and agonies, when it seems about to collapse, the Lord will fortify it. let us be on guard, then, against the many temptations that will befall us; for judging by what is happening in the world today, it seems that God wishes to completely wipe out all memory of His Church, that He does not want its name ever to be mentioned again in this world. But He has revealed that He will always preserve some remnant of it, which He will restore when the time is right. When troubled times befall us, when it seems that chaos reigns everywhere, let us look to the Lord's promise that He will so strengthen us that all our debilities will be transformed into power and might. The Lord has made it clear we will find our strength in Him, not in ourselves.

Micah emphasizes that if God is to so strengthen us, He must reign in our midst. If we do not accept God as our King, everything will go to rack and ruin. Certainly the House of David foreshadowed God's presence to reign among His people. But the

244

wickedness and unfaithfulness of the kings who followed threw everything into chaos. Nevertheless, because God has revealed Himself to us through the Son, we may rest assured that He is always ready to take us by the hand and deliver us, provided that we grant Him total and complete authority over us. If we refuse God's grace, He in turn will reject us and give us over to Satan to be our master. By the same token, when men comply fully with God and totally subjugate themselves to Him, then they may boast it is God who governs them.

Consequently, Micah says that if the Church is to enjoy the good things God promised it, He must reign there. Psalm 46 really takes up the cause here when it says that we must fear not when we are in the midst of troubles and obstacles, when we are besieged by all the crafty schemes the wicked can cook up against us. Why? God has taken up residence among us. Furthermore, this Psalm specifically says that such residence consists of a kingdom, to make it plain that if we reject God, He will punish our ingratitude and we will not share in His power. What is the major stipulation of God's promise to aid us? We must accept God as our King, which means He must have sovereign authority over us. Then, I say, men can boast that they are the People of God and that He dwells among them.

What is the presence of God, save the Word, by which He reveals His will? Consequently, if we do not rebel against His will, if He enjoys complete and total control over us, then He will protect and sustain us. It is the epitome of all well-being

245

when we obey God everywhere and in all matters. If we do not enjoy such happiness, the blame falls on none other than our own ingratitude. God is present in Christ for one reason only: To rule all the world. The Word will go forth from Zion to be shed on all the earth, as Micah says. Our Lord has only one wish and that is to rule over us. If we are so foolish as to reject His grace, it is just and fair that He deprives us of the blessings He promised and that we experience what great unhappiness comes from being separated from Him. Furthermore, Micah does not say that God wishes to reign only for a day or such-and-such a length of time; he says that God wishes to reign forever. What advantage is it for us to assume that tomorrow the Lord might default on the sustenance he has given us today? For a time we might be at ease not knowing what is going to happen; but eventually that proves very unsatisfying. When God reveals that He will continue to aid us to the end of our lives, indeed even beyond our days because He will protect us in death as well as life, what more could anyone ask of Him? If we live in the midst of terrible upheavals, if it seems God has forsaken us, this is all our fault because we have rejected Him. On God's own end of it, He wishes only to continue governing us as He so began for the sake of our salvation.

However unworthy we may be, God dwells among us. He, through His infinite bounty, will surmount all our evil and build His Kingdom among us. It is more than necessary His Throne be among us, for it supports us in all our weaknesses and infirmities. That is why it is said that the blessings He sheds upon us are grounded solely in His infinite mercy. But let us not abuse God's patience. The fact that He pardons our sins and supports us in our depravity should not become an excuse for us to give free rein to evil. Jesus Christ cannot be our King unless we accept Him as such. He will take pity on us poor sinners, provided we do not reject His grace and rebel against Him. God will reign among His people forever. Zephaniah says that God will make His people respected and honored throughout all the world. Like Micah, he stresses that God will give the Church such strength that it will be able to defend itself against all those who would afflict it. After he has said all this, he adds, "You will have a name by which you will be respected throughout all the world." What will bring this about? Are some men truly more honorable than others? No! The reason is simply that the glory of God will reign among His people forever. Men will enjoy fame and renown only if they comply fully with God and allow Him the absolute authority He is entitled to.

Micah continues, "You, Tower of the Flock and sanctuary, it will come to you, daughter of Zion, the first kingdom will come." When he speaks of the Tower of the Flock, there is no doubt he means Jerusalem. But more needs be said here. Perhaps he speaks this way because Jerusalem was lacking in honor and respect and would even be more shamed yet. Perhaps, when he speaks of the Tower of the Flock, he has in mind the Genesis account of the

247

Tower of Edar, as if to say, "You were a great and marvelous city. You were the place of God's Throne. You were the royal seat of His kingdom. Now, however, you will become a little village; but in the end, you will be rebuilt." There is no point in getting into a long harangue over whether or not he had this similitude in mind. Let us stick with what is certain and that is this: He calls Jerusalem the Tower of the Flock because it was the nest where the remnant of God's people were gathered together. Our Lord preserved the seed of His Church, and Jerusalem was the nursery for His children.

When Micah says, "And you, daughter of Zion, your first power will come," it is tempting to assume he is looking forward to a restoration of Jerusalem's former position of political supremacy. Perhaps, then, "first power" means "corporal power and splendors." However, what is uppermost in Micah's mind is a retreat for the small remnant that remained in Judah. That is why he so aptly describes Jerusalem as a "sanctuary," as if to say, "True, you will see chaos everywhere. Our enemies will cause great havoc in our land. There will be terrible desolation. But God will preserve a little nest for His own. Jerusalem will be the barn in which God will store the seed He wishes to preserve."

Earlier it was said that Micah taught during the time of Isaiah and that Micah, being the elder of the two, was the first to die. It should come as no surprise, then, that he too speaks of the Tower of the Flock. At the time of Hezekiah, the kingdom of Judah was pillaged and sacked by enemies, Jerusalem was besieged. Sennacherib, resting assured of total victory, made up his mind to devastate the land. As Isaiah tells it, after he got his army in place, and with his eyes firmly fixed on Mt. Zion, he raised his hand against the people, roaring and thundering against them, threatening to destroy their Temple, as only one totally confident of victory can do. But Jerusalem was spared for the moment. Subsequently, however, the city was sacked, the people exiled. Although the Church was totally devastated, God did preserve one small remnant of it. That is why Micah says that however Jerusalem may shrink in size, it will be the Tower of the Flock, that God will collect His people there to preserve them.

Micah adds that "the first kingdom will return, indeed it will come to you." He uses two verbs having the same meaning, because he is speaking of something totally incredible: Seeing such awful desolation, how could anyone ever believe that the kingdom would be restored and the city rebuilt? Nevertheless, he says that God will bring order out of this chaos: "The first kingdom will come." At the time of David and Solomon, God greatly exalted this kingdom. Subsequently, it shrunk greatly. At the time of Rehoboam, son of Solomon, 10 1/2 tribes had deserted. Only a small throng of men remained. There was no longer any government or police. In the end, the kingdom totally collapsed. Nevertheless, Micah says that God will restore the kingdom of Judah, indeed "the first kingdom." However, it would

249

not be restored to its former condition. Rather, it would be so exalted by God that Micah says, "You will never see anything else in the world like it. No, not even the glory of Solomon will compare with what God will bring about after He has redeemed you from your servitude and delivered you from Babylon."

We no longer have the kingdom of the House of David, but a far greater one; we have the truth of all these shadows of things to come. The Son of God reigns over us in person. He is our Emmanuel, as the Holy Spirit so named Him, which means God is present, we are united to Him, and He dwells in us. Our condition is far better and much more excellent than that of the Patriarchs. Not only do we have men of David's lineage but we have our Redeemer, the Son of God, who wishes us to be His people and flock. True, He does not dwell among us corporally; but His strength and the grace of His Spirit are shed everywhere upon the world. Although we cannot see Christ, He is here, present among us now; and He will make us know His presence, through faith and hope. Rest assured that whenever He comes to our aid, we will not perish. Without Him, how would we be able to resist against Satan and all the temptations he throws our way? How would we be able to exist in the midst of so many enemies whose only desire is to destroy us totally? It is very necessary, then, for God's hand to be close to us through our Lord, Jesus Christ. Yet, we see the Church is dying through its own decadence. This is purely our fault because we would not permit Him to govern us, as was mentioned earlier. Because of the wickedness and ingratitude of men, Christ seems to be receding farther and farther away from us, so we are no longer able to look upon Him. The vast majority of men hold the Gospel in great contempt; and everywhere we look, we see things are as perverse as they could possibly be. What is the cause of this, save our sinfulness? But will this discourage us? No! For we know that Christ, who contains the living reality of His Kingdom within Himself, has been exalted and that the Gospel has extended God's salvific power to all men. So let us wait patiently upon the Lord to restore this first kingdom, which as yet remains abolished.

True, there has always been some seed and some remnant; but the ingratitude of the world necessitates that they be as hidden underground, that no one be permitted to see how the Lord reigns. Nevertheless, we must not give up hope that God will deliver this first kingdom from its desolation. Although this will not come to pass in this world, we always look forward to the Last Day, when our Lord, Jesus Christ, will come in the majesty of God, His Father, accompanied by all His angels. In that day, we will see the greatest restoration ever. Indeed, Solomon's kingdom will not even begin to compare with the majesty of the one to come.

So Micah's message for us today is one of great hope. He says twice that "it will come," to emphasize that we must trust completely in God's promise to restore the first kingdom and adopt us as His children. So let us rest assured that God will always provide a refuge for His people. Let us remember that however the Devil may strive to destroy all the world, God will take pity upon the faithful who invoke His name. However it may seem that everything is going to rack and ruin, however it may seem that Christ has rejected us and vanished from our midst, let us not give up hope that God will put things back in order again. The Lord has promised to restore the first kingdom, so let us be purged of all distrust and incredulity. We may not be convinced upon first hearing of this promise; but Micah has repeated it in order that we may return to it and be convinced upon second hearing that Christ will be exalted and all the world will obey Him. Let us fix our eyes upon the Last Day, when Christ will come in the majesty of God, His Father, to be exalted over all creatures. Let us wait patiently for this day. When we see His Kingdom is not exalted in this world, let us look beyond it to the Last Day, when He will appear in order to restore all things.

Consequently, Micah adds, "Why do you cry, daughter of Zion? Is your king no longer with you? Has your counselor perished? It is truly necessary you cry and lament, for you must depart from the city and live in the fields. You will go to Babylon. But your God will redeem you from there. You will be delivered from the hand of our enemies." Now, when he asks, "Why do you cry?" This is to warn the faithful of the terrible affliction about to befall them. True, this would not come to pass in his time; but still it was necessary for the faithful to be armed well before the blows began to fall. If our enemy has his sword unsheathed and is ready to strike us, there is no time to say,

"Wait up. I have to get my gear together." We must be totally prepared before our enemy attacks.

Now, God submitted His people to a very great temptation indeed when He permitted Jerusalem to be pillaged, the Temple to be demolished, and the kingdom of the House of David to be abolished. God had said, "I will establish a throne which will stand firm. Also He had said, "The race and line of David will go on forever." Now the complete opposite was happening. It seemed that God did not wish to abide by His promises. So the people said to themselves, "We're finished! Our situation is hopeless. David's kingdom was our refuge. The king was our breath of life, as he is so described in Jeremiah's Lamentations. Now that we no longer have him, we have nothing to look forward to but our own destruction!" The faithful were terribly perplexed, so it was very necessary to arm them against all such temptations, as I have just said. That is why Micah asked, "Why do you cry?" To give them advanced warning. True, he also said that the kingdom will be restored, but he made it plain this would not happen for a very long time. In sum, he says, "True, you will know the mercy of God upon you; but do not think this will exempt you from all affliction, for it is necessary you be taken into captivity and be cruelly enslaved. Prepare yourselves for these coming chastisements, for your wicked ways must be corrected. But do not despair, for God will take pity on you."

Micah says, "Cry, because you no longer have a king," and with good reason; for the hope of the people rested solely upon

253

the House of David, which foreshadowed God's reign among His
people, as we have already seen. Today, because Jesus Christ has
appeared to us to take possession of us, we have the truth. In
those days, however, David's successors were but a foreshadow of
the Son of God. So it is not without reason that the life of the
people depended entirely upon the kingdom. Now, however, Micah
says to them, "Cry, for your king has defaulted you," as if to
say, "Up to this point, God has led you and established a kingdom
among you as He wished you to be governed. But now you will be
deprived of such grace. You have good reason to groan and cry,
for God will permit great desolation to befall you."

When would it profit us if we were so hardened that we felt
nothing whenever God raps us over our heads? He afflicts us to
warn and admonish us of our sins, so that we will not be deprived
of His grace and that His horrible vengeance will not befall upon
us. It is a good thing we suffer misfortunes; for in so
suffering, we are sufficiently moved to beg God's pardon and to
become truly displeased in ourselves for having offended Him. On
the other hand, if we are so hardened that we refuse to recognize
it is God who chastises us and why, then, I say, we are merely
playing games with Him. He will not tolerate such blasphemy and
will visit horrible vengeance upon us.

Most of us are ill advised on the question of suffering. We
fail to realize that if God gave us everything we could ever hope
for according to the flesh, we would not care for anything else.
Look at idolatry. Well we will see that where idolatry reigns,

corrupted and perverse practices come to substitute for truly serving God. His salvific teachings are obscured by lies and false, diabolical doctrines. As long as the world is at ease, it cares nothing for God, His truth, or the like. The world will never amend its ways; it just gets worse and worse. Ambitious men are totally obsessed by their pride and ambition. Gluttons will not abandon their gluttony. Adulterers wish to be left alone to wallow in their own shit. Indeed, the world will always be obsessed with its carnal desires and will never know how unfortunate it is to be deprived of the Kingdom of our Lord. So let us listen carefully to the Holy Spirit, who speaks through the mouth of Micah, asking, "Why do you cry, daughter of Zion?" as if to say, "You have good reason to cry when you find the Son of God no longer reigns over you. Although you possessed all the goods in the world, you will never be more unhappy than when God has abandoned you." That is the key point to bear in mind.

In what does our happiness consist, save that the Son of God governs us and is our Prince? Not only is He the supreme repository of all our good things but also of our life, for in Him alone do we have being and movement. All the goods we receive from God will be cursed unless Jesus sanctifies them by His presence and makes them serve to our benefit and salvation.

The word "counselor" deserves special attention. Although Micah applies this title to the king, who was only a foreshadow of Jesus Christ, he means that it is more fittingly applied to Him, through whom we have full knowledge and the reality of all that was foreshadowed under the Law. Christ reigns over us in order to be our wisdom. So let us not make the mistake of taking our own heads to be sages; let us follow Christ's advice. Let us be confident that everything will go well for us; for if Christ is named Counselor, He will not fail to carry out His office. Let us not assume that we will remain ignorant simply because all wisdom is contained in Christ alone; for we may share in all His wisdom, provided that we thoroughly ground ourselves in Him. True, we will often be so perplexed that we will be at our wit's end, as the expression goes. But we can always count on good advice from Christ, provided that we pray it please Him to counsel us. That is why Saint Paul says Christ has been given us for wisdom. That is also why Isaiah 11 says that the spirit of wisdom and the spirit of understanding rest upon Him. Jesus Christ did not receive the gift of wisdom and judgment because He had need of it for Himself but in order to shed it upon those such as ourselves, who are sadly lacking in this regard.

So above all, let us recognize that we can have neither wisdom nor counsel unless we go to the Son of God. If, however, we lack such humility, we will never comply with Christ's teachings; nor will we tolerate His governing. Well we see how the vast majority of the world refuses to be governed by the Son of God. The reason is simply that most people prefer to rely on the vain wisdom of men. Why is the Gospel rejected? Simply because men passionately trust in what they dream up in their own heads. That is what alienates them from salvific teaching. So let us be humble and recognize that all our senses are nothing but vanities and lies. We have great need for the Lord to lead us through His Holy Spirit, for we cannot take one step without stumbling. That is why Micah says we need not fear anything if we have Christ, for it is His office to counsel us.

Micah continues, "Cry, lament, for you will leave the city and live in the fields. You will be taken to Babylon. But you will be delivered from there. The Lord will rescue you from the hand of your enemies," as if to say, "My friends, you must prepare yourselves for this coming affliction; for God has made up His mind that Jerusalem will be destroyed and you will be stripped of your heritage. All this must come to pass. Therefore, be prepared to receive this chastisement. But console yourselves with the fact God will deliver you from there."

One of Micah's tasks, as we have seen, is to arm the faithful against the strong temptation that is about to befall them. They know themselves to be God's chosen people, but soon they will be totally abandoned by Him. Micah knows that in that day his people will become quite desperate and ask in astonishment, "What is happening to us? What will become of us?" That is only to be expected; for if we can no longer hope for salvation in our God, are we not the most miserable nation on earth? So Micah strives to console them and strengthen their faith by emphasizing that God will sustain them.

The other of his tasks is to provide the people with a remedy. He admonishes them to groan and cry, that they might

257

come to say, "Alas! We have failed. Let us turn to our God, begging His pardon." The people may yet receive God's grace, may yet avoid their impending captivity, provided that they amend their ways. But none needed Micah's call to repentance.

Micah, then, provides us with some extremely important advice to follow. Indeed, he is speaking not only to men of his own time but to us as well. If we do not tremble at the threats of God, we will feel His blows upon our heads. If His first blows do not serve to amend our ways, He will redouble His blows until we are totally crushed and broken. So let us not be like stubborn mules when God corrects us; let us receive His chastisement as something very necessary and beneficial to our salvation. Let us come to acknowledge our own sinfulness, for it is the epitome of all ignorance when we wallow in our sins and vices. God's words of reproach are followed by blows of His hand in order that we fully realize how terribly angry He is with us. So let us be ignorant but humble ourselves, cry and groan because we have so grievously sinned. Let us look to Micah's consolation; "Your God will deliver you," and recognize that all our chastisement will have a happy ending, provided that we return to God. Micah's consolation is not addressed to all men but only to those who return to God in true faith and repentance. If we do that, we will know God to be our Redemptor and true place of refuge in our times of greatest adversity.

Following this holy doctrine, we prostrate ourselves before the face of our good God, acknowledging our sinfulness. We pray that He so awaken us to our own poverty and misery that we turn to Christ, who alone is the repository of our good things. May we, who are stained and soiled, come to the living fountain which is Jesus Christ to be cleansed. May He so reign in our midst that His great powers are more and more manifest among us. May we totally subjugate ourselves to Him and not be so unfortunate as to reject His grace. May each share in His blessings according to his needs. May God shed this grace not only on us but upon all the peoples and nations of the world, etc.

All-powerful God, celestial Father, through your Son who has united into one body your Church, which has so often been dispersed and broken into pieces. Give us the grace that we remain forever in this unity of faith. Give us the strength to fight continually against all the temptations of the world. May we never stray from the Path of Righteousness, no matter what troubles we encounter. We are exposed to so much death, so we ask in your name that we not be so overwhelmed by fear and fright that all hope is extinguished in our hearts. May we look with our eyes, our spirits, and all our senses to your infinite power, by which you raise the dead and make things out of nothing. May we, in death, look to eternal salvation. May we, in the end, share in the fountain of life, this eternal joy, which has been won for us through the blood of your only Son, our Lord, Jesus Christ. Amen.

* * *

## (17) Monday, December 22, 1550

You will go to Babylon. You will be delivered from there; the Lord will deliver you from the hand of your enemies. Now men are gathering together against you saying, "Let her be condemned and let us keep our eye on Zion, etc." Micah 4.

Following up on our train of thought, it is necessary to turn now to Micah's consolation of the faithful: Their time of affliction will have a happy ending. True, for a time, God will lay a heavy hand on us because of our sins. We must bear His harsh treatment patiently. Only by afflicting us, can God overcome our passions. His afflictions, then, are very beneficial for our salvation. If it is necessary to afflict us more for the sake of our salvation, He will not hesitate to do so. But there is always hope and consolation in the midst of our suffering. Look to Micah's promise!

He says, "You will go to Babylon, but you will be delivered from there. The Lord, your God, will rescue you from the hands of your enemies." At first glance, this seems like a very strange thing to say. One could well ask, "If God is merciful to them, why did He send them into captivity in the first place?" Certainly it does seem strange that God loves these people and yet He holds them in such contempt that He spells out their doom by sending them into captivity. On one hand, the people can see nothing but signs of God's great wrath against them; on the other, Micah declares His great love for them. But, as I have just said, it is very necessary for God to chastise us. If we think of the bounty and grace of God solely in terms of our present condition, if we are unwilling to look beyond the tips of our noses, we will never know that God is our Father and Savior. Our faith must so elevate us that we look toward things very distant, incomprehensible, and hidden. That is Micah's point when he says, "You will go to Babylon, but you will be delivered."

Although Micah is speaking specifically to the Jews, he is also speaking a universal truth: God will never fail to be our Father and deliver us from all evil. However He may find it necessary to afflict us for a time, He will deliver us in the end. Because of our sins, we cannot escape misery and poverty, death and the grave. But do not doubt for an instant that God has His hand ready to aid us and will receive us in all mercy. Hold fast to Micah's promise! The hardships we suffer daily tempt us to think that God has abandoned us and is in point of fact our major enemy.

We would soon become totally disheartened, had we not as our bastion this truth: Just as it was necessary for God to exile the people to Babylon to chastise them, so it is necessary for us to undergo many hardships in order to recognize the power of our celestial Father. If God did away with all our miseries, if we never had to endure the slightest hardship, how would we ever come to know His bounty? It would seem that what we had was simply due to good luck; we would attribute nothing to the power of God. It is very necessary, then, for God to allow us to

261

suffer extreme hardship. When everything about us seems to be going to rack and ruin, then we come to know the hand that will deliver us. It is through afflictions, then, that we learn to glorify God. So it is necessary for us to undergo many afflictions. Then, God will deliver us. We stand upon His solemn promise: "Your God will deliver you." God will protect us in life and in death, provided that we trust fully in Him. Micah says His power extended even to Babylon. He delivered His people from there, although it was totally beyond human comprehension how this could be accomplished. God's promise was not in vain to the ancients, so be confident He will deliver us today.

When you see that God permits His Church to be oppressed, trampled down, and cruelly persecuted by tyrants, remember Micah's promise that God will deliver His people from Babylon. Do not doubt that promise holds for individuals as well. When anyone of us get into such a terrible jam that he does not know which way to turn, let him look to the Lord and have faith He will deliver him from his Babylon. God's promise is not in vain, for we know that He fulfilled His promise through Micah and delivered His people. Be confident, then, that He will do the same for us today.

But do not look just to Babylon; look beyond it to death; for after we have all undergone so many ordeals in this present life, we will all go to the grave. What do we really know about death, save that all men must perish and turn to dust? We know that the body rots away; but in regard to the soul, we have to be guided by faith alone. As Solomon says, human wisdom cannot tell whether or not the human soul goes in the same direction as the souls of horses and other beasts. Our hope is grounded in God alone. As it is His office to deliver His people from Babylon, so, too, He will deliver us from death and Hell, however impossible that may seem. This is why Micah says, "The Lord will deliver you from the hand of your enemies."

Because men are full of incredulity, Micah adds, "So be it, by the hand of the Lord," as if to say, "My friends, if it seems to you that you will remain in Babylon forever, if it seems you will never depart, trust in the power of God and you will never be disappointed." Because God has promised to deliver us, we have good reason to trust in Him. That, in a nutshell, is Micah's point.

He continues, "Men will assemble themselves against the Church, saying, 'It will be condemned; and our eyes will rejoice, for we will see Zion made desolate.' But they do not understand God's thoughts; nor do they know His plan." Here, he is arming us against a very common source of temptation. The infidels strive to discourage us and make us lose faith. Whenever we are afflicted, they really hound us, saying that God is against us, as so it would seem to them. Even our Master, Jesus Christ Himself, was hounded this way. When He was on the Cross, the infidels said of Him, "He believed in God, so let God save him!" The basic tactic Satan uses to lead us astray and corrupt us is to so destroy our confidence that we no longer invoke God's name and become so frightened that we think our situation is totally hopeless. Once the Devil gains such a foothold on us, we are finished. Satan has seduced many a man through the all-out efforts of the infidels to discourage them and make them lose all faith in God.

Since this is such a dangerous temptation, God must arm us with His strength if we are to resist against it. Here, God is arming His people through Micah's words, as if the prophet were saying, "My friends, prepare yourselves for a very rough war. You will have many cruel enemies. Because you are God's children, you will be persecuted throughout the world. Your enemies will boast of the power they have over you. They will say that God is against you. They will drive you to despair. They will say to you arrogantly, 'Well now, we see how trustworthy your God is. Zion will be wiped out!' How Satan will assault you through the infidels, who are his henchmen and instruments! But you will resist; you will stand firm against all his assaults. For those who speak against you do not know God's plan. You must not, I emphasize, conceive of God's will according to the opinions of men; for they are blind wretches who do not know what God will make of you."

It is nothing new for the Church to have enemies in the world. That has been its condition from all time, as it has been said that "the evil ones fought me since my youth; they have plowed upon my back." That is the voice of the Church of God speaking universally, saying that it has always had adversaries. So let us prepare to endure many miseries, hardships, and injuries inflicted upon us by men; it is certain that the vast majority of men are dominated by Satan. Since they are the sworn enemies of God and Jesus Christ, our Captain and Chief, how can we make peace with them? True, it is our task to make peace with them; but when we have done all that we could and yet they rage all the more against us, there is nothing left for us to do but to put into practice what it says in Psalm 110, namely that we march with Christ to rule over our enemies. Since Christ is our Master, we must fight in this victorious battle. We will be surrounded by enemies and stabbed by them as if we were in a field of thorns. That is why we must be warned ahead of time in order to be better taught patience and forbearance.

It is the Devil who prods the wicked to tempt us to despair. The devices they use against us were not made in their own shops; they were made by Satan, who uses these men as his bellows to blow the fumes of Hell into the world. Since Satan has such cunning ways to seduce men, we have to be constantly on our guard against him. Remember the example of Job. When his friends supposedly came to console him, they tried to drive him to despair. They asked him, "Where do you find that God ever treated His faithful as harshly as He does you? Do you truly believe that He cares for you? It would seem He has totally rejected you." What could the poor man do but be crushed and bewildered? Satan also submitted Christ to similar temptations.

David said that similar reproaches were made against him, by which he symbolizes the plight of all the faithful.

Since it is Satan who tempted Job, David, and even Jesus Christ, who is the Master of God's children, there is no doubt it is all his handiwork when the infidels trouble us and try to discourage us from our faith in God. Their sole aim is to ruin us; they are very displeased the Church of God has not fallen into such decadence as they had proposed for it; their only wish is that the Church go to Hell. When we are afflicted, they mislead themselves into thinking they will triumph over us. When they see the blessings God shed upon us, they become enraged out of spite. They declare themselves to be the sworn enemies of God and His Word by cooking up all sorts of lies about us to make us appear loathsome to all the world: One day we are going to be sacked and pillaged; the next we are going to be thrown headlong down to the bottom of Hell. In brief, they are mad dogs whose only wish is that we be totally destroyed. So what other recourse have we, save to take up the arms God has given us through Micah? If we do not hold out against such temptations, the blame falls squarely on our shoulders, for God has amply armed us.

Let us examine how God has given us a clear path to victory. Micah says that the infidels do not know God's plan. He means, as I have just said, that we must not measure God according to the standards of the infidels, for they are poor blind wretches. What do they really know about God? What do we really know about

God? If we are honest about it, we have to admit, "We are not sure what God intends to do with us. All we see today are signs of His great anger and vengeance. We do not know if He will continue to persecute us to the very end." But God's plan for the Church is revealed through Micah. If God had not so spoken through the prophet, we would be compelled to say along with Scripture: "Who is His counselor? Who can climb high enough to know His thoughts? For these things surpass all human understanding." Micah, however, reveals that God does not wish the Church to remain in the dark and has in point of fact given ample warning as to what its future holds. True, he was speaking to a people already well schooled in salvific teaching. Today, however, we are in a far better position to understand God's plan. In addition to the Law and the Prophets, which the Patriarchs had, we have Jesus Christ, whose holy mouth has spoken to us. Still, we can and do become extremely confused about God. Micah warns us about this, as if to say, "My friends, you will have mortal enemies whose only wish is to exterminate you from the face of the earth. Your end will seem at hand. When endure great misfortune, they will drive you to despair by mocking you, saying, 'Where is your God now? Do you truly believe He will come to your aid?'" Consequently, he assures us that God is always close at hand, provided that we hold fast to His promises in Scripture, by which we know He still favors us.

Micah's teaching is of great benefit to us; for in the midst of our suffering, it serves to remind us of God's plan. But what exactly is this plan? God, knowing how much we can stand, will not permit us to be tempted beyond our limits. Furthermore, He afflicts us solely for our own benefit. The evils God sends upon us are His reproaches for our sins, so let us bear our hardships in all patience, as was noted earlier. Let us take care that we profit from His admonitions and do not remain hardened. If we persist in our evil ways, if we resist His will, certainly we cannot expect Him to fulfill His promises. Our Lord wishes to take us by the hand and clasp us to Himself, but we snatch back and rebel against Him. Do we wish to show that we know His plan? Then, the instant His rod falls upon us, let us recognize our offense and let us thoroughly ground ourselves in His promises, which are the remedies against all the evils that befall us. That, I say, is what we must do above all else.

God always afflicts us in only moderation, and as He knows to be expedient for our salvation. He will never lay such a heavy hand on us that we are crushed to death by evil. It is necessary to repeat again God's promise that He will not tempt us beyond our limits and, as Saint Paul says, without their being a favorable outcome. Still, we must amply prepare ourselves for battle.

God's plan applies to the body of the universal Church as well as to each member. God intends the Church to remain until the end of the world. True, judging by appearances, the Church has often seemed to be in rack and ruin and about to totally collapse. But God's plan calls for it to remain as long as the sun and the moon are in the sky. Here are two daily witnesses, then, that the Church will never perish. When we are in the midst of the greatest conceivable trouble, when it seems that the earth and sky themselves are about to collapse, we must hold fast to God's promise; His plan is immutable and so will be carried out, no matter what obstacles or stumbling blocks there may be. True, the opinions of men cannot guarantee that the Church will endure. But as God has so spoken, there is no doubt it will remain forever. God's plan applies to each member as well. In times of greatest trouble, when it seems that all is against them, each can say, "Lord, you have promised never to abandon us. We are consoled by your plan. Trusting fully in your bounty, we cling to your Word. We will never be conquered, neither by the efforts of man nor by all the assaults of Satan."

True, we are often trampled underfoot by men, but that does not mean that we cannot get up again. We have such a strong foundation that we can never be conquered. God's plan is not something secret or hidden; it is His infinite bounty, which He amply reveals through Scripture. We, then, have good reason to say, "Nothing can happen, save what God has ordained for us, so we are free of all doubt." True, the ways in which God will deliver the Church are totally incomprehensible to us. God permits this in order to test our faith. True, we may be surrounded by such chaos, that we cannot help but conclude, "All is lost!" Yet we should be more than certain and know that the outcome will be favorable for us. So let us cling to God's promise and allow Him to test our faith by not revealing to us at once the method by which He will deliver us.

Micah continues, saying, "Rise up, daughter of Zion. The Lord will give you the peoples of the earth as sheaves (or bundles) or wheat. You will flail and stomp them as so one threshes the wheat." Micah is speaking here not of threshing by the flail alone, but of threshing by both the flail and the hoof. His point is that although the infidels are puffed up with pride and think they will easily devour God's children, they face a very different fate, one undreamed of by themselves: They will be thrown on the threshing floor, and "God will give His Church the hoofs of iron to smash and break them." But bear in mind that we too will be thrown on the threshing floor. God does not leave His children to lie fallow but afflicts them in many ways. That is why the Church of God is compared to a threshing floor when it is said that the wheat will be mixed with the chaff. Why would Scripture speak this way, save that we also must be trampled down? God's children as well as the infidels will be stomped down and then flailed with the rod. The chaff will be thrown on the compost pile to rot and the wheat will go to the grainery. Although afflictions are common to all men, God has so planned it that He will always gather His children to Himself. Although all men will be stomped and flailed by the hand of God on the threshing floor, the infidels will yet be thoroughly thrashed in another way. They are nothing but chaff, and the afflictions they suffer in this world are merely a warning that

God is their Judge and will sentence them to eternal death. In contrast, we are afflicted in order that God may receive us and that we may attain the immortal celestial glory He has promised us. Note well, then, that God does not exempt His own people when He throws all the peoples of the world on the threshing floor. It is said that chastisement begins in the Church. Judgment must begin in the House of God, says the prophet. So let us not assume we will be exempt from the rod; in the end, that will serve our best interest.

It is, of course, completely against the grain of the infidels' thinking to assume that they will be flailed. In their arrogance and rebellion against God, they pay no heed to the hand of God and believe that they have a special pact with the dead, as Isaiah mentions. If you speak to them of God's judgment, they merely mock at you. Not for an instant do they ever think they will be thoroughly thrashed and rejected as chaff. But on our end of it, we must contemplate through the eyes of faith the destruction and damnation of the wicked and the reprobate. As I said earlier, when we are in the grips of death, we must look beyond this life to God's promise of salvation. We must look beyond the heavens above to see what God has promised us and to recognize that He eternally holds us in His hand to protect us. When we see the prosperity and triumphs of the wicked, we judge them to be very happy, fortunate people. But we must look beyond all this and think upon how God will condemn them in the midst of their triumphs. Because they deceive themselves, they will be

271

subject to sudden, violent destruction. When they say, "All is well," that is when the hand of God will strike them down.

When Micah says, "Rise, daughter of Zion, stomp upon the peoples of the earth, for God will give you hoofs of iron to crush them under your feet," it is tempting to think that God is encouraging His own people to be very cruel. So it would seem at first glance. Indeed, when the Jews read this passage, they thought God had given them the sword to cut the throats of all the Pagans. The Jews were a barbarous nation, which God had assigned to the ranks of the reprobate. They were mad dogs whose only desire was to kill and spill blood; they were insatiable gluttons whose only desire was to pillage and plunder their neighbors. "Right here, in this passage," they said, "God has promised us all the riches of the Pagans." They deceitfully interpreted passages promising the Messiah to mean they would be given free rein to plunder all the goods of the world.

Christ, however, has clearly spoken to the contrary through the prophets. He has made it plain that His people will not be victorious next week or next year, as the Jews mistakenly assumed; for the Kingdom gradually emerges through a prolonged period of struggle starting with the deliverance from Babylon and continuing on to the Last Day. The Church, then, will undergo prolonged persecution by the infidels, though it will eventually triumph over them. In order they be smashed and broken, the Church has been armed with hoofs of iron, that is to say, so hard that none can stand up against them. Furthermore, the

272

Church's victory will be a victor of faith, as it is said, "Be patient!" The key, I say, to our victory over the enemies of God and all the reprobate is that we patiently wait upon the deliverance God promised us. It is through patience that we conquer those who afflict us, as will be discussed tomorrow, God willing.

We must know our calling and we must stick to what God has commanded; we must guard against corrupting His promises into something totally contrary to His intentions. It is our calling to lead men to the threshing floor to feel the rod of God upon their backs, for the Gospel is the rod to break the pride and rebellion of men and to beat down the lusts of the flesh, which are the enemies of God. We must battle against all those who are enemies of God and His Word. We must take great pains to flail with the rod of the Gospel those who are hardened and refuse to be led to the knowledge of Christ, as Saint Paul says this is the purpose of preaching. God, I say, has put in our hands the rod and the iron hoofs, to smash and break the hearts of all rebels. Furthermore, the Word is called a sword because we must kill all souls to sacrifice them to God. This soul death means that men will renounce themselves and turn from everything contrary to God to what is agreeable to Him. In the end, then, this death will open men to eternal life.

When Micah says that "their riches will be dedicated to God," he means that the whole world will convert to God. In part, this promise has been fulfilled through Christ's action

273

within ourselves. When we had no knowledge of God, our Lord came and drew us to Himself, teaching us through His Word all that we needed to know to serve fully His honor and glory. This promise continues to be fulfilled each day, but this point will have to wait til tomorrow.

Following this holy teaching, we prostrate ourselves before the face of our good God, acknowledging our sinfulness. We pray it please Him to so govern us that we no longer follow our chaotic, evil appetites. May we resist all the temptations of the world and remain steadfast in our obedience. May we, when afflicted, look to His plan and providence. May we, in this way, constantly resist all Satan's efforts to sway us from the Path of Righteousness. May we persist on the Path until we reach our immortal glory and the Celestial Kingdom, which He has promised us. May He shed this grace not only on us but upon all the peoples and nations of the world, etc.

* * *

(18) Tuesday, December 23, 1550

Surround yourself with troops, O daughter of the troop. They have besieged us. They will strike the Judge of Israel on the cheek with a rod. And you, Bethlehem Ephratah, least among the thousands of Judah, from you will come to me the ruler of Israel, who has been everlastingly going forth, etc. Micah 5.

Yesterday, we began to see how God will dedicate to Himself the riches of all His enemies. Whenever our Lord gives us the grace to be numbered among His own, it is always on condition that we serve Him. This condition is fulfilled through the power of the Holy Spirit working within us to transform our wicked ways into something good and useful. Although Scripture says that each must dedicate himself to God, none can accomplish this, save that God Himself takes matters in hand. When a man gives himself to God, he must totally deny himself: All the goods and facilities of the world must be applied contrary to their customary usage; that is, they must be used solely for the purpose of serving and honoring God. True, God only makes the good things of the world; He in Himself has absolutely no need of them. He wishes us to serve Him solely because His will is that we serve the neighbor.

Yesterday's passage makes a very important point for us: If we wish to be faithful, all our goods must be dedicated to God. This means we must not use them in profane ways. We must not waste and misuse them through extravagant indulgence in the voluptuous delights of the world or through vain ambition to

275

acquire great wealth and the like. We must use them as God so intended they be used. Then, all our goods will be solemnly dedicated to God. The Lord has revealed to us that we serve Him when we use thoughtfully, thankfully, and temperately all that He has put into our hands. He wishes us to diligently attend to the needs of our neighbors. When a man uses the goods of this world in order to serve God, he will recognize that all these things come from On High. He will not eat like a pig, who knows not the hand that feeds him. The very bread he eats will bring him to recognize the celestial Father, who nourishes him. And then when he is moved by charity to aid his neighbors, there, as I have said, is a man who has dedicated his riches to God. Although God in Himself gains nothing whatsoever from these riches, still He will be gracious enough to accept from our hands whatsoever we give the neighbor in His name, that is to say, according to His will. Whatsoever we eat or drink, though it is consumed purely for our own benefit, is dedicated to God, provided that we live by a clean conscience and apply the whole of our life to serving Him. When that is the case, all the creatures we use will serve as sacrifice God will graciously accept.

God, out of His inestimable bounty, has ordained that all His gifts serve to the benefit of our salvation, provided we receive them in the spirit of true thanksgiving, as I have said. On the other hand, when men, out of their ingratitude, refuse to recognize the good we have done them, our efforts are not in vain. Nothing is lost or wasted here, for God will bless our good deed as if it were done for the benefit of His own person. Is this not sufficient witness of His great bounty towards us? Does this not inspire us to make far better use of the goods He has given us?

The Hebrew word Micah uses for wealth also means rapine and plunder. It is well chosen because it emphasizes that God will dedicate to His honor all that has been prophaned, polluted, and rejected by Him. So then, if we wish to say that we are truly faithful, we must employ all our goods to serve God. And that can be done only if we totally renounce ourselves and dedicate our whole life to God.

Today, however, Micah renews his threat of impending captivity. He says, "You, daughter of the troops, you will be besieged now. They have laid siege against us. They will strike the cheek of the Judge of Israel" (that is, the prince), as if to say, "You, Jerusalem, though you boast of your greatness and power, you have abused these things. Your leaders have abandoned themselves to all forms of evil. You are like an army that pillages and plunders everywhere. Now you will be given a dose of your own medicine!" He adds that "they have laid siege against us," to show their fate was already sealed. Speaking of the Assyrians and then the Chaldeans, he says, "They have struck the cheek of the Judge of Israel." In Hebrew, the word "judge" means "governor," as we noted earlier. So he is saying they will strike the cheek of the King of Israel. This means the king will be treated with the greatest disrespect, for there is no greater

277

insult than to be hit in the face. Jeremiah tells us that King Zedekiah had to stand trail as a criminal and that his eyes were poked out after he had been forced to watch the throats of his children being cut. Micah's point, then, is that the hope Jerusalem has in its king will prove to be in vain, for the king will be grievously shamed.

However, he does add this note of consolation for the faithful: Although the Lord will exercise terrible vengeance against Jerusalem, which was the royal seat of the kingdom, He will set up a new government, one far more excellent than the first. This will be brought about in a most extraordinary way. "You," he says, "Bethlehem Ephratah (as she had both a first and a last name), you are now so small that it would take great effort to make you count as a provostship among the princes of Judah." He speaks of the thousands, because each provostship consisted of one thousand persons. He says, "You are so small that you do not count as a provostship" (as we would say today). You are only a little village of no real prominence now, but I will bring out of you the ruler of Israel. His reign will be for all eternity." So he is really saying in effect, "You will no longer have a mortal man, as you have in the House of David; for I will rise up a new king who will be of the blood of the line of David but who will also be eternal, namely our Lord, Jesus Christ, who, born of the Virgin Mary and from the line of David, is a man such that He is also the eternal Word of God." That is the promise Micah makes to console the Faithful.

This is a very important passage to bear in mind. Our Lord chose Jerusalem to be the living symbol of His Church. Indeed, there would have been no Church in the world at the time, had it not been for Jerusalem. The kingdom, Temple, Altar, and all the rest were intended to foreshadow the Kingdom of our Lord. Had the Jews recognized this grace God had shed on them, had they worshipped Christ and witnessed to His presence among themselves, God would have so multiplied His grace upon them that all these shadows would have been replaced by the reality of the Kingdom. Instead, they gave free rein to their evil impulses, rebelled against God, and broke His commandments. "Why should we worry?" they said. "Have we not the Temple of God, the Altar, and the kingdom?" They boasted of these things but chased God from their midst, yet they believed God was obligated to do everything they demanded. That is why Micah tells them that their Temple, kingdom, sacrificing, and the like will profit them nothing; for Jerusalem will be razed because of all the extortion and violent crimes that have been committed there.

There is an important lesson here for us. Whenever God puts men in positions of power and authority, they think themselves a cut above all the others. This is a vice I addressed earlier and one of which we see examples daily. Men in high positions think that the whole world was made just for them. They no longer think of themselves as men; they think they are living miracles, yet they abandon themselves to all sorts of cruelty and inhumanity. When we see how they wrong, extort, harm, and

279

violently injure others, we have good reason to complain; but we fail to realize that we too are evil and prone to this vice. If God has us live modestly, this is to our advantage; for we are all too prone to use for evil ends the good things He has given us. If we are not rich and famous, be content, appreciate that God is keeping a tight rein on us. Watch out, those of you in high positions! Do not let your titles become an excuse for you to become wild armed men, ferocious beasts who pillage and devour all they can trap. God strongly condemns all such violent acts. Those who harm their neighbors will be given a dose of their own medicine, as it is said, "You who pillage now will be pillaged in turn." Although that is said specifically of Babylon, our Lord says it is a just punishment levied upon all. We see such punishment take place daily, although we may not recognize it for what it is. Most kingdoms, principalities, and manors have been acquired through murder, bloodshed, cruelty, pillage, and the like. Do we think God will let these crimes go unpunished? Our Lord may overlook them for a time, but He does not forget them. He will make that clear enough in the end.

But let us not stop here. Look at how nothing in the world ever lasts. Look at how everything is in continual turmoil. Look at how people are suddenly reduced from riches to rags. We see how the world changes every day; and although we may not recognize these changes to be the workings of God, they are in point of fact ample testimony to Micah's warning: Those who abuse their God-given powers and turn to plundering their

280

neighbors will receive like treatment in return, if not in their own persons, then in the persons of their successors. So we must walk in fear of the Lord and wrong no one, if we wish to be treated kindly by God and to enjoy the peace He has promised. If you are wealthy and if you wish God to bless both your children and their inheritance after your demise, then abstain from all extortion. The Lord will treat you and your kindred as you have so treated your neighbors. If you have sucked some blood from your neighbors, they will in return quaff down the blood of you and your kindred. If you have nibbled on your brothers, they will in return devour you and your kindred. May we so profit from this teaching that such horrible vengeance does not befall us.

Remember Jerusalem, remember Micah's words: "You, daughter of the troops, although you are renowned to be The City of God, your glory is a lie, for you are corrupted and polluted by your own malice." Most importantly, remember why he spoke this way: Jerusalem was the city God had personally chosen; it was The Holy City, the place of God's Throne, a veritable paradise on earth. Yet it became so corrupt that he condemned it as the root of all evil, said it was nothing but a den of thieves, as we also read in other passages.

So when God calls us to be His people, let us walk in fear and obedience. God has sanctified us, and the Holy Spirit has engraved the sign of His children upon us. So let us continue to walk in such purity that we never allow ourselves to backslide or be separated from Him, no matter what happens.

Micah says, "They have laid siege against us and have struck the cheek of the Judge of Israel." He says "against us," because he considers himself to be a member of the body constituted by the people. Although he would not see the fall of Jerusalem in his own lifetime, he wished to be a member of the Church of God even in death and therefore wished to share in the terrible affliction that would befall it. He is teaching us that whenever God punishes the wicked, the good must also suffer. Although both the good and the wicked will share a common temporal affliction, the outcome will be very different for each of them. God will insure that the afflictions His own endure work for the benefit of their salvation and He will deliver them from death. Our Lord has promised the faithful: However they may be afflicted and whatever evil schemes the wicked may cook up against them, He holds their well-being and salvation near and dear to His heart, as Saint Paul says in Romans 8. But Micah warns: Because we as a people constitute a body, each of us must feel and bear in patience all the blows, all the afflictions God lands upon us. They serve the constructive purpose of spurring us on to fight against all wantonness and to restore law and order. Not only, then, may we serve to save souls who should have otherwise gone to Hell but we will appease the wrath of God.

When the question arises how God can be fair in punishing the innocent, the answer is very simple: Nobody is ever so innocent before God that He can find no reason to punish him. When God treats people kindly, He is in point of fact sparing them from well-deserved punishment. Take, for example, someone considered to be the most holy and innocent person in all the world. If God were to punish him as he so merited, without going to extremes, He would have to totally destroy him. Nobody ever has any reason to complain to God that He is too harsh and severe. It is perfectly fair for the good to be punished with the wicked, for they are members of a body where there is only impurity, contempt for God's Word, adultery, wantonness, drunkenness, and a vast array of other forms of mischief-making. True, not everybody is that bad; true, some will make an effort to fight evil; but it is also true that nobody stands up and says with any real degree of conviction and zeal, "How can we sit here and let God's Word be mocked in our midst? How can we be so nonchalant? We say that we are the people of God, so let us rise up and fight against evil with all our might!"

It is pitiful how cold and apathetic we are. It is not only those in high public office but all those with some degree of power, however small it may be, to maintain order who turn a blind eye towards evil. We are cold as ice; we simply numb ourselves to the evil that goes on here daily; we turn our backs upon it because we do not wish to take the pains to seek out effective remedies. We are all culpable from the most powerful to the least among us, which is why we receive nothing but our just desserts when God's punishment lands on each and every one of us.

So then, let us get busy and work hard to prevent evil! Let us go to the rescue of wayward souls. Let us not despair of our failures but patiently accept all God's chastisement. Let us trust in Him to convert evil into good. Let us always remember that all our afflictions will have a happy ending because He will insure they serve to the benefit of our salvation.

This brings us to Micah's consolation. He says, "And you, Bethlehem Ephratah, you are small among the thousands of Judah, but from you the ruler of Israel will come to me," as if to say, "When God punishes those who stray, those who are puffed up by foolish pride, He will not forget His Church. He will keep His promise so those who trust in Him will never be disappointed in their hopes. When God's terrible vengeance is visited upon all the earth, when it seems He will destroy the world by thunderbolts, let us trust in His bounty. Let us trust in Christ's promise of salvation, and we will never be disappointed."

As I have said, this passage contains a vitally important teaching for us. How would we survive amidst the great troubles and confusion of the world if God did not fortify us by His strength? When God says that our salvation is secret, He does not mean that it has been mislaid someplace; He means He has it right in His hand; and He means that we can in fact come to know our own salvation, provided we persist in our faith and in our invocation of His holy name. The prophet Joel makes the same point. He says that when all the world will be in chaos, when the earth will tremble and the sun will be hidden, when the stars will fall from the sky and other horrifying signs will occur, whosoever invokes the name of the Lord will find salvation. So let us thoroughly ground ourselves upon the foundation God has given us. Let us never abandon our hope of salvation, however it may seem that all is lost. Today there is more need for this teaching than ever before, seeing the current state of the world. What do we find in the world today, except trouble everywhere? If we find a place to rest, what assurance have we that we can remain there? Where can you find some small corner of the earth that has been at peace for any significant length of time? Nevertheless, our salvation is eternal; for God has promised to govern us not just for a day or so but forever. Indeed, our faith must surpass death itself. We must look far beyond our present life if we hold fast God's promise of salvation.

When Micah says that God will bring forth salvation out of Bethlehem when Jerusalem is destroyed, he means that we must never abandon hope in God, no matter how it may seem everything is lost and damned. Suppose, for example, that God were to gather together all His people from the far corners of the earth and make His Church flourish as before, so that one could say, "God initially revealed Himself only in Judah, but now His Gospel has spread throughout the world." Now, suppose this Church were to perish. Still, our faith should surmount whatsoever we may see happen in the world. God put the faith of His loyal followers to the test in just such a way when He destroyed Jerusalem. They saw only chaos and destruction everywhere; yet they were able to say, "Salvation will come from Bethlehem," which was but a small village where no one in their wildest dreams would have expected to find salvation. God has ways to restore His Church that transcend all human powers of comprehension. If we are told that something wonderful is about to happen and if we understand the means by which it will be brought about, then we have great faith that it will come to pass. Without such understanding, we just simply will not believe it will come to be. Our Lord, however has totally deprived us of any insight into His methods. For one thing, He has no need of any manmade devices to perfect His work, that is, the salvation of the Church. For another, He wishes to test our faith and to further glorify His power. In sum, He is warning us not to trust in creatures for our salvation but in Him alone. That is why Christ came from Bethlehem.

Micah's promise was fulfilled! Saint Matthew, Chapter 2, cites Micah's words, and with good reason, for it shows the truth of his promise. Jesus Christ was born in Bethlehem. How? In what palace? The Son of God was born in a lowly state; He could find no room or lodging in this village and so was turned away to the stable, as if He were rejected as being unworthy of the company of men. This lowly birth makes it apparent that God gave

His Son all the power to save and redeem the world. His birth is a living symbol of the universal condition of the Church of God. Just as Jesus Christ, Saviour of the world, was born in a village where one least expected to find salvation, so He will deliver His Church when there will be only chaos and confusion everywhere. When it seems that all has gone to rack and ruin, He will make His Church flourish and triumph.

Christ was born in Bethlehem in a miraculous manner in order to show the world His coming is governed solely by the providence of God and to give ample proof that He is the promised Christ. When Joseph and Mary went to Bethlehem, they had no idea what would happen. They did not go to Bethlehem with the intention that she give birth there. They had no idea Micah's prophecy would be fulfilled in this way. They went there solely because Joseph was under an edict to return to the place of his birth to be enrolled in the census. Since he was from the line of David, he had to go to Bethlehem to be registered in the census along with the others of his line. This, of course, was all the working of God's providence in order to fulfill Micah's promise: "You, Bethlehem Ephratah, you are small among the thousands of Judah, but God will bring forth from you the Governor of Israel." This is such ample proof that Christ is the true Redemptor that one need look no further. Even the blind themselves could see that Christ was the Savior of the world, as Saint Matthew says. Even the Scribes, those poor wretches who were the enemies of truth and envenomed against God and His teaching, knew that the

Redeemer must come from Bethlehem. When Herod asked them, "Where will the Messiah be born?" They answered him, "It is written by the prophet: 'You, Bethlehem, in the land of Judah, you are not least among the lines of Judah, for from you will come the one who will govern my people of Israel.'"

No longer would Ephratah, or Bethlehem, be an insignificant little village too small to be numbered among the cities of Judah, as it was in Micah's day. Christ's birth there gave it sovereign glory over all the rest, which is why Micah says, "You are not least." The Lord chose such an insignificant village to make a very important point: The majesty of the Son of God is not of this world. Neither does He seek personal gain from the world nor is He conditioned by it. We have no bearing on our salvation, which comes from Him and Him alone. Since we have only malice and perversity within us, it is Christ alone who, through the bounty of His Father, gives us all that we could ever hope for in Him.

Now we arrive at Micah saying, "I will bring forth from you (or I will bring forth from you to me) the ruler of Israel." Clearly this is God speaking through the prophet, for he says he will bring forth from there the ruler of Israel. Note that this prophecy further confirms what I have just said: God has revealed it is His task alone to save the world. There is nothing of salvation that men can claim for themselves. Everything must be left to God alone. It is not up to us to prompt the Redemptor or His redemption. We are full of all iniquity and we can do nothing on our own, except to damn ourselves. Redemption comes solely from the hand of God and His bounty. That is why Micah says, "I will bring forth from you."

Although the infidels have made up many gods and many lords, we have only one God and only one Lord, Jesus Christ, as Saint Paul says. Micah says that the God we worship in spirit will reign in Israel. Now, exactly what does Christ's lordship require? He must be exalted; all creatures must pay Him homage and fall on their knees before Him, as it is said that men and angels must humble themselves before Him and that even demons tremble in His presence. Christ is Lord in order to be exalted and have a name which surmounts all the honors of the world, as Saint Paul says to the Philippians. But He wishes to reign over us purely for the sake of our well-being and our salvation. He did not become human and descend to earth for His own benefit, for He was and is eternally God. He has no need of His God-given superiority over man. True, He wishes to have total power and authority over us. Indeed, He wishes the demons in Hell to tremble at His majesty. But that does not mean that He wishes to frighten us off from Him. As I have said, He wishes to rule us solely for the benefit of our own salvation.

If we wish Christ to govern us continually, we must not be a rebellious people. We must willingly subjugate ourselves to Him. It is not enough merely to say that we are His people and His Israel. We must prove by our actions that we are truly His people. Our lives must be a testimony to our baptism by the Holy

Spirit, such that it can be said of us as it was of Nathan, "There is a true Israelite." Let us walk in all purity and simplicity, as God has so commanded. If we want to be His Church, if we want to be His flock, He must rule us as our Shepherd. To encourage us to ground ourselves deeper in the Lord, Micah says that He "has been everlastingly going forth." However He came from Bethlehem, which is only a little village, His Kingdom will be eternal. Micah stresses this point in order to strengthen our faith. The rest will have to wait until tomorrow.

Following this holy doctrine, we prostrate ourselves before the face of our good God, acknowledging our sinfulness. May it please Him to make us so know His grace that we are strengthened more and more. May we be so governed by Christ that we bear no hate or grudges against our neighbors. May we preserve peace and harmony among ourselves. May we employ all our efforts to do good to others. May we no longer provoke God's wrath against us and feel the severity of His punishments, by which He threatens all those who abuse the name of His Church. May we ground ourselves in the Kingdom of our Lord, however small and insignificant it may seem by the standards of the world. May we abandon all the vanities and voluptuousness of the world. May we take our refuge in Him alone, trusting that He will gather us together in Heaven, though our salvation is now hidden from us. May He shed this grace not only on us, but upon all the peoples and nations of the earth, etc.

All-powerful God, celestial Father, we continually provoke your wrath against us, and you continually chastise us with blows of your hand to humble us and to teach us to subjugate ourselves and willingly obey you. Give us the grace that we do not falter under your blows. May our hopes be raised by the Mediator you have sent us to reconcile us to yourself and to aid us when we are in need. May our hope in your Son give us the invincible courage to withstand all the hardships of the world without ever becoming weary. May we rejoice in our victory and may we in the end come to share in the blessed rest that awaits us through Jesus Christ, our Lord. Amen.

* * *

(19) Wednesday, December 24, 1550

Therefore, he will abandon his people until she who undergoes the travail of labor gives birth. Then the remnant of his brothers will return to the children of Israel. He will abide and he will govern in the power of the Lord and in the majesty of the Lord, his God, etc. Micah 5

Yesterday, we saw how our Lord will come to the rescue of His Church. All men have offended God, and all men will be punished. Nevertheless, He will preserve a remnant, as He wishes His Church to be eternal in the world. However, the church will not have an impressive, glorious appearance according to human standards. He will restore His Church in an invisible way, not with great pomp and ceremony. Our Lord is a living symbol of the Church. He was not born in Jerusalem, the city of greatest renown, the city of the Altar and Throne. God sent His Son to be born in the stable of a village so small that it counted for nothing at the time. This was to teach man that God will in fact restore His Church in a miraculous way, in a way totally incomprehensible to human understanding, when all seems to have gone to rack and ruin.

Because men are so prone to judge by appearances, Micah emphasizes that Christ's birth does not detract from His majesty or lessen in any way His power, for, he says, He has been everlastingly going forth, as if to say, "True, when God will send His Redeemer, He will be of humble origin and despised; but do not think Him to be any the less worthy because of that, for He goes forth eternally." Christ is not only a mortal man but the Son of

292

God, who has appeared to us and to whom belongs all glory. Micah warns us not to measure Christ according to human standards, for we must look beyond the flesh and come to recognize that He is our eternal God. He is not only speaking of the being of Christ, but of the grace He forever sheds upon His people. As the Apostle says, He is the same yesterday, today, and forever. Christ has never been hidden in His celestial glory; He was known by the Patriarchs as the Savior of the world and as the Head of the Church. They know of no salvation--save by Christ, whom was promised them and in whom they put all their trust. We must do the same, for Christ is our end and perfection. That is Micah's message for us today.

One could well ask, "How exactly does it benefit us now, that God will send His Redeemer from Bethlehem, a town of no import?" In response, I say those of Micah's time could have well asked, "What real consolation have you given us, Micah? You say the Redeemer will come; but as this will not be during our lifetime, it will certainly be of no benefit to us." Micah would have had a ready answer to such an objection: "Although the time is not yet right for Christ to come as Mediator, nevertheless God will not fail to govern us in the meantime. My Friends, the Lord has revealed that He will send the Mediator to restore all things. Let us trust fully in this promise and rejoice in the midst of our afflictions. When it seems that we can endure no more, when we are totally destitute and at the end of our rope, then He will reveal His power to us. Our Redemptor will not come until our situation is totally hopeless and we seem about to perish. He will be born in a lowly way in Bethlehem. Although He will be of humble origin and although He will not share the pomp and ceremony men associate with kings, do not fail to trust in Him. If this does not profit us right now, so be it! Although He has not yet appeared in the flesh, still we share in His grace. True, He has not yet revealed Himself to us and come to live among us; true, He has not yet endured the death and passion to reconcile us to God; true, He has not yet shed His blood to wash us; true, He has not yet been resurrected from the dead to give us eternal life. But despite all this, He is in fact already our Redemptor; and we will come to know our redemption, provided that we put all our trust in Him."

We have, then, more than ample proof of our faith. Not only has Christ come forth eternally, so that His own always knew Him to be the Redeemer, but He has fulfilled all that He promised to do to be our Savior. Trust in His grace! However the world may seem in such turmoil that the Church is about to perish at any minute, trust that our Savior was born in Bethlehem and will restore the Church in ways totally incomprehensible to us. This may not happen at once, however; but, I say, He will eventually restore the Church, despite the fact we totally lack the means to do so ourselves.

Micah says that "He will abandon them for a time, until she gives birth," as if to say, "The faithful should prepare to endure great suffering and they must not fail to trust in the promise of their redemption." This point was made earlier, namely that whenever God chastises us for a common vice, it is necessary His wrath fall upon everyone. True, some may not have as grievously offended God as have others; nevertheless, the whole body must be punished. No one is exempt from God's chastisement. Micah, then, warns the faithful that for a time they will seem to be totally abandoned by God. God, of course, will not truly abandon them, but they will not recognize that He is close at hand, ready to give aid. When they look both high and low, all they will be able to say is that God has abandoned them and no longer cares for them. It is the infirmity of our flesh that makes us so distrust God that we believe He is no longer our Savior and Father. That is why Micah tells them they will be abandoned by God for a time, as if to say, "My friends, God will permit you to be afflicted by your enemies. You will know no joy in you sufferings, for God will seem to have abandoned you and to care for you no longer. Prepare yourselves for this day, that you may patiently endure such great suffering."

Micah's warning does not hold merely for his time; it holds for all time. If we abandon ourselves to evil, if vice reigns everywhere among us, rest assured the hand of God will land upon us. True, God will sustain us eternally; but it is also true that, having put up with our offenses for a very long while, it is high time He exercises His office as Judge. What would happen to us if He let us go on piling up evil on top of evil? Would that not soon enough lead to our total destruction? God must chastise our vices when we offend Him. The fact that God is our Father and Savior does not mean He will refuse to punish us when we have provoked Him. When we remain hardened and persist in our wicked ways, I emphasize it is necessary for God to so afflict us that it would seem to our physical senses He has totally abandoned us.

But how can we be expected to endure such terrible affliction? Micah provides us great consolation. He says this terrible period of affliction will only be temporary, as if to say, "The infidels and the reprobate, feeling God's heavy hand upon them, will see no end in sight. They will be totally destroyed. True, they will think there will be an end to trials and tribulations, but they will sadly deceive themselves. They will never escape from the hand of God. When they have surmounted one terrible affliction, another will befall them. God afflicts them continually; there is no letup to their afflictions. But it will not be this way with us, for the Lord declares that we be afflicted only for a time." What great consolation it is to know God will abandon us only temporarily! The prophet Isaiah also says that the time will not be long; for God is angry with us only for a moment, whereas He is eternally merciful to us. God's mercy far exceeds the rigor of His punishment when it is a question of His faithful. He is angry with them only for an instant, for a mere flick of His wrist. As it says in the Psalm, "His anger lasts but for a moment, but His mercy lasts for life." The passage I just cited from Isaiah also confirms this point. So then, whenever God strikes us, let us recognize our sins and accept the fact He afflicts us for good reason. In this way, we will be able to console ourselves, knowing that God will punish us only for a time.

Because we are impatient and so fragile that we cannot endure the blows of God's hand, Micah cautions us that God may not work as fast as we would like. He speaks of a woman in labor, which is a common metaphor in Scripture. By the word "travail," he signifies the hope we must have in the midst of our afflictions. If we have no hope, if we become totally desperate, we cannot be said to undergo travail. A woman undergoes the travail of labor in the hopes of giving birth.

Micah says that she will give birth, so her longing will not be in vain, her hope will not be frustrated. This is Micah's consolation for the faithful. God will never fail to aid them, provided that they turn to Him with burning desire for help. To better understand Micah, look at what Isaiah says about the hope of worldly people when God threatens and punishes them. They look here and there, expecting aid from all sides. They really take the bit in their teeth, totally confident they can save themselves. But all they really do is rebel against God and vex Him. In the end, they will learn how they have deceived themselves by vain hopes. Isaiah says, "We have undergone terrible labor pains, but in the end we only farted." Certainly we can say the same for many of our hopes. He also says, "We have conceived like a barren woman." What exactly does he mean by this conception? He is speaking of the rashness of men who think they can get themselves out of their troubles without God's help and therefore do not look to Him as their refuge. They trust in creatures and so puff themselves up with foolish pride that they are as big as a woman about to give birth to two infants at once. That is why he says, "We have conceived, but we have only farted." Note that he counts himself among the people, although he does not consent to their evil ways. Consequently, he says, "I see that you have conceived, but that will serve you nothing in the end. You undergo the pain of a woman near birth, but why? You will only fart, and God will put your ideas to shame." That is what happens to men when they put their trust in themselves or in creatures rather than in God. Their foolish pride puffs them up like toads; but after their arrogance has put them to all sorts of toil and trouble, all they can give birth to is a fart.

However, even if we totally subjugate ourselves to God and are pliable under His hand, still we will be subject to the trials and tribulations of the world. God will punish us for our sinfulness and rebelliousness. But we have a consolation that those who trust in the world do not: We know our punishments are more than necessary and that God will not permit our ordeal to be in vain and our hopes to be frustrated. If we patiently bear our afflictions, invoke God, trust Him to aid us in the midst of our greatest afflictions, and look to Him as our sole refuge, there will be a happy outcome to all our sufferings. Our situation is like that of a woman who, having undergone the pain and agony of labor, rejoices in the child she has brought into the world. That is how the Lord will make things turn out for us, provided that we patiently wait upon His aid.

Consequently, Micah adds that "he will persevere and be steadfast in the name of God and in the glory of the Lord, his God." Here, he is deepening his promise of salvation through Bethlehem, by emphasizing that the office of Redemptor is eternal. He says that "He will abide" or "He will be steadfast," as if to say, "God will not send a Redemptor who will vanish the very instant He has appeared. He will not spend just a couple of days with people to lighten their burdens and then quickly depart, leaving them to languish. No, the redemption God will bring to His people through Jesus Christ will be forever."

He adds that Christ will rule as a Shepherd and not as a tyrant who oppresses his subjects, as we saw yesterday. All we have to do is comply with Christ and we will be governed justly and fairly. He emphasizes that Christ's power is full of gentleness, consolation, and joy. Our Savior will not torment us by cruel tyranny but will care for us as a shepherd would his flock. He will do so in the name of the Lord, His God; for God Himself will sustain the kingdom He has given His Son. Because we have no real conception of God's power and therefore do not trust in it as we should, Micah speaks of the "glory of the Lord," as if to say, "When I speak to you of the name of God, do not think that it is a small thing. Be ravished in admiration. Be grounded so much the more deeply in God's love! God has revealed His majesty in the salvation of His own and He gave ample proof of this when

He sent His Son into the world." Like Saint Paul, Micah wishes to emphasize the great humiliation suffered by Christ. He says that the Redemptor will reign "in the power of the Lord," because Christ, who is eternally God, renounced all His privileges as God, abased Himself to become a man, a servant, in order to lead souls back to God from even the depths of Hell itself.

Next Micah says that "he will be our peace and we will remain undisturbed under him." He means that the Kingdom of God will so safeguard us that we will never need to worry. We will always be at ease because we will be beyond the reach of our enemies and because death will have no power over us. Again, however, he takes up the matter of afflictions. He promises the faithful a life without fear, not a life without war. But however battles the faithful must fight, they can rest assured of total victory. He warns His people that the Assyrians, the sworn enemies of Israel, are on the way. He says, "Our enemies will enter our homes. They will trample everything underfoot. However, we will regain our own ground, for we will raise up against them seven shepherds and eight captains who will destroy the lands of Assyria and of Nimrod." This latter territory extended its reign to include Assyria, as we know from the Genesis account. The people, however, thought otherwise; they did not trust in Micah's promise of the coming of the Lord and they did not believe they would be victorious. When they saw how strong and powerful their enemies were according to worldly standards, they could not understand how they could possibly win. But Micah assures them that God will give them the grace of having shepherds and captains to lead them to victory. By the words "shepherds" and "captains," he means a well-ordered army. By the numbers "seven" and "eight," he is speaking in terms of an expression commonly employed in Scripture to signify a sufficient quantity.

To profit from Micah's teaching, let us remember that Jesus Christ will abide. That is important because otherwise we can have no real assurance. If we live one day at a time, if we do not know what will happen tomorrow, we are as if suspended in midair. That is how the Papists live. They are compelled to doubt God's grace, for they do not believe there is any way to determine whether or not they merit it. Consequently they cannot rest assured that God loves them. They are founded upon nothing but confusion, for they put in doubt what we know to hold as sure and certain. True, we are often in direst circumstances, due to the fragility of our nature and to the vices that reign in us. But that does not mean we must doubt God's promises or hold them certain only for a day or so, for our faith must extend beyond death itself. What a horrible punishment it is for men when they can be assured of God's bounty only for a time. Let us ground our faith in the Kingdom of the Lord, which is eternal. Because this Kingdom is not something perishable or transitory, we must not doubt that Jesus Christ will so persevere in His efforts to save us that we will all be saved in the end. Micah says that Jesus Christ will abide, as if to say, "My friends, I have spoken to you of a King who will be ordained by God. But do not think that he will be a King in the manner of

301

men, that He will be subject to death, that His Kingdom will perish." Christ, by His death, acquired eternal life for His own. That is the true victory and triumph He obtained over the Devil, the world, and sin. Christ was given to us for the express purpose of ruling over us forever. Let us put all our trust in Him alone; for in life, and in death, He can so arm and fortify us that we can resist all temptations once we are under His protection.

Let us also remember that Christ is our Shepherd. This means God does not wish to rule us harshly, so that we would seek only to flee from Him; He wishes to govern us in love and kindness. Micah is quick to emphasize that Christ has come neither to terrorize us nor to rain down thunderbolts against us; rather He has come to be our Shepherd and care for us as His sheep. If we are truly His sheep, that is, if we humbly and patiently obey Him, then He will truly sustain us and procure for us our salvation. The task of any good shepherd is to safeguard his flock. If men charged with the care of beasts look after them, certainly Christ, who is the fountain of all mercy and kindness and who is charged by God with the care of ourselves, will look out for us so much the more. Surely Christ loves us more than a man does beasts. He has given ample proof of His great love for us: He risked His life, suffered grievously not only in body but in soul, and even endured the torments of Hell for a time in order to deliver us. Do we not, then, have good reason to trust in Him to so sustain us against all assaults that we will always be victorious?

Although Christ appeared in this world and put on our human nature, He preserved all His divine majesty and power within Himself. That is the meaning of Micah's words "in the name of God and in the glory of the Lord, his God." So let us take care to think of the bounty of God in such a way that we do not diminish its grandeur and power. Let us come to recognize that Jesus Christ, who has come in the name of God, His Father, wishes only to employ His strong arm to sustain and protect us. It is very necessary for us to have such faith in Christ, for where are we now? What is our present condition? The whole world is like a forest full of robbers, like a sea agitated by winds and storms. In brief, the world is like a gigantic abysm ready to swallow us up at any moment. Where would we be if we are not grounded upon God? What would remain of us in the world? Indeed, we survive in the midst of great troubles, by the power and grace of God alone. True, we have many enemies who are so well equipped that they could devour us as easily as a wolf does a sheep. But since God is on our side, we need not fear. Jesus Christ is our Shepherd; He will govern us not in a human way, but in the name of the Lord, in the name of God, His Father, who sent Him to us.

What marvelous consolation! God, I say, has applied all His glory, grandeur, and majesty to our salvation. How deeply He cares for us! Who could ask for anything more? Yet we are so easily shaken and so fearful that all it takes is a leaf to tremble or a tree to fall and we fear all is lost. Although God Himself has guaranteed His promises and although Christ Himself has assured us

303

He will never fail us, still we do not fully trust in the Lord, as we read in Saint John 10. So when Satan drives us to despair, when he tries to deceive us and destroy our faith in God, let us take special care to cling to this promise that Christ will govern us in the name and in the Glory of the Lord, His God. If we firmly believe this, we will be able to repulse all Satan's assaults. True, Satan will erect many stumbling blocks to make us trip and fall into Hell. But if we truly believe that Christ will sustain us in the majesty and authority of God, there is nothing we cannot conquer. In the very midst of our enemies, we will be fortified by the power of God to drive them back. In the midst of war, God will be our wall and rampart. Our faith will be our shield, so that we will see life in the midst of death. So let us ground ourselves in God and trust fully in His promises. Then, we will know total peace and fear nothing, though our enemies attack with all their strength and though it seems they can destroy us at first blow. That is why Micah, as well as Saint Paul, says that Christ is our Peace. Indeed, these and other Biblical passages call Christ our Peace, for He comes to us solely to enable us to share in this Peace, which can be had only through Him.

Seeking to make this grace of God so much the more praise-worthy, Micah adds that "it will be extended to the ends of the earth," as if to say, "God had revealed Himself only in Judah and there made His bounty known, but today it is made available to all the world." God had made great promises to the Jews alone, but now all people can share in them. The name of God can be invoked everywhere, for there is no longer any distinction between Jew and Gentile. I say distinction because there is no longer any particular nation that can say, "We are the People of God." All peoples are called to know God. His grace is shed on all people without any exceptions whatsoever. Christ has offered His grace to us, that we might share in it. However, this does not mean that we will be exempt from all the trials and tribulations of the world. We will have to endure much suffering, just as the faithful underwent great agony when they were taken into captivity. Yet they did not renounce their faith in God, and neither must we. If we permit God to guide us by the hand of His Son, it is certain we will suffer grievously; but we must not forget that God will deliver us from all our afflictions and will show us in the end that our hope in Him was not in vain.

It is a pity that today there is more infidelity and impiety in us than ever before. Our Lord sheds as much grace upon us as we could possibly want, yet we continually trample it underfoot. There is such vicious impiety in us that it seems our only desire is to vex God. All one sees is blasphemy, scandals, and wantonness everywhere. I see such enormous impiety in Geneva that it seems this city is the mouth of hell itself. True, many in this city claim to be Christians; but this is all a facade, a mockery of God; for when you look deep within them, all you see is hypocrisy. I am not sure if there is even one out of twenty among you who truly believes that God has spoken to us. True, in the past, you were quite foolish, intoxicated as you were by the silly superstitions and Mass of the Papists. But today you are even bigger fools; for the Work of God is a two-edged sword to pierce through the heart and prod those who are steeped in their vices. But precisely the opposite happens here. You are so cold and indifferent that it seems you have never heard of God. Each of you is obsessed purely with his own self-interests. There is neither righteousness nor justice among you. What a pity that everything is totally out of control. Adultery is just about taken for granted. Those with the power to maintain law and order, those responsible to chastise and punish the iniquitous, are content to share their cloaks with them and be stained by their filthy shit. Try and outlaw shameful bawdy songs that speak only of adultery, and those who boast of being such good Christians will protest that people have a right to sing such songs. They will say, "It's fine with us if men want to sing dirty songs, just as long as they do so in their own dens of iniquity and don't drag their shit into the Church." But if that is what you think, you have no scruples whatsoever and you are trying to make adultery honorable. You are nothing but whores. Yes, I say whores even though I am speaking to men; for you are full of nothing but mockery, hypocrisy, and contempt for the Word of God, prophecy, and preaching.

Following this holy teaching, we prostrate ourselves before the face of our good God, acknowledging our sinfulness. We pray that it please Him to so open our eyes to our faults that we become totally displeased with ourselves and ask for forgiveness in the name of Jesus Christ. May He not refuse to pardon us but so guide

306

us by the Holy Spirit that we never come to doubt our salvation, even in the midst of all the trials and tribulations of the world. This we say of one voice:

All-powerful God, celestial father, from the very beginning, you have sustained your Church and never abandoned it. Although its disloyalty and revolt seemed to banish it from your presence, you remained faithful to your covenant and continued to shed your grace upon it down through the ages until the Redeemer of the world appeared. May you continue to shed your grace on us today. However we have provoked your wrath against us and are worthy of being totally rejected by you, may you so humble us that we may receive the sustenance of your Word. May we so ground ourselves in the promises of Scripture that we surmount all our enemies by our patience. May we remain the master of our passions until such time as you deploy the invincible force you have given your Son to put down Satan and all the evil ones and to fortify and shield us against all the troubles they will throw our way. Amen.

* * *

## (20) Thursday, December 25, 1551[*]

And the remnant of Jacob will be in the midst of many peoples as the dew of the Lord and as the showers upon the grass, which do not wait upon men and do not trust in the sons of men, etc. Micah 5

Yesterday we heard the Lord's promise that if we accept Christ as our King, He will give us both capable leaders and the power to resist against assaults from all sides. Micah spoke of the seven shepherds and the eight captains, which signifies we will have enough good men to lead us, provided Christ is our King. If we wish God to establish law and order among us, if we wish to be governed by His hand and guided by the Holy Spirit, and if we wish to have leaders equal to their tasks, then we must exalt and serve Christ's Throne alone. Indeed, that is our chief end. We are often destitute of good leadership. We look all around ourselves and we are compelled to ask, "Why is it everything seems to be breaking down on us? Why is it we have such poor leadership and no real protection?" We do not have to look far for the answer: We have not accepted Christ as our King. The blame rests squarely on our shoulders; for when men refuse to share in God's blessing, they have no real power to resist their enemies. In brief, they are destitute of everything necessary to maintain their own well-being.

---

[*] Calvin's Geneva began the new year on December 25. Furthermore, following Gal. 4:10, Calvin's Geneva celebrated all holidays only on Sundays.

Micah says that the remnant of Jacob will be like the dew of the Lord, like the rain which falls on the grass, making it sprout, grow tall, and thrive, without being cultivated by the hand of man or any artifact. Nevertheless, he also says that the remnant will be like a lion among savage beasts, ready to devour all. It would seem, then, that he has contradicted himself. Nothing is sweeter than the dew, which gives sustenance to the earth so it can produce our food. Our Lord compares the faithful to dew and then to lions and savage beasts that devour one another. I say it is a contradiction to claim that they are like both a gentle shower and savage beasts. But if we are the Children of God, then we must come to resemble Him; otherwise, we would not be His children. Now, God is gracious and loving to good men, but the wicked and the perverse know only His great wrath. The same thing is true of Christians. Good men will find them to be full of love and kindness; but the wicked, aroused against them, will find them to be savage beasts. This, of course, is not the true nature of God's children anymore than it is the true nature of God to be harsh and severe. But when men become perverse rebels who refuse to accept His bounty, then He is compelled to treat them harshly, as we read in Psalm 18 and as we find in the curses of the Law. God's children are the ambassadors of His grace; they are responsible for its dispensation; it is through them that the Lord multiplies and expands His grace throughout the world. When our Lord sheds upon us the graces of His Holy Spirit, they are not be exploited by us

309

for our own private benefit; they are intended to be shared with others, to be applied to the benefit of our neighbors.

To better understand what Micah means by the remnant, note that it was necessary for terrible desolation to befall the people. Only a very small segment of those who called themselves the People of God was privileged to be preserved. We, then, must be very careful how we act; for God will not shed His mercy upon all those who call themselves Christians and bear the sign of baptism, just as He preserved only a very small remnant of those who claimed to be His people. So, as I have just said, we must be very careful how we live. God has called upon us all to be His people; but as many have provoked His wrath and abused His name, He has chosen very few. Isaiah, Chapter 1, says, "If God had not taken pity on us and preserved a small remnant, we would have been as Sodom and Gomorrah." And in the tenth chapter we read, "Though your people were as numerous as the sand of the sea (that is to say, of infinite number) still only a small remnant will remain." Micah, who lived at the time of Isaiah, makes the same point, saying that God will preserve only a small number of people out of the vast multitude to which He revealed Himself. Therefore, whenever we fear we are about to perish and be lost forever, let us console ourselves with the realization that we are in God's hands and that He will not fail to govern us by His Holy Spirit. Let us remember that however His wrath may be kindled everywhere, He will take pity upon us and number us among this small remnant.

Now we are in a position to understand why Micah says, "This remnant will be like the dew or rain which falls upon the earth, making it thrive without man having to turn his hand." The reason is that absolutely everything depends upon the grace of God. Micah, then, is revealing the true calling of the faithful: They are to share with their neighbors the grace God has shed upon them. The Children of God, I say, must be of a charitable nature. The hand of God is always extended not only to aid men but also beasts, for His mercy extends even unto them, as the Psalm says. God is so generous that there is no place on the face of this earth that has not enjoyed His bounty. There is no doubt, then, that we will enjoy His bounty in abundance; for He has done us the great favor of bestowing upon us the honor of being His children. So if we wish to really prove that we are Christians, each and every one of us must dedicate himself to serving the neighbor. Indeed, Micah's point is that it is very expedient for God to preserve some remnant of the Church, because the well-being of all others depends upon the Church alone. Why? The Children of God are the ambassadors of His bounty. Enlightenment, joy, and well-being, all these things are possible only because those to whom God has revealed Himself share their salvific knowledge with others. The Children of God are the light of the world, as it has been said. Saint Paul says to the Philippians, "Go and teach this nation of infidels righteousness and justice." The infidels are poor, blind wretches who grope their way along, only to trip and fall into Hell. God has made us lampposts to light their way to the path to salvation

311

and to the life He has promised. Our Lord multiplies His grace upon us in order that we share it with others. He reveals His wisdom to us in order that it be made known throughout the world. Isaiah makes the same point, for one and the same Spirit of God spoke through the mouths of these prophets. Isaiah says that when God will have destroyed everything, nevertheless a small remnant will remain and bear fruit throughout all the world. Both these prophets are telling us that if we wish to be the Children of God, we must share with all the world the grace God has shed upon us; we must be like a rain which nourishes the earth so it may bear fruit.

So then, we must be willing to receive the rain God sends upon us through the Lord. When the Children of God reveal to us through their doctrine and behavior the path of salvation, it is as if God brought to life a barren land whose only source of nourishment is On High. Let us not be like rocks; let us not repulse God's grace by our hardness. But only very few of us are willing and able to profit from God's grace. The Gospel is very poorly received among us. When the Gospel is preached in purity to us, it is as if God sends rain to make the earth fertile. When we see it raining, we say, "Look! It's raining wheat and wine." We say so because we have such a keen interest in our stomachs. But when God sends us this spiritual rain, this rain, I say, that is not for the nourishment of our stomachs but for the nourishment of our souls so we may share in the immortal celestial glory of Jesus Christ and become true heirs to God, how is it received among us? Either we ignore it altogether or we hold it as an object of great contempt because it seems like such a bother for us. We wish God would leave us alone and not call upon us, for our nature is totally contrary to Him.

How many of us can stand being admonished and exhorted to come to God? The vast majority of us only grumble, gnash our teeth, and become very vexed against God and against those who admonish us for our own benefit. This comes from our ingratitude, which blinds us to the fact that God rains on us in order for us to bear fruit. God wishes us to so profit to his glory that everything in creation serves to the benefit of our salvation. But we refuse everything; we will not swallow one single drop of His rain.

So much the more, then, must we pay careful heed to Micah's point that God so dispenses His grace through men. God does not descend from Heaven; He does not appear in a visible form to shed His grace upon us. He works through men, who are the instruments He has ordained to dispense His grace. When the hand of God comes to our aid through men, let us not be so foolish as to reject this blessing He has offered us. Let us come to understand how we may profit from it: If we have a sweet and gracious disposition, it is certain God's teaching will be as a sweet and gentle rain to us. David, speaking of the Word of God, said that it is sweeter than honey. If we do not reject the Word, we will find it quite to our liking and we will also find the faithful to be so kind and generous that we will always have a harmonious relationship with them.

On the contrary, note carefully that Micah says if we do not receive the rain, if we refuse to be like the grass that cries out for water to grow and bear fruit, then the Children of God will be like lions to us, like savage beasts to devour us. It is not their nature to be such. The reason is our own malice. In God Himself, who is the fountain of all mercy and kindness, we will find only harsh and severe treatment if we reject His grace. Indeed, not only God and His children but all creatures will stand over and against us when we reject God's grace. Not only will God permit the Devil to torment us but we will find nothing but cruelty in God and His children. Whether we look high or low, in the heavens above or on earth, we will find that there is nothing that does not stand against us. Now, this is a horrible threat and one that we must think long and hard on; for it amounts to Micah saying that if we do not obey God, we will be destitute of everything, as in fact we are, what was ordained for our life and salvation will become our condemnation, the very bread we eat will become mortal venom. In brief, God's grace will serve only to multiply our afflictions and hasten our downfall. Micah, however, does not fail to give us the remedy, of which I have already spoken: Let us come to profit from this singular grace God has shed upon us to become His instruments, His ambassadors to distribute His grace to all men. Take a good look at our condition. Are there any among us who can boast they are worthy of the grace God has shed on them, especially as He has shed it so abundantly? Our Lord, of course, does not intend us to keep all His grace for ourselves. He wishes

314

us to be ambassadors and dispensers, so that others might share in the grace He has shed upon us. Has He not bestowed an honor far too high upon us when He not only sheds His grace upon us but also wishes us to be a brook by which this grace flows to others? That, I say, is the very special privilege conferred upon the Children of God by Micah.

Furthermore, our Lord will give us such strength that our enemies will be defeated. However they may plot and scheme against us, however they may seem like ravenous wolves about to devour us, our Lord will give us such great strength that we will be victorious. Our enemies will be subjugated to us and we will have them under our thumb. True, for a time we must suffer in patience. This period is necessary for us to learn the virtues of self-discipline. But after we have so suffered and dedicated our lives to God, we will know well that Micah did not speak in vain when he said the remnant of Jacob will be like a lion among savage beasts. The wicked, after they have plotted and raged against us, will find that all their efforts were in vain. In the midst of life, they are in death, as I have said of all those who refuse God's grace. On the contrary, in the midst of death, we have life, provided that God takes us by the hand and safeguards us. However the Gospel may be oppressed by the tyranny of the wicked, however they may be filled with such great diabolical rage that it seems we will perish, let us cling to Micah's promise that we will be like lions; that is to say, God will give us the strength to resist all the assaults of our enemies after we have endured the afflictions He sends upon us to humble us.

After having so consoled the faithful, Micah adds, "In that day, says the Lord, I will destroy your horses and chariots. I will destroy all your cities and fortresses. I will bring an end to all sorcery and fortune-telling among you. I will destroy all your graven images and idols. Never again will you worship what you have made with your own hands. I will uproot the groves of tall trees from your midst and destroy your cities." Certainly Micah seems to threaten severely the people when he says that God will destroy their walls, fortresses, arms, horses, and chariots. But in point of fact, he is calling them to rejoice; for he means that God will eliminate all stumbling blocks that might prevent them from coming to Him in wholehearted obedience and seeking in Him alone their well-being, joy, and glory.

True, cities and fortresses in themselves are not evil things, but consider how men abuse them. Can men have fortresses without being inflated by foolish pride and without coming to put all their trust in worldly things rather than in God? So whenever men find they are aided by worldly things, they cannot help but put their total and complete trust in them. That is why the Lord says He will destroy all the horses and chariots, as if to say, "Well I know you will not come to me as long as you cling to those worldly things you think will aid you, for you believe all your salvation and well-being lies in them alone. That is why you are damned." When creatures separate us from God, what happens to us? Are we not quite unhappy? Are we not as lost within the earth's abysms? Whenever creatures separate us from God, so much the greater is our condemnation. Even if we had everything we could ever hope for, still we would be unhappy. All the good things we possess curse us.

Our Lord, seeing that we are prone to trust in worldly things, says that He will strip them from us in order to give us a clear path to Him. Worldly things are like bandages over our eyes. Now, when a man's eyes are bandaged he cannot tell whether he is being led into an old ruin to be exposed to the wind and rain or whether he is being led into a forest full of robbers and savage beasts or whether he is being led into a well-furnished house where he will be well treated. So he refuses to take a step until the bandages are removed. It is impossible to lead him with his eyes bandaged. This same thing is true when our Lord calls us. We know that our survival depends upon God governing us. Otherwise, we are prey to a thousand different ways of death, and creatures, though intended for our usage, will curse us. Yet, we are unable to follow God one single step of the way because our eyes are bandaged. And there is not one bandage covering our eyes but more than a thousand: Some of us are full of nothing but pride and ambition; others are given to loan sharking and rapine: still others are prone to adultery, wantonness, and scandalous behavior; and although we are totally destitute in ourselves, the slightest aid we receive from the world so puffs us up with pride that we think we do not need God's grace. But God will cut away all these bandages by revealing

317

to us our own poverty and total dependence upon His grace, in order that we come to Him with an ardent heart.

This unbandaging is what Micah has in mind when he says, "I will destroy your chariots and horses, your fortresses and cities." He means that the Church is truly restored and rightly governed when God has so turned us away from worldly things that we go directly to Him, put all our faith and confidence in Him, and no longer depend upon creatures. True, God permits men and creatures to aid us. But, as I have just said, our nature is so perverse and vicious that were God to give us worldly goods to our heart's content, we would become so captivated by them, so stupefied, that we would no longer see a wink of God. Consequently, God strips us of all worldly goods so they no longer serve as obstacles blocking our path to Him.

The question arises whether God wishes His own to be so destitute that we must be stripped of absolutely everything if we wish to be true Christians. The answer is easy enough. Micah does not say that God will strip everything from His faithful when He restores His Church; he says God will deny them only a superabundance of goods, as heretofore it was this superabundance of good things that seduced and led the people astray. God will provide us with worldly goods, but in moderation only. If God were to give us a superabundance of goods, we would become instantly carried away, as I have just said. For example, a man subject to gluttony and drunkenness should be served only very moderate portions. A small child should not be fed according to his appetite. Why? If he were allowed to eat to his heart's content, he would do so until he bursts, as he totally lacks the discretion to know when he needs to be fed. This same principle applies to all other behaviors. A man subject to drunkenness should be served wine only in moderation; if he were given the whole jug, he would get drunk. So it is with our souls: If God were to give us an abundance of worldly goods, we would instantly become intoxicated by them, for we know no moderation. Therefore, God has to cut way down on our rations of the very things which are necessary for ourselves and which are not evil in themselves.

Note that in Deuteronomy God expressly forbid the kings from amassing great numbers of horses and chariots. Why? Our Lord knew that men are inclined to be so carried away by an abundance of goods that they no longer pay any attention to Him. He did not wish to give the kings occasion to trust in creatures; He wished them to remember that it is God alone who strengthens, sustains, and protects them. It is good, then, that God strips us of all abundance, which would otherwise block our path to Him. This is His way of unbandaging our eyes so we may see the light and follow Him. If God sends poverty and indigence upon us, this is far more to our benefit than would be prosperity. True, we will undergo great affliction. Indeed, we will suffer and grumble all the more, as we are prone to be very impatient. But we must always bear in mend that prosperity would soon enough pervert us so we would only blaspheme God. Today, we see well how those in prosperity rebel against God, thinking they no longer need Him and are no longer

319

subject to Him. They make themselves into idols and multiply their evil until they have reached the heights of all iniquity. Prosperity is far more dangerous for us than poverty, for we are all too inclined to trust in worldly things. Note carefully that Micah is speaking here of things which are not evil in themselves, provided that they are used properly; that is, men must not go to extremes with these things, as they are prone to do. He says, "I will destroy your chariots, rid you of your horses, and smash down your fortresses." All these things are good in themselves. God created horses for the usage of men. But, as I have just said, although all these things are good in themselves, God must strip us of them because of our perverse nature: The good things God gave us to bring us to Himself serve only to turn us away from Him.

Next, Micah says that God will do away with all sorcerers, astrologers, fortune-tellers, and the like, as these are evils God strongly condemns. There are two important points to bear in mind here if we are to profit from this passage. First, the true restoration of the Church necessitates God abolish and chase all evil from our midst. Secondly, this restoration requires that we be stripped of good things whenever we abuse them by applying them to evil ends. Do we wish Christ to reign in our midst? Do we wish to share in all the good things He has for us? Do we wish Him to save us? Then, according to Micah, all evil must be abolished from our midst. By this, he means that we are as yet still prone to corruption and vices and will be so until God finally purges us of all evil. This is readily apparent if we take a long, hard look at ourselves. We are as yet prone to self-love, which so intoxicates and blinds us that we completely overlook our moral turpitude and therefore fail to be horrified by it. We are so carnal that what is evil seems good to us. That is why we do not recognize our vices and sins and fail to become displeased with ourselves. Therefore, Micah warns us that God will destroy all statues, graven images, and the like. This is a common teaching throughout Scripture; but at present, Micah's words will suffice to remind us that all that men consider to be true perfection is nothing but an abomination before God, as we read in Saint Luke, Chapter 12. All that men consider good God will reject and hold in abomination.

Micah could have spoken of adultery, murder, rape, larceny, and the like, but he did not. Is that because God approves of these vices or overlooks them and so will not punish them? No! These are such great evils that we cannot help but be horrified by them and strongly condemn them. True, there are men so perverse that they would try to justify these evils. But in the end, their conscience will get the better of them, and they will be compelled to confess these are very wicked things. On the other hand, when it comes to superstitions, it is very difficult to convince us that these things are evil: They are things we have invented to please ourselves and we take great pride in our workmanship. That is why Micah speaks out so strongly against the idols and false gods forged by the superstitions of men, saying that God will destroy all these things. He says God will uproot the groves of tall trees, because that is the place where people went to worship idols, thinking they were worshipping God. But the Lord said to them, "You do not honor me there, you honor the Devil."

Now, as I have already said, these are things evil in themselves. But God will not abolish just the evil things from our midst; He will purge us and correct our ways by stripping us of things good and necessary in themselves. It is necessary for God to curtail our supply of things necessary to sustain life. Look at how the wealthy are so imprisoned within their riches that they cannot get to God. The only way God has of freeing them is to seriously curtail their wealth. That, I say, is a good example of how God works with us. He does not strip us of everything; He does not render us totally destitute; He provides us with goods, but only in moderation.

Let us be very careful how we act. Let us remember that we are full of nothing but shit and corruption until God purges us. Let us recognize that God must purge us not only of our vices but also of beautiful things in order to thoroughly cleanse us.

Micah emphasizes that only God alone can cleanse us. Why? Men are so perverse that they cannot liberate themselves from their idolatries. Therefore, it is necessary for God to step in and strip them of everything. Indeed, when we realize how truly perverse we really are, we should not find it surprising that our Lord strips us of even the good and beautiful so we will not have even the slightest occasion to do evil.

I see that there are more of you out there than are accustomed to attending my sermons. Why is this? It is Christmas Day. But according to whom? Poor beasts! What treachery, that you would celebrate Christmas today! Do you think you are honoring God by this? How truly obedient do you think you are to God? Consider carefully the fact that you wish to make today a holiday. True, you have been told time and time again that it is good and necessary to take one day out of the year to review how the birth of Christ was to our benefit and to recount the history of the nativity, as will be done this Sunday. But if you think you can serve God by setting up special holidays, you are worshipping idols. True, you think you honor God, but in point of fact you honor Satan. Pay attention to what the Lord has to say. Did not Saul wish only to serve God by sparing Agag, king of the Amalekites, the best oxen, the fattest cattle, and everything else worth saving? Full of devotion to God and with the best of all intentions, he said, "I wish to serve the Lord." But what was the response he received? "You are a sorcerer, heretic, and apostate. You say you wish to honor God, but He condemns you and disavows all that He has done for you." God will do the same to you because one day is not better than any other. Days do not matter when it comes to speaking of our Lord's nativity; we can speak of it on Wednesday, Thursday, any day. But when you are so wicked that you wish to serve God according to your whims, that is blasphemy; you have forged an idol, however you may think you are acting solely in the name of God. And when you try to serve God in useless ways,

323

that is a very grave fault, one that will attract all the others until you have reached the heights of all iniquity. Note that our Lord not only strips us of things bad in themselves but that He abolishes all occasions that might lead to superstitions. When you realize that, you will not find it strange that celebrating Christmas on this day has been abolished and that on Sunday we will celebrate Communion and recount our Lord's nativity. But if this vexes you, it is simply because you do not know Jesus Christ, you do not understand how to be one of His subjects, and you do not realize that God removes all the stumbling blocks that turn us away from Him. Well you sense how your wicked courage has failed you, for you have been failed in your evil attempt to celebrate Christmas today.

Following this holy teaching, we prostrate ourselves before the face of our good God, acknowledging our sinfulness. We pray that He so open our eyes that we know all the poverty within ourselves. May in this way we be inspired to come closer to Him than ever before. May we totally renounce ourselves and all our wicked desires, that we comply fully with His commands. We pray in all humility that He so guide us by the Holy Spirit that we never become separated from Him. May we realize that it is in Him alone that we seek and find the plentitude of all goodness and wisdom. May He shed this grace not only on us but upon all the peoples and nations of the earth, etc.

* * *

324

(21) Friday, December 26, 1551

Hear now what the Lord says: "Rise up and plead before the mountains. Let them hear your voice: 'Hear, your mountains and your strong foundations of the earth, the judgment of the Lord; for the Lord has a dispute with His people and will speak out against Israel, etc.'" Micah 6

Yesterday we saw how the Lord returns us to himself by purging us of all superstitions and also by stripping us of things that are not bad in themselves but might be an occasion for evil. Regarding superstitions, men simply refuse to believe that these lead them astray from God; for there is a common opinion among us that God will find good whatsoever men do with the intention of serving Him. On the contrary, however, God will not rescind His commandments and will hold in abomination all that men do when they take the law into their own hands. We cannot be true Christians until God purges us of all idolatries and superstitions. However these things may be objects of great piety and devotion to us, God must cast them out of our midst. Because we are so wicked that we trust in creatures and become fixated upon worldly things, these also must be cast out of our midst in order that we go directly to God and put all our trust in Him.

Micah wishes this message to be taken with the utmost seriousness, so he says that the Lord will pour out horrible vengeance upon all those people who have not heard it. Although our Lord has provided only one people with his salvific teaching, He says He will spare no nations. He intends this as a warning to

325

the Jews to take care, lest they be found without excuse before God. If the pagans, these poor blind beasts which God has allowed to go astray, are punished, what will happen to those whom He took such great pains to teach by His very mouth? Will they escape punishment? Certainly not. God threatens such horrible vengeance upon the world in order to warn the Jews that they will be the very first to be brought to account because of their rebellion. Because they refused to hear God, they will feel His heavy hand upon them; they will receive well-deserved punishment.

Micah says with yet greater vehemence, "Hear, I pray you, what God has to say, for He has commanded me to summon the mountains and the foundations of the earth, for he wishes to bring you to trial." God wishes this trial be public and of such great solemnity that all will attend. In that way, the people will be without excuse. Micah says, in effect, "I hereby summon before the court all creatures without sense or reason, to bear witness against you." What is the case God wishes to prosecute? The ingratitude of His people. He says, "My people, what have I done? How have I wearied you?" as if to say, "Are you not unhappy to have abandoned me and to no longer have me as your God? Have you forgotten what all I have done for you? Did I not deliver you from Egypt, leading you by the hands of Moses, Aaron, and Miriam? Did I not protect you against Balak and Balaam? When I have shown you what great love I bear for you and how deeply I care for you, what possible excuse could you have not to obey me and subjugate yourselves to my Word? Can you truly testify against me? All you can really say is that

I have done so many good things for you that it is impossible to number them." That is the main point to bear in mind in today's lesson.

When he exhorts the Jews to hear the Lord, he does so not only to impress upon them His God-given authority but also to warn them it is no small matter to have God as an adversary, as will be revealed shortly. The prophets all shared a common manner of speaking: "The Lord says to you, the mouth of the Lord has spoken, the Lord has revealed to me." Micah, however, has a special reason for speaking this way: He pities His people because he sees they are bound for Hell and do not realize how horrible it is to fall between the hands of the living God. So, seeing their great stupidity, he warns them, "I pray you, hear what the Lord says to you." Bear in mind, as you have so often been reminded, that the prophets did not haphazardly usurp the name of God. They were sure and certain that God had in fact spoken to them. The name of God is sacred; we must not mock it by taking the attitude that on one hand God has revealed to us all that we say before men but on the other that we are not certain and fully resolved in our own minds that God has spoken to us. If we take this attitude, we will be rendered culpable before men and angels for having defamed the name of God. Let us guard against all such temerity. The prophets claimed that God is the author and guarantor of what they have to say, because their messages were engraved and sealed in their hearts by the Holy Spirit. They had no doubt whatsoever that they were sent by God and that He put words in their mouths just as one would give a messenger his instructions right down to the letter.

When God commands Micah to speak to the mountains and hills, perhaps He means to men who enjoy positions of great power. Mountains are a common prophetic symbol for men of power, as we find to be the case so often in Jeremiah and Isaiah. The princes and kings, the magistrates, and justices are likened to mountains because they stand over and above all other men. Although we know God reproaches the high and mighty, we also realize that He calls everyone to account, rich and poor, big and small; for God is Judge of the world and makes no exceptions for persons. Let each man be ready to present himself before God, for He is the Judge of all mankind. All men, whether they enjoy positions of power or whether they have none, are reproached, threatened, and exhorted by the Lord. Why, then, do prophets focus primarily upon men of power and authority? Because when they sin, their sin is not exclusively a private matter but causes great scandal by which all is corrupted and perverted and everyone is led straight to Hell. When a man of no real social position sins, so what? He will soon enough pass away and be forgotten. But when those in authority are wicked, the Devil has a field day corrupting everyone. That is why our Lord focuses upon those in positions of power. Indeed, they are so puffed up with pride that they think themselves a cut above all other men and will not tolerate the slightest criticism. They try and use their high position as a shield against God. Consequently, our Lord speaks out quite harshly against them to humble them and put them in their place. In brief, those who fail the most grievously, indeed to the ruination of all others, are those who wish only flattery and cannot tolerate the slightest reproach. But our Lord, the sworn enemy of all pride, has declared war against all men of power and will really knock them down a peg or two.

Nevertheless, when all is taken into consideration, Micah is speaking literally, not figuratively, when he says, "Speak to the mountains; let your voice reverberate through the abysms of the earth to the strong foundations of the earth itself, that is, to its foundations of rock and stone, witnessing of that which I accuse my people and of that which I ask of them in pleading against them." Now, it is nothing new that the Lord commands His prophets to speak to the earth and mountains. At first glance, it seems very strange indeed that God would speak to creatures who have neither sense nor reason. We can well imagine Micah asking, "What is the purpose of preaching to the earth, for it cannot see a wink? Why should I speak to the mountains? That certainly seems like a lot of work for nothing." However, God is not speaking to the mountains or the earth for themselves; He is speaking to them in order to speak so much the more vehemently against us. It is His way of reproaching us for our hardness, rebellion, and stupidity, by which we are totally unmoved by whatsoever He has done for us. He is saying, in effect, "I created men and gave them intelligence. They are the ones intended to receive my Word. I demand they thank me only by having the courtesy to listen to me. I have given men very special gifts: They have reason and intelligence; they can understand what is said to them. Yet they do not wish to listen to me. What else can I do, then, but go speak to the rocks, the mountains, and the earth?" Likewise, Isaiah said, "Listen, sky and earth, give ear to me." He knew well that the sky and earth would not hear a thing he had to say; he spoke to them solely because people paid no attention to him: "Since I am not heard by men, I will go speak to insensible creatures." This was spoken to the great shame of men, who, while gifted with reason, are more insensitive to God than are the brutal beasts. Likewise Moses, seeing the great evil of the people, said, "I call upon the sky and earth to witness that I give you this day the choice of life or death," as if he were saying, "Though the angels refuse to speak and the faithful refuse to witness against you, still the earth and sky alone would suffice to condemn you; for the voice of God is so powerful and so penetrating that it can split apart rocks and stones, and yet it cannot reach your hearts. How do you expect God will deal with you? Will not all the creatures rise up in judgment against you?" That is Micah's point.

As we have already seen, our Lord did everything possible to reproach His people in order to return them to Himself. But all His efforts were in vain. Therefore, Micah says, "Behold, the Lord commands I make public your summons before the court, for He fully intends to institute proceedings against you." When a man is a fugitive from justice, his name is placed on wanted posters everywhere, so there is no place for him to hide. The Lord is using this very tactic against His people. They are a rebellious lot who refuse both to hear the prophets and to obey their summon to appear before the court. They are like wild beasts; indeed, they are like lions ready to tear apart and devour everything. Since they refuse to appear before the court, the Lord summons the mountains, the earth, indeed its very foundations, as if to say, "These people refuse to receive me, obey me, and subjugate themselves to me. They reject my Word and rise up against my prophets. They are so hardened that I cannot get through to them. Therefore, I am compelled to bring them to trial. Since they refuse to appear before the court to answer for the charges against them, I hereby summon the mountains to testify as witnesses against them." Micah makes all this known to the people in order to shame them, as if to say, "True, you hear my words; but how can you profit from them? Where are your hearts? Where are your spirits? For a very long time, I have exhorted you in the name of God; but I might as well have spoken to rocks. Indeed, even rocks themselves are far more responsive than you; for at least they reverberate to the sound of my words. But you, you are so hardened that you will not listen to a single word that God commands I speak to you. When I speak to you, you might as well be a hundred thousand leagues away from me. You have no love for God or His Word; the Devil has so blocked you off from God that He cannot get through to you. I hereby proclaim that God has summoned you before the court, that your trial has begun; but you remain oblivious to all this and think that you can flee from God's justice. I warn you that God does not speak in vain when He says you will not escape His hand. I warn you that however it may seem that God overlooks your sins, He is your Judge and will make you feel His heavy hand upon you, for you have refused to believe in His Word."

Let us take care that we do not find ourselves in a similar situation. When God speaks to us, let us not give Him occasion to complain that we are so hardened that He might as well go speak to the earth and to creatures who have neither sense nor reason. Since we are gifted with intelligence, what excuse have we when we hear less of God than would a rock? Do we think our ingratitude will remain unpunished? God has given us the gift of reason, that we may hear and understand the Word, which manifests His love to us and which is the source of our salvation. So let us receive and trust fully in the Word. Let us profit from this priceless gift of the Word, that God be honored and glorified by us. Let us not give God occasion to abandon us and turn to creatures who have neither sense nor reason.

Note carefully why Micah says, "Let the strong foundations of the earth hear God's judgment!" He means that there is nothing so hard and strong that it will not tremble when God rises in judgment against men. After speaking of the mountains, he might have mentioned just the earth alone; but he wishes to speak of something yet even stronger, so he speaks of the very foundations of the earth itself. He does so to emphasize what a terrible thing it is to have God for an adversary: Men will be scared out of their wits; all creatures will tremble; the earth will shake all the way down to the bottom of its deepest abysses; there will be no metal so hard that it will not be bent. Are we not more than foolish, then, if we do not fear God summoning us before His court? Men wish to enjoy themselves. However God may warn them that it is not a time for rejoicing, they will not abandon their merry-making until they feel His heavy hand upon them. However His Word may lack authority and respect among them, in the end they will be unable to escape His hand. Just as a larcen may for a time escape punishment but in the end will be brought before the judge, so it will be with us. And remember, we will not be brought before an earthly judge but before God. Where can we flee that we can escape the hand of God? As it says in the Psalm, if we had wings to soar to the clouds above and fly beyond the seas, God would well be able to find us. If we were hidden in the abysms, the arm of God would reach us. So let us not transgress; let us quake in our boots whenever God threatens to take us to court. "The wrath of the king is the message of death," says Solomon. What are worldly kings in comparison to our sovereign King? They are only flies and frogs, compared to Him. So how is it possible for us not to be frightened when God threatens to take us to court?

Whom will God bring charges against? His own people! If it were merely a matter that God were prosecuting only the Pagans and idolaters, we would have reason to say, "This should not bother us in the least. We are the People of God. He has chosen and elected us. We are in His safekeeping. We have nothing to fear when He brings to trial His enemies." Yes, that certainly is what we would say alright. But when it is a matter that God brings His own people to trial, this should make our hairs stand on end. No men are so glorious that they are exempt from God's judgment. We are the People of God, which is the greatest honor that can be bestowed on men; yet we are not excused from God's punishment; He will not fail to prosecute us whenever we rebel against Him. We will be the first brought to trial; we will be without any defense, for who could possibly win his case when he has to plead against His Creator? What terrible day this will be for us! So beware how Satan has blinded and bewitched us: If a man hates us, or wishes evil upon us, or threatens to sue us, we are instantly worried and we will seek out every possible way to remedy this situation. We will not rest as long as mortal man constitutes a threat to us. But when God is our adversary, when He threatens to bring criminal charges against us and prosecute us to the full, we remain at ease, thinking the whole thing is a joke. But in the end God will make us know He does not speak in vain.

So let us remind ourselves again and again of Micah's warning that God will prosecute His people. Let us also remember that God is fair and just in doing so: Since God has chosen us, we must be totally dedicated to serving Him and glorifying His name everywhere and in all things. Otherwise He will have just cause to prosecute us for our ingratitude, by which He is dishonored. So much the more God sheds His grace upon us, so much the more must we walk in fear and humility. But this is not to say that we must walk in doubt of our salvation. We have every reason to be confident of our own salvation, provided that we hold Christ to be our Prince, that we are thoroughly grounded in His mercy, and that we are so united to Christ that absolutely nothing can separate us from Him. But such confidence must be accompanied by a deep sense of humility. We must guard against giving free reign to evil by making light of it, saying to ourselves, "Whatever evil I do, I can easily enough appease God." That is why we should come to fear abusing God's grace, hearing that He fully intends to prosecute His people.

We receive daily God's message of salvation. That is the whole point of the Gospel. Saint Paul says, "I am the ambassador of God in the name of our Lord, Jesus Christ. I beg and plead with you to be reconciled with God." Whenever and wherever the Gospel is preached, the message is this: "God wishes only that the world be at peace with Him." If we decline His offer of peace, we declare war on Him. However we may be called the People of God, He will not fail to prosecute us for our ingratitude. I have already warned that all our subterfuges and cunning will serve us nothing before God. True, before a human judge, a man may win a bad case by all sorts of trickery and conniving. But that will be to no avail before God, who will see to it everyone is brought to account.

Remember, as I have just said, there are two basic reasons why we cannot win our case before God. For one thing, God is so wise and mighty that none can successfully oppose him. For another, there is not one single excuse we can find that will justify us before God. True, men believe that they are armed with more than enough alibis to defend themselves against God. But God can easily enough shoot them all down by saying merely, "True, you think you are righteous men, but I say you are traitors, for you have abandoned me." That is what Micah means when he says, "My people, what have I done to you? How have I wearied you?" Likewise Jeremiah says, "My people, what iniquity have you found in me that led you to abandon me?" So we see how we will for sure be convicted if God brings us to trial.

If we accept as a foregone conclusion that God will hand down a verdict against us, now, then, should we live? Here, Job is a shinning example to enlighten us. Although he claims to be a man of clean conscience, sanctity, and loyalty to God, he says, "When I come before my Judge, I will be without excuse, for I am more than culpable. For every point that I might raise to justify myself, God would find a thousand others to condemn me." He says that he was an eye for the blind, an arm for the lame, a father for orphans; he says that he was kind to animals and always had his hand outstretched to help the poor, that he oppressed no man, and that he never rebelled against God. Yet he also knows that men are all sinners full of nothing but shit and infection; he realizes that we all deserve to be convicted by God, that we are all worthy of a thousand deaths. So he says that nothing remains for him to do but repent and confess his sins. Likewise David, though God said he was a man after His own heart, protests, "Lord, do not bring your servant to trial"; for well he knows that he is more than condemnable in every respect.

336

Here, then, are two men who are like angels from Paradise, and yet each realizes that he would be more than damned if God brought him to trial. So what will happen to us? That is something we really need to think about. We know that God has shed His grace upon us, called us to Himself, and wishes us to be His Church. Yet we know that we have defaulted upon our promise to be faithful. So what can we really say of ourselves, except that we have broken the covenant God has made with us and look to Satan as our master? This is precisely the complaint Jeremiah made against his people when he said, "Go and see if there are any other nations in the world that abandon their gods even though they are idols. Yet I am unable to keep a tight rein on you. Although I have given you sufficient proof that I am the living God, although I have demonstrated my power to you so many times, still you will not obey me. Is not the loyalty and devotion of the Pagans alone sufficient to condemn you?"

Jeremiah's words are very relevant to us today; for he was addressing a people who had abandoned themselves to superstitions and idolatry, who had rejected the pure truth of God, and among whom all the vices came to reign by and by. Now, when we take a good look at ourselves today, do we not see that we are just as disloyal to God? Have we not falsified our baptism by all our idolatries and abominations? God delivered us from Hell in order to be united with Himself. But how successfully have we fulfilled this calling? True, we boast loudly that we wish to live by God's teaching alone. But when we examine our lives carefully, we find they are about as compatible with the teachings of the Gospel as is fire with water. Have we not, then, good reason to fear the sentence our Lord will pass against us? As I have said, God makes no exceptions for persons. Furthermore, our Lord will punish us for our ingratitude when we abuse the good things He has given us, just as He punished the Jews; for we have taken the place of the Jews and are given the grace of which they were deprived.

Now we come to the point where the Lord says, "My people, what have I done to you? How have I wearied you?" God has a serious grievance against us; and if we examine matters closely enough, we find He has good reason to be upset with us. Our minds boggle at the vast evil within us. Our minds also boggle when we see how God's bounty surmounts all our offenses, providing us with an infinite number of blessings. Indeed, God has shed a veritable abysm of grace on us in body and soul. God is anything but stingy. Saint James says that God gives abundantly to all and that He does not in the least object to filling men to the brim with His riches. But Micah here says that God deeply regrets what He has done for His people. However, this is not due to anything within God Himself. He does not wish to withhold goods from people. Indeed, it is completely against the grain of His nature to be ungenerous. The problem is that we have provoked Him. So if we wish Him to continue giving us good things, we must use them as He so intends, namely that they serve to glorify His name.

God reproaches the Jews in three ways. First, He says, "I delivered you from the land of Egypt, from the house of servants, that is to say, from the servitude in which you were detained." Secondly, He says, "I gave you Aaron, Moses, and Miriam to lead you." Thirdly, He says, "I fortified you against all your enemies. Remember how I delivered you from Balak, who had conspired with Balaam to destroy you. When you remember these things, you are compelled to praise the aid I have given you." True, the Lord could have reproached the people for many other things He had done for them, but He is just speaking here of some of the more important ones. It is, of course, a magnificent act of grace that God nourishes and sustains us. These alone are enough to show how obliged we are to God and how praiseworthy are His grace and bounty. When Micah speaks of God delivering His people from Egypt, leading them by Moses and Aaron, and safeguarding them from the machinations of Balak, he is emphasizing that God has shed yet even greater grace upon us, taking us to be His people and watching over us. Indeed, God has shed very special graces upon us that He has not upon other peoples. That is Micah's reason for speaking of the deliverance from Egypt rather than of those blessings that God confess upon men in general.

The Lord adds, "I gave you Moses, Aaron, and Miriam," because they were the leaders of the people. Although Miriam was only a woman, she was gifted with grace in order to be a source of strength and support for the women, as we know they are far more needy in these respects than are men. Although Moses and Aaron were in charge of governing and teaching the people, Miriam provided an invaluable service for her sex, as the women were more

339

inclined to confide in her than they were in a man. God provided
for all the needs of His people. That is why we read in Exodus 15
that Miriam led the women in singing the praises of the Lord after
they had crossed the Red Sea. Micah mentions her to show that God
had provided for all the needs of the people. There were two
Governors for the men and a Governess for the women. None of the
people, then, had any reason to say, "We do not know what to do;
we are abandoned here." God always had His hand ready to help
them.

Let us apply what we have just learned to our own situation.
As I have said, we have taken the place of Micah's people. It is
as if we have been grafted onto a good olive tree, some of its own
branches having been cut away and we taking their place. These
branches, I emphasize, were cut away because of their ingratitude.
So if we are ungrateful, as were the Jews, we too will be cut off
from the rich nourishment provided us by the tree. If we do not
profit from the good things God has given us, He will not spare
us, especially as He has shed more praiseworthy grace upon us than
He did upon the people of Israel: He was not merely content to
choose us as His people, He gave us His Son as a sure and certain
sign of the great love He bears us. Furthermore, He has seen to
it that the Devil and all the armed forces of Hell can do nothing
against us, as He has ransomed us by the death and passion of His
Son. Since He began our salvation, He has sustained us daily by
His grace; so we can be sure that He will continue to multiply His
grace upon us, provided that we praise the mercy He has shown us

and provided that we are truly repentant and beg His pardon for our sins, which He has promised to remit in the name of and through our Lord, Jesus Christ.

Following this holy teaching, we prostrate ourselves before the face of our good God, acknowledging our sinfulness. We pray that He open our eyes to know better the blessings we receive from His hand. May we recognize to what end He daily multiplies His blessings upon us in body and in soul. May He be our gracious and loving Father and treat us as His well-beloved children. May we no longer so provoke His wrath against us that He brings us to trial. May He give us the grace that we use His blessings according to their intended purpose, namely that His name be glorified throughout all our life. May He shed this grace not only on us but on all the peoples and nations of the earth, etc.

* * *

(22) Saturday, December 27, 1551

What shall I bring when I present myself before the Lord and bow before the sovereign God? Shall I bring offerings and year-old calves? Does the Lord wish a thousand sheep or ten thousand beasts from the grassy valleys?, etc. Micah 6

Yesterday we saw that God continues to shed the grace upon us that He did upon the ancients who lived under the Law. Indeed, He will shed far more marvelous grace upon us, provided that we are not ungrateful and therefore merit twice the punishment He inflicted upon the people of Israel.

God is a generous provider and does not in the least resent being asked to give abundantly. But we must be careful not to abuse His generosity by misusing His gifts so as to dishonor His name.

In conclusion, we saw that God not only delivered us from Egypt but that He also delivered us from far worse slavery yet. He has delivered us from Hell itself; for we were all slaves to sin, bound by the Devil's chains. So let us praise the great blessing God has shed upon us. Our Lord, Jesus Christ, does not exercise His office as Redemptor only temporarily; He will safeguard us forever. He continuously teaches us and leads us along the path to salvation: He incessantly fulfills all the requirements of a good shepherd. Are we, then, not more than hardened if we are not thankful to Him? We feel His power flowing through us to strengthen us and fortify us against all enemies. Satan has a thousand ways to damn us; but Jesus Christ, having all power within Himself, protects us against him. We are so well armed that the Devil can gain no ground with us, no matter how hard he tries. Remember, as God had good reason to complain against the people of Israel for their ingratitude, so much the more will He be displeased with us today if we do not apply His blessings to the benefit of our salvation in order to glorify His name, which is our chief end, according to the Scriptures.

Now Micah turns to the fact that the people think they can appease God by ceremonies and the like. Here, he is pointing out how hypocritical we are because on one hand we will acknowledge our sins but on the other we will resort to quick and easy ways of purifying ourselves before God, as if God must conform to our standards. True, we admit that we are sinners and that we must confess before God. Indeed, God has so impressed upon us the grievousness of our sins that we are more than convinced of our own sinfulness. Nevertheless, we are always seeking easy ways to appease God. Each of us is prone to say, "I do not deny that I am nothing but a miserable sinner, but look at all I am doing to appease God." We are so full of pride and deceit that it seems to us we can bandage God's eyes, appeasing Him with some frivolous thing. No doubt the people responded to Micah's question by saying, "True, God has bestowed upon us infinite blessings; true, we have not always appreciated them as we should. But that is really no reason for you to condemn us as you do. You say that we have offended God by disobeying Him, but you also have to take into account all the sacrifices and things we have done to compensate

God. You have to look at both sides of the coin. Sure, we have failed God in many respects; but at the same time, we have done many, many things to make up to him for our failings." Sin now, pay later. That is how the whole world thinks.

Micah puts down all such hypocritical practices, saying they will not return us to a state of grace once we have provoked the wrath of God. He says that men have sacrificed in vain, for God wants neither sheep nor any other beasts. He will not be appeased by either what might be translated as a thousand beasts from grassy valleys or cakes made with oil that are offered up in sacrifice. So Micah is saying in effect, "If you emptied your stables and offered up all your beasts as sacrifices, if you offered up in sacrifice all that your fields yield, still that would not appease God, that would not serve as a payment made to Him to erase your sins. When you sacrifice your children, as you are accustomed to do, that is only an abomination in the eyes of God. Our Lord neither requested nor wished sacrifices to be made in themselves. He wishes sacrifices to be made only as a symbolic gesture that you truly repent of your sins. Our Lord ordained sacrifices for the express purpose of teaching you to be horrified of your sins. The death of the sacrificial object was intended to remind you that you yourself are in the midst of death because of your fragility and because you are all culpable before God. Sacrifices, then, are valid only as a confession of your deep need to be redeemed and cleansed by God of all your spiritual shit. But you do nothing of this. You think all you have to do is offer up an animal, and God is well paid off. You do not sacrifice in righteousness and truth, yet you think your sacrifices will settle the score with God. I tell you your sacrifices are totally worthless. Look at what God demands of you. First, you must be fair and just to your neighbors. That is what the word "righteousness" means. Secondly, you must be merciful and help others. Thirdly, you must obey God. Do not be prideful, for that will make you rebel against God. Walk in all humility. Accept patiently all the blows of His hand. These are the main things God wishes of you. But you do completely the opposite. Don't try and con me into believing that your sacrifices are some sort of shield against God. They are worthless; they will not prevent you from being convicted for your ingratitude." Micah's message, then, is that God will strip away all our frivolous facades and bring us to acknowledge our own sinfulness.

We, as all men, have a jaundiced eye that can see only the good in ourselves. Therefore, God must force us to acknowledge our sins; otherwise, we would continue in our rebellion and become so much the more hardened against Him. What is the basic way we try to resist against God's judgment? Hypocrisy is the sole method we have to beat a retreat from God when He calls us. We always have, I emphasize, all sorts of silly cover-ups on tap. We think these will so shield us that God will be unable to see a single thing in us. As it is a matter here of ceremonies, note that men have had these from the very beginning and have presumed them to be an effective shield against God.

The sacrificial rituals of the Jews provided more of a facade of an easy acquittal before God than those of other religions, for the sacrificial ordinance of the Jews contained the promise: "In doing this, your sins will be forgiven." But they completely overlooked God's rationale for sacrificing. Instead of taking it to a confession of sin, they thought it was an easy way of appeasing God. But however men may wish to flatter themselves, they must admit that no man has ever been so perfect that God could not condemn him in many ways. There never was a man so prideful that in the end he could not be forced to admit that he was deeply indebted to God. And yet we counterfeit money to buy God off. By that, I mean we try to appease God by some silly trinket, saying, "Well! When God has this, won't He be pleased." True, the Jews had some justification for their sacrifices insofar as God himself had commanded them to do so. But the sacrifices they offered were bastard and corrupt sacrifices, for they paid no attention to the point and truth of sacrificing. Our Lord did in fact ordain sacrificing. Why? Whenever a man sinned, he was to go to the Temple and kill a beast. Blood was spilt in order for him to be able to say to himself, "Alas! What am I really? Here is a poor innocent beast dead in my place. What do I truly merit but eternal death? Do I not deserve to be destroyed and cast down to the bottom of the abysms of the earth before God and man?" Sacrifices were intended to encourage the poor sinner to return to God, saying, "Alas! I wish no longer to provoke the wrath of God. I wish Him to live in me to strengthen me. I wish to so live in the world that He lives in me and governs me by His Holy Spirit." Sacrifices were ordained, I say, to call men to repentance and to make them realize the deep need they have for God to kill their wicked impulses so they may lead a holy life. And they were to be a profession of faith in Jesus Christ: "I have sinned. My mortal enemy is my God. I will remain at war with Him until I am reconciled to him by the promised Redemptor." So even though Christ had not yet appeared, the Jews were to trust in Him to shed His blood for the redemption of all souls. But they did none of this. Instead they said, "I have sinned. To make amends with God, I offer up this sacrifice in the manner prescribed by Moses." So they gave free reign to their evil impulses, thinking they could be easily acquitted before God by some small ceremony.

Look at how that has been the case with Papism right up to the present. They will not acknowledge a hundredth part of their faults. Although their heads are so full of wickedness that their eyeballs are about to pop out, still they refuse to come to terms with their own sinfulness. Yet they are unable to deny that they are sinners and have offended God. Nevertheless, they play with God as if He were an angry child who could be easily appeased with a rattle, a straw dolly, or a ball. To make amends with God, they have their grand ceremonies, their stations of the cross; they will mumble a Pater Noster, light a candle before an idol such as Saint Barbara or the Virgin Mary; they will abstain from eating meat, fast on the vigil of some holiday, chant a mass; they sincerely believe all these things will appease God. It is obvious they are totally possessed by the Devil, for they say, "True, we have offended God, but we compensate Him well for our offenses. Not only do we perform works of reparation but we do more than is necessary by performing works of supererogation. Although God did not command these things, we do all this to appease Him." They try to barter with God, not realizing they have vomited up the greatest blasphemy of all.

It is because of such great arrogance on their part that we have a dispute with them. We say a man must throw himself completely upon the mercy of God; we say we are lost and damned unless God takes mercy on us in the name of and through our Lord, Jesus Christ. On the contrary, the Papists say they are saved by their merits. They claim they are pardoned before God because they have made proper payment. We seriously challenge everything they say, but this is all in vain. They are more hardened than ever, for the Devil has bewitched them.

But how do things really go on our side? We have the same seed of hypocrisy within our natures, though it bears different fruit. Many among us think that they may easily appease God by merely listening to a sermon or saying a Pater Noster. As long as one puts on a good show, that is deemed sufficient to placate God. Many of us think that God has His eyes bandaged and can see no further than our ceremonies. We are foolish enough to believe that we can measure God according to our standards. So we must remember that we are carnal beings and therefore cannot see all our sins unless they are very obvious, thick enough to cut with a knife, as the saying goes. We can recognize a slight fault if it is very apparent; but because we are carnal beings, we do not have eyes powerful enough to look inside ourselves and to see the sins that God condemns. That is why we gnash our teeth, grumble against God, and are quite vexed with Him. The Lord has an eye that can see where we cannot see a wink. So we must not measure our sins according to our weights and measures, for we stand before the judgment of a God who is totally other than the thoughts of men. Furthermore, we are all prone to self-love, by which we are blinded to our faults, although we have no difficulty at all recognizing them in our neighbors. If a neighbor throws a little mud at us or shakes his finger at us, we take this to be an irremissible crime and are grievously offended. We make mountains out of molehills. Yet when it comes to offenses grievous enough to send us to Hell, we shrug these off as of no importance whatsoever. That is what we do every day. So let us not assume that God judges according to our standards. Let us be stripped of our self-love, that we may see things as they really are. Whenever God warns us that we have grievously offended Him and provoked His wrath against us, let us not make the mistake of assuming that our sins are easily pardonable; let us realize that we have so grievously offended God that we deserve to be thrown down an abysm five hundred times deeper than Hell itself. Think long and hard on these points.

There is absolutely nothing we can do to appease God to pardon our sins. What could we possibly find in the world to give God as compensation for having offended His majesty? If men and the

349

angels of Paradise brought all that they could bear to God, still this would not suffice; for we have perverted the true justice of God, which is sacred and must not be violated. When we offend God, there is only one way to obtain pardon, and that is we confess our faults and do not seek to justify ourselves. The medicine for our spiritual ills is to be found in Jesus Christ alone, who shed His blood to cleanse us. That is how God's wrath was appeased. That is why He will be merciful and forgive our sins, provided that we go to Him in the name of His Son alone and not by our good works.

True, Micah, in this passage, does not speak of the remission of sins through Christ. But if we follow his train of thought far enough, we will find he reaches the conclusion that we cannot be reconciled with God any other way than through Jesus Christ.

I have already said that God ordained sacrificing, yet it seems Micah rejects sacrifices as something to no avail, indeed as something of which God strongly disapproves. That is because the Jews did not sacrifice in the way God has so ordained. I have already said that sacrifices were intended to bring people to repentance and to faith in Jesus Christ. On the contrary, the Jews thought that the ceremony itself was sufficient to appease God. So the prophets had many battles with the Jews over sacrificing. The Jews believed that they were grievously wronged when the prophets spoke out against their sacrificing; for as I have said, the Law required that all those who had sinned must go and sacrifice at the Temple. In addition to the annual sacrifice, which was a very solemn ceremony, there were daily sacrifices, which were much plainer affairs. Imagine what a solemn and reverent procession it must have been on the day of the annual sacrifice: the High Priest followed by the king followed by all those privileged to enter the Temple. Yet the prophets cry out after them, "Hey! What do you think you are doing? This is all an abomination. The Lord says to you, 'You are polluting the very pavement up to my Temple. You are doing nothing I have ordained. I have no use for your sacrifices. In fact, I detest them immensely, for you have rejected everything that God has commanded.'" Certainly it would seem the prophets had done the people a great wrong. But bear in mind what Moses says, "When you offer a calf, it is as if you have killed a man." The people were shocked that the prophets, who all spoke as if by one mouth, would compare sacrificial rituals ordained by God to outright murder. It is no wonder there was great friction between the prophets and the people. David says, "Do you think that I would tell you if I were hungry? Is not the world and all it contains mine? What do you think you are doing when you sacrifice stinking grease on my Altar?" Isaiah says, "I do not wish animal sacrifices; I want you to be merciful and charitable toward one another. Your sacrifices mean nothing to me." Jeremiah also spoke out harshly against sacrifices. Indeed, all the prophets were in accord on this point and they all encountered great opposition from the people, who were totally unable to answer their objections.

So remember, as I have just said, God is not at all like us; He does not fixate upon visible things; He does not judge according

351

to the flesh. When we make something that seems very good to us, do we really think that God is as delighted with it as are we? No, certainly not! Note well, then, that visible acts, such as ceremonies, are nothing but smoke, though God has instituted them, unless men recognize and honor His truth there. But because men are carnal beings, they try to go to God according to their own imaginations, not realizing this is precisely what turns them from Him. They do not stop to consider the faith they must have in Jesus Christ, for they are too preoccupied with what they can see by their eyes.

If sacrifices ordained by God are an abomination whenever men fixate upon the external appearance and therefore ignore the reality of Jesus Christ, what about the foolish things men invent on their own? Papism is full of all kinds of sacrifices and oblations which the Papists believe God will find acceptable. But who instructed them to do all these things? They cannot find one single line in Scripture that says God approves of what they do. They have invented all these things themselves; or perhaps it is more accurate to say that all these things have come from Satan's workshop. How, then, can the Papists truly believe that they can appease God? They are seriously deceived in their belief that they can serve God by their own inventions; they completely overlook the Lord has said, "Who told you to make sacrifices? I never told you anything of the kind. Do not bring your sacrifices to me!" Certainly God is right in rejecting sacrifices; for all creatures are subject to Him, so He has no need for them to be given to Him.

Sacrifices are not at all what God wants, as I have already said. They must be abolished. How the Papists deceive themselves! Their reparations and merits are founded on truth alright, the truth that these things are going to send them right straight to Hell with the devils. The Papists have abandoned themselves to all evil; they think they appease God and are easily acquitted before Him through their mass, which is a diabolical abomination. As I have said, they think they can easily appease God by fasting for a day, abstaining from meat, trotting off on pilgrimages, mumbling before idols, and running from chapel to chapel. Yet they turn right around and renounce the passion and death of Jesus Christ through their abominable mass. They seek remission for their sins before a mummy's case and I don't know what all else. Have they not done enough to be damned five thousand times over? So let us remember that if God rejects all that He ordained by His Law, because people came to fixate on external appearances, He has even stronger reason yet to condemn all the foolish inventions of men. In fact, these things are so readily deserving of God's condemnation that He need not trouble Himself to open His mouth to do so.

Micah adds that "God has taught you what is good," to further confirm his case against sacrifices. Although some read this passage as "I will teach you," the more common translation is "He has taught you what is good, that is, to be just, merciful, and all the rest." Micah's point here is that men deceive themselves willingly, for they refuse to do what God has commanded of them. This refusal is the source of all superstitions, for our Lord has

353

never left the world in the dark, never failed to declare, "Here is my will." True, He did not teach the Pagans anything, but that is because they had already turned their backs upon Him; we know that God, from the very beginning of the world, revealed to all men how He wished to be served and honored by them. When the pride, malice, and hypocrisy of men turns them from God, they cannot excuse themselves by arguing they do not know God's bounty. Out of their foolish pride, they come to believe that they are wise enough to decide themselves how God is best served. So Micah's point is that the Lord is always just and fair. If we fail to obey God, we can say only that we have failed willingly and knowingly. The blame is always on our shoulders.

True, we are more condemnable than those who never received such instruction; but still the fact remains that no men are excusable before God, for all are given some taste of His bounty and Word. What Micah said to the Jews goes for us: "You, a man, have the Law of God. He has sent you His prophets to instruct you sufficiently in it. Who is to blame, then, save yourselves, if you do not understand His will and do not wish to live according to His Law?" What, then, will happen to us, who have a far more ample revelation of God? Beware, I say, how the pride and hypocrisy of men turns them from God. Look at the Jews. They wished to appease God by their sacrifices of animals, cakes, and bread. They made up their own sacrificial rituals and even sacrificed their own infants. All this came from the fact they refused to obey God and accept His teaching, as it had been revealed in the Law. True, all first-born males were to be dedicated to God unless they were bought back. However, the Jews, turning from God's teaching, took this to mean that must sacrifice their infants to Moloch. So it is said that our Lord has made clear what he wants. That is what is good. That is what men must do. That is the service God accepts as true obedience.

There are, then, two things inseparably bound together: the commandment God has given us and the knowledge that it is the standard of all excellence. It is as if the prophet had said, "You have the doctrine of God by which you must be governed." It is certain that whenever God speaks, we are instructed in all perfection; so it is not licit to add anything of our own. And why is this? God has revealed what is good and does not do a halfway job of teaching us. So anything we add of our own, anything which naturally appears good to us, is nothing but shit. Think long and hard on this point; for if we try to add something of our own, this amounts to claiming that God has not taught us what is good. Note carefully, then, that the prophet has brought together here two inseparable things: the standard of all excellence and the knowledge that God Himself has revealed it to us. Do we know God's will? Then this amounts to saying, "Behold what is good." God commands us to do this and that; in so doing, He shows us what is good, what he approves of. So we must always remain humble before Him. Although we do not see why He commands one thing and forbids another, although we do not understand the reason, we must not

355

complain. God knows what is good and why He commands the way He does.

Let us not be like the Papists, who are always trying to add something to what God has commanded of them. If they only realized how they blaspheme God, whose office it is to decide what is good and what is evil, and to reveal to us what we must accept or reject. So when God reveals His will to us, let us fulfill all that he demands. As Saint Paul says in Romans 12, the true service of God is that we conform to His will. Now, God wills that we renounce ourselves, that we no longer live according to the world or according to our chaotic desires and emotions. So if we serve God according to our standards, we can no longer boast of truly serving Him. Indeed, He will make us know we are condemned. The Papists may think, when they are engaged in all their tomfoolery, that God will come down to earth to laugh and share in their merry-making. Everywhere they have such beautiful ceremonies and objects that it seems as if one is transported into Heaven itself. But Saint Paul says, "Do you wish to serve God in a way He will find acceptable and approve? Then, you must conform to His will." The Papists do nothing of the sort. What they call serving God is nothing but superstitions invented by themselves. Papists sin doubly, for they will not openly admit of their rebellion against God. Rather, they resort to all sorts of cover-ups to shield themselves against God. These, in turn, give them license to abandon themselves to all sorts of evil. Mass, which is a diabolical abomination, is one prime example of the cloak they throw over their shit.

Even among ourselves, there are still those so possessed by the Devil that they think they do God great service when they abstain from meat on Friday or Saturday and when they fast in the manner of the Papists. Although they think they are truly serving God by these practices, He has rejected them and said that those who do so are worthy only to be called a dog and placed among the ranks of the brutal beasts. They think they are serving God, but our Lord says they are serving the Devil. We cannot serve God in the least when we wish to do so according to our own standards.

So let Micah's words be firmly engraved in our memories: "O man, I have revealed to you what is goodness and what the Lord wishes," as if to say, "You will be unable to excuse your sins by saying that you believed you were doing the right thing. I reveal and make manifest to you in the name and authority of God what is goodness. So you have no reason to complain to God, for He has revealed what He demands of you." Then he tells us what God demands of us: "Be merciful and just with your neighbors, and walk in all humility before your God." That, I say, is how God wishes to be served. So let us be kind, gentle, and merciful; let us show that He has truly imprinted His image within us and that we are truly His children, who resemble Him.

Note, then, that Micah's teaching makes two major points. First, if we are to truly serve God, we must come to Christ, without whom we are lost and damned. Secondly, we must treat our neighbors fairly and justly. Before God had revealed these truths to us, we were blinded by our sins; we believed that we could truly serve God by our own inventions; we thought that we could gain an easy acquittal by doing some small thing to appease God. The ways we tried to serve God under Papism were just so much tomfoolery on one hand but no laughing matter on the other. We committed horrible blasphemies. The Lord says that all we did was nothing but abominable shit. We cannot enjoy God's blessings unless we serve Him truly, and we cannot serve Him truly unless we are guided by Christ and the Holy Spirit. So Micah recalls us to the teaching of the Lord, in order that, knowing the Father's will and serving Him as is fitting, we may obtain true remission for our sins and be strengthened in all our infirmities.

Following this holy teaching, we prostrate ourselves before the face of our good God, acknowledging our sinfulness. May He bring us to the realization that we must completely renounce ourselves if we are to comply with His will. May we not snatch back when He takes us by the hand to be His own, as is witnessed through the Word. May we honor Him by totally subjugating ourselves to Him and to His teaching. May we, seeing our terrible infirmity, look to Christ as our aid and remedy. May we live in justice and peace with our neighbors. May we in the end attain our immortal glory, in which we will be united in perfect harmony, as the Lord has promised. May God shed this grace not only on us but upon all the peoples and nations of the earth, etc.

All-powerful God, celestial Father, we know to hope in you because you have called us so lovingly and mercifully through your Law and Gospel. Give us the grace that we may not turn a deaf ear to your commandments and promises. May we obey you everywhere and in all matters. May we so subjugate ourselves to you and so attune all our senses to you that we show by our behavior we live according to the standards of goodness and sanctity established by your Law. May we so cling to your promises that neither the world nor flattery nor Satan's deceptions turn us from the love you have revealed to us through your Son, by which you strengthen us daily in the teachings of the Gospel. May we, in the end, come to enjoy the plenitude of this love through our celestial heritage, which has been won for us by the blood of your Son. Amen.

* * *

(23) Monday, January 5, 1551

The voice of the Lord cries out to the city. A man of wisdom will fear His name. Hear the rod and him who will witness to it. Is not the house of the wicked full of ill-gotten treasure? Does not the scale bear false weights? Micah 6

Micah is emphasizing here how poorly received the Word of God is among His people. Many times he has warned them and called them to repentance, yet they paid no attention. True, a few listened and amended their ways; indeed, they continue to tremble at God's threats, even though they are no longer culpable. But the vast majority of the people remain hardened. So Micah complains to the people, saying, "Hear the rod and him who proclaims it," as if to say, "Don't delay another minute. Don't wait for God to strike you. The instant He threatens you, obey Him, comply fully with His will, and be pardoned." But the people pay no attention; they are hardened and stubborn; they cling to their false weights and iniquitous measures; they are full of nothing but extortion, violence, fraud and malice.

Note well that those who do not hear the voice of God have very little intelligence. Indeed, there are very few people intelligent enough to know to fear the name of God and to receive His Word in all humility. So when Micah says that a man of intelligence will fear the name of God, he means that the vast majority of his people will not retain a single word he has said. As far as they are concerned, all he has done is utter sounds that vanish into thin air. They do not know the majesty of God;

they have no idea it is God who speaks; they have no real conception what it means to subjugate themselves to Him.

In Micah, the word "intelligence" signifies righteousness or trustworthiness; for we know that a man is trustworthy if he can distinguish between good and evil. So Micah is saying that if a man is righteous and if he allows himself to be instructed, he will come to fear the Lord. But there are very few men of this high caliber among his people. The majority are quite hardened and very stubborn; they refuse to be instructed; they are totally hopeless.

When Micah says that God cries out to the city, he means that He does not teach in secret or speak in some obscure language but that He speaks His warnings in a loud and clear voice. Indeed, His voice is like a trumpet sounding the call to battle. But however our Lord may speak to shake men up, very few hear Him. So if we allow ourselves to stagnate in our sins, we will not be able to excuse ourselves by claiming that God did not sufficiently admonish us; for God cries out loud and clear to us; His voice reverberates everywhere. So if men do not hear God's voice, it is purely their own fault, for they have stopped up their ears. None can excuse themselves by saying, "I plead ignorance; I never once heard from God." Men stop up their ears willingly in order not to hear God. As it says in Proverbs, Wisdom cries out everywhere. Solomon means by this statement that God cannot be accused of ever having left any men in ignorance. So ignorance is a punishable offense by God, for it is out of willful and deliberate malice that men do not hear the voice of God.

Note that Micah is emphasizing that it is a very special gift to be able to fear God and to profit from His teaching. This gift is not bestowed upon all men, especially as the vast majority are so hardened and stubborn. Very few men in Micah's day truly feared God. So what must we do? Micah tells us that he could find but few men of true faith, and we know our souls are all too prone to become obsessed with vain things. So let us make a special effort to humble ourselves and pray to God that He keep a tight rein on us to hold us on the right path so His teaching will not be in vain with us.

Now, let us be very clear on what exactly it means to hear the voice of God. Certainly we cannot claim to have heard the voice of God if we think of it as just so many sounds from the mouths of men. Rather, we can claim to have heard the voice of God only if we have some to honor and fear His name. Bear in mind that Micah emphasizes the word "fear." He could have said merely, "The voice of God cries out to the city, but very few hear it." But instead he said, "They are very few who fear His name"; that is to say, there were very few people who had not totally abandoned themselves to evil. The reason he uses the word "fear" is that if we truly receive the Word of God, then we will be in total awe of His majesty, as I have just said. God has revealed Himself to us; so if we reject Him, do we not deserve to be destroyed for our ingratitude? Will our plea of

362

ignorance be able to excuse us then? That is what Micah means when he says the man of intelligence will look upon the name of God. The verb he is using here has two meanings and can be translated as "look upon" or "fear." However, when all is taken into consideration, it is very apparent that he intends the word "fear" here. In sum, Micah is saying that when God speaks through his prophets, He speaks in a voice loud and clear enough to be heard everywhere, so that none can claim ignorance.

Consequently, Micah says, "Hear the rod and him who ordains it will strike you" or "the one who ordains it will strike you." This passage can be translated in various ways, for the word used by Micah sometimes means "witness" in Hebrew. It might read "him who will witness" or "him who has summoned you" or "him who has assigned the date for your trial" or "him who will assign a date for your trial". The whole point here is that the people had been warned countless times that God would bring them to trial and yet they persisted in their wicked ways. So that we are not led askance from this point by all sorts of diverse interpretations, bear in mind there is no doubt he is speaking of the rod. What he intends to say is simply, "Hear the rod and him who set the date when it will strike you." The verb he uses here means "to set a date," as when a date is set for one to appear before the court or when through mutual agreement a date is set when payment must be made or the terms of some instrument must be met. Sometimes the verb means "to witness," but that is not what he means here. He is saying, "Hear the rod and him who ordains it to strike you," that is to say, the people have been given a limited amount of time to think on their impending punishment and amend their ways or they will feel the hand of God upon them when their time is up.

The question arises as to why Micah says, "Hear the rod" rather than "feel the rod," as elsewhere the prophet says, "Behold the hand which strikes you." The answer is that it is not a matter here of God actually punishing the people; He is only warning them of their impending punishment. Micah makes this clear when he speaks of "him who ordains." He does not speak of "him who sends the rod" but of "him who sets the date." When he says, "Hear the rod," he is warning them of impending punishment; so the blows have yet to fall. Fools think that God will never touch them, until He lays His hand on them. So men are well advised to return to God when they are warned of impending punishment. Just as it is necessary to use the whip on the horse and put the bridle on the mule, so, too, it is necessary to use the rod upon the backs of fools, as Solomon says in Proverbs 26. The prudent man, then, is well advised not to wait for God to strike him. The instant he hears God is angry with him, he should say, "Alas! I have offended God. I take his threats very seriously. I am not at all vexed against God, for I realize I must humble myself and return to Him to beg His pardon." The instant we see some sign of God's wrath, let us come to recognize the offenses we have committed against Him and ask for mercy. That is Micah's main point here. Certainly it is a very important one for us to bear in mind. We have rebelled against God and thrown off His yoke, so it is now or never that we make up our minds whether we will return to God or be punished. Let us not be so stupid and foolish that we pay no attention to God until He strikes us. It is not in vain that God threatens us, reveals His wrath, and warns us of our faults. If we do not heed His admonitions, we will feel the blows of His hand soon enough.

It is a very special grace that God sheds upon people when He warns them. He does not shed this grace upon everyone. Our Lord is not obligated to say ahead of time, "You have sinned, so I must take steps to discipline you." Who said this to Sodom? It was destroyed without having received any preaching or instruction whatsoever from God. Our Lord did not shed His special grace upon that place. So let us come to appreciate what an inestimable blessing God bestows upon us that He will warn us of our sins, call us back to Himself when we have gone astray, and awaken us when we have been lulled to sleep by our sins. Behold, I say, what special grace the Lord sheds upon us when He admonishes and exhorts us in order that we might turn away His wrath. This grace is available only to those who have the Law, prophecy, and the Gospel. These serve to remind us each day of our sins, so that the Devil cannot blind and bewitch us. Our Lord exhorts and threatens us to encourage us to repent. When we are told, "Hear the rod," let us remember that God is the Judge of the world, whose responsibility it is to remind us daily of our sins. Let us not be vexed by this special grace God sheds upon us; let us openly confess our failings and beg God's forgiveness. Let each take special care to look long and hard at his own sins; for whenever we are reproached for our sins each of us is prone to blame his neighbor and totally ignore his own wrongdoings. But each must look to himself, each must face his own trial and own individual sentence; for the only way each of us may be reconciled to God is to recognize and confess himself such as he truly is.

Micah says, "Hear the rod and him who ordains it will strike you," for it is no laughing matter to have God against us and yet we pay no heed to His warnings. We are so perverted in our thinking, that a single threat from a mortal man will frighten us more that all the warnings God gives us. What is the reason for this, save that we are more than stupid? That is why Micah speaks of "him who ordains," as if to say, "You are so blinded and hardened that you attribute neither majesty nor glory to God. Whenever He speaks to you through His prophets, you think that you have heard a mere fable or else you think you can appease God as easily as you can a small child. Is this the kind of authority God has over His creatures? Pay attention to who has set the date for the rod to strike you." We are prone to reject the Word of God because we do not see angels descending from the heavens above or God appearing in person to speak to us. Because God speaks to us through mortal men, His teaching lacks authority among us. Nevertheless, we should be sure and certain that God has spoken to us, despite the fact He uses mortal men as His instruments. That is what Micah means in this passage, as if to say, "Although I have incessantly warned you, you refuse to believe my words. But soon enough you will know that God has a hand strong enough to accomplish all that I have told you. Know, then, that it is God Himself who ordains the rod to strike you." So let us realize that God can and does speak through men who do not speak for themselves but are inspired by the Spirit to reveal God to us. If we are so shortsighted we cannot recognize the fact that God uses men as His instruments, then let us pray we be so enlightened that whenever a minister preaches the Word, we are able to look beyond his words, beyond the minister himself, and see that it is God Himself who speaks. Then, we will truly receive the Word, and we will come to obey God and pay Him due homage.

Micah continues, saying, "Still the fire burns in the house of the wicked, for the treasures of iniquity, the false measures, rape, loan sharking, and the weights of iniquity are there." Here, he is pointing to the hardness of men, by which they have no fear of God whatsoever. The word "fire" here has many diverse interpretations. Some take it to mean men; others interpret it as do we, namely that it means admiration, although this certainly is not a common meaning for the word "fire." But in this passage, Micah is saying that men are so marvelously hardened that God's word cannot gain an inch of ground with them. When he says the fire burns in the house of the wicked, he is speaking out of admiration for their hardness, as if to say in astonishment, "Is it possible that men will let a fire burn in their houses?" This fire is kindled when men resort to false weights and measures. Their malice, violence, and extortions are the flames which will consume themselves. Micah is astonished by such brutality in men. If one cried, "Fire!" we would not waste a minute running to our homes. If the fire were twenty houses away from us, it would seem that it was already right on top of us. Yet we will feed a fire in every corner of our homes and not realize the grave danger we are in. It is truly astonishing how sluggish and nonchalant men are. True, we may not see this fire at first glance, for it sleeps beneath its cinders. But the wrath of God can awaken it in an instant. When we are nice and cool, that is the moment when God will burn us alive. So it is not without reason that Micah asks, "How is it that the fire can still burn in the house of the wicked?" as if to ask, "How is it possible when men have had their ears so thoroughly beaten by the incessant cries, exhortations, and admonitions of the prophets, and when God has threatened them so many times, that this fire still burns? One would have hardly thought this to be likely." So beware what horrible condemnation hangs over the heads of those who refuse to tremble at God's warnings and reject His admonition.

Note that Micah is not speaking out of his own sense of wonderment; for God by His Spirit is speaking through him to reveal what a monstrous, horrible, and unnatural act it is when men behave as stubbornly as they do. Indeed, even the angels in Paradise are ravished in admiration for our obstinacy and hardheartedness. So what else can be said of men, except that they have less sense and reason than brutal beasts? God's voice is powerful enough to make rocks and even harder things burst apart, yet it fails to budge men a single inch. So pay heed, I say, to Micah's warning, for he speaks not according to human understanding but according to God: Men, by their monstrous obstinacy, continually kindle the fire of God's wrath against them, though they know it not. When they least expect it, He will consume them in His flame, as I have just said. This passage gives us ample reason to be far more cautious than we are accustomed to when God warns us. The metaphor of the fire should be uppermost in our minds. Scripture uses it frequently and with good reason; for it teaches us to fear the signs of God's wrathful vengeance just as we would be fearful when someone cries out, "Fire! Fire! There is a fire burning." Because the Lord so cries out to us, we cannot claim ignorance as our excuse. We will not be destroyed because we lacked sufficient warning. Our own consciences will testify that we have been given more than ample warning.

Micah says that the fire of God's wrath is kindled by false weights and measures that cheat people by being far smaller than they should. Actually he speaks of rocks here, for in those days they used rocks for weights. He speaks of the "weights of abominations," because God holds in abhorrence all that we do to

369

defraud and cheat our neighbors. So if men were to have asked him, "Where exactly is this fire?" He would have answered, "Wherever you use false weights, wherever you resort to extortion and fraud, there you kindle the fire of God's wrath and the vengeance of God to consume you." True, for a time, the fire may sleep beneath its cinders; but do not think it is ever extinguished; God can fan it back to life when we least expect it, as we see every day. Those who live by fraud, loan sharking, rapine, extortion, and violence, what are they really after, except great wealth? It seems to them that they profit more by offending God than by living righteously. Who wants to live righteously today, who wants to treat his neighbors fairly, when it seems you cannot get rich that way? The prevailing attitude is that if you want to get rich, you have to hang your conscience on your cloak like a pendant. This is all the Devil's handiwork; he has poisoned the minds of men; he has bewitched them into thinking there is no other way to get rich than by doing evil. But Micah warned that those who use false weights and measures have lit the fire which will one day consume them.

True, they may not be consumed at once; but Micah's words will come to pass. If our eyes are attuned to what goes on in the world, we will readily see that those who use false weights may enjoy great wealth for a time but that in the end they will loose everything. Is this not what we see happening daily? Why is there so much upheaval in the world, save that God has cursed all ill-gotten goods? It is because the world is such a deceitful, dishonest place that everything is going to rack and ruin, and chaos reigns everywhere. Our Lord has warned time and again that He has not pronounced such a curse against us in vane. But we do not listen. Yet we certainly do our share of complaining; and rightly so, for things today are more chaotic than ever. Indeed, there is such terrible upheaval in the world today that many sons are deprived of their inheritances. Nevertheless, we rarely, if ever, inquire into the reason why the world is in a continual state of turmoil so that we might find a remedy. All the world's problems come from the fact there is neither honor nor honesty among men. Indeed, men would sooner poke out each other's eyes than aid one another. Men are addicted to violence, rapine, loan sharking, and defrauding one another through false weights and measures. Let us pray that God does not permit us to be dishonest with our neighbors. Let us remember that we have been given ample warning that false weights are an abomination before God. If we resort to them, it is certain that God's vengeance will fall upon our heads. God is not lazy; He will fulfill out His office as Judge of the world.

Fraud, deceit, and iniquity are all abominations before God. They will not remain unpunished. The hand of God will destroy the world. Yet the world, because of its infidelity, believes nothing of this. We profess to be Christians, yet the vast majority of us are in doubt about God. Walk about the streets of Geneva and you will find there is about as much righteousness and honor among men as there is among dogs. Our shops are nothing but robber's dens in which the customer has his throat cut. If you look among the laboring classes, where certainly you would expect to find a far more innocent way of life, all you see is cheating and fraudulency. The preacher cries out everyday, but who profits from his teaching? He says in a loud, clear voice: "False weights and measures are an abomination before God. The day will come when you will have to stand trial before Him." But nobody really gives a damn. The majority of people believe there is no longer any God to judge them. The wicked man says in his heart, "There is no God," as we read in the Psalm. Why? He knows in his conscience there is truly a God, but he wishes to believe that God does not see a thing he does and so will not punish him for the iniquities he has committed against both Him and other men.

But those of us who truly fear God will refrain from all fraudulency and deceit because we know that God is our Judge. When we find men using false weights and measures, we will do everything possible to remedy this situation; we will warn these men that although they think to live in safety and comfort, they are in grave danger. We must be a shinning example to all the world by our fair and just treatment of one another. Knowing that we have done otherwise, let us turn to God in true repentance. Let us pray that He so govern us by His Holy Spirit that His wrath is never kindled against us.

Following this holy teaching, we prostrate ourselves before the face of our good God, acknowledging our sinfulness. May He so awaken us to our vices that we become totally displeased with ourselves and seek to mortify the evil lusts of our flesh. May we recognize that our sins merit His wrath and judgment against us. Yet, may we not despair of the mercy and bounty He has promised to shed upon us. May we come to God, confident Christ will fulfill His promise to reconcile all the elect to God, His Father, in order that we may share in eternal life. May He shed this grace not only on us but on all the peoples and nations of the world, etc.

* * *

Your rich men are violent; your inhabitants have spoken lies; their tongues are full of deceit in their mouths. Therefore, I have begun to strike you and send you to rack and ruin, etc. Micah 6

Yesterday we saw that Micah focuses upon the wealthy because they have such ample opportunity to oppress the poor and to abuse their positions of power and authority. They must take great care that they do not resort to fraud and violence in order to steal away the basic necessities of others; for they will ignite a fire in their houses that will consume themselves and all their lineage.

However he may give the wealthy special attention, he does not fail to chastise everyone. Indeed, he says that the city of Jerusalem and the lands of Judah are full of corruption, that the inhabitants are liars; that their tongues are full of deceit and venom. So he is not speaking of just one or two persons here; he is saying that the land is so totally corrupted that he cannot find one honest man anywhere, as will be explored more fully in the next sermon. Now, when we hear that the people God had chosen became so corrupt and perverse that they went to total rack and ruin, we are warned that a similar fate could befall us. So let us pray that God does not permit us to persist stubbornly in our wicked ways, lest we be destroyed. May He shed such grace on us that we no longer provoke His wrath and vengeance against us.

Micah says, "I will afflict you by sending chaos and desolation upon you." The verb form "I will afflict" is a derivation of one which means "I will begin" or "I have begun to strike you down to send you to rack and ruin." But in the context of the passage, it seems best to translate it as "I will afflict"; for Micah is warning them that God will not punish them lightly but will destroy the city of Jerusalem and all the land. Thus the word "affliction," which we identify with illness, may seem out of place here; but bear in mind that Micah is speaking metaphorically, just as we often liken prosperity to health. So Micah is saying that whereas God had led his people to prosperity, now He will knock them down and destroy them, as it came to pass. God had warned them many times but to no avail; so He decided to multiply and make yet more grievous their punishment, which is why He sent them into exile, as we have seen. This punishment should make it perfectly clear to us what an intolerable abomination it is to God when we cheat our neighbors by loan sharking, violence, and false scales. God intends us to be honest, fair, and just with one another. So whenever men resort to fraud and violence, they succeed only in kindling so much the more God's wrath against them. Remember, we individually need not commit crimes against our neighbors, to be condemned by God; for the Lord punished all of Judah, which should make it perfectly clear to us that we kindle the fire of God's wrath against us just by our membership in a society which tolerates fraud and violence.

Micah, wishing to spell out the exact nature of God's punishment, says, "You will eat but you will not be full; your affliction will be in the midst of you." This was a punishment handed down from the Law of Moses. Indeed, the prophets understood themselves to be applying the teachings of Moses to their own times. So we are well advised to be very circumspect in our actions; for God, who is Judge of the world, does not change. When we see that He punished His chosen people, we can well expect He will lay a heavy hand on us.

Micah means that although we have an abundance of good things, we will be unable to satisfy ourselves. So let us not make the mistake of assuming that bread has any power in itself to sustain us. We could have an overwhelming abundance of goods and yet be famished once God breaks the staff of life, as it is called; that is, once He strips our goods of their nutritive power. How does bread nourish us, save that God has blessed it to serve us? So once God curses men, they will know no contentment; they will be famished, though they are bursting at the seams with goods. Certainly we find this to be true of all greedy men. Although they have amassed vast amounts of goods, still they burn with unfulfilled desire. They are insatiable gluttons who can never get enough and whose appetites know no limits. That is how the Lord curses and persecutes all those who seek their profits through rapine, loan sharking, and crooked deals. And it is more than fitting punishment, since they think true happiness consists solely of amassing great wealth.

It is astonishing that we could be in famine in the midst of plenty; but we must remember that God has the power to break the staff of life; that is, He can strip all our goods of their nutritive power, so that we will be famished, though we have eaten well, and that our bellies will seem full only of air rather than food.

We see, then, why Christ taught us to ask God, His Father, for our daily or everyday bread. For although we would have goods in abundance, indeed far more than we would ever need, they will not nourish us unless God blesses them. So let us be content with what God is pleased to give us. If we have but little bread, still it will suffice to nourish us, provided that God blesses it. Let us not be greedy and worry over acquiring great wealth; let us be grateful to God and ask His blessing upon what little He has given us. Remember, those who are ungrateful and do not ask God's blessing are eternally cursed such that they will never be full, no matter how much they eat.

Micah says that "your affliction will be in the midst of you," as if to say, "There will be no need for an enemy to persecute you, for your affliction will be within you." He means that God has secret, hidden ways of punishing us that do not require Him to marshal up a huge army to persecute us. Although all creatures are favorably inclined to serve us, they will curse us once God condemns us. There is no need for an enemy to persecute us from without, for we will have famine within ourselves and therefore be unable to profit from creatures. All

God has to do is withhold His grace from us, and innumerable evils will press in upon us. Although the Lord speaks here only of famine, He is referring to the passage in Moses where it states that once the coffers of God's wrath are opened, afflictions beyond measure will befall the incorrigible ones. So let us heed Micah's warning; for when we least expect it, when we feel to be the most secure, that is when the vengeance of the Lord will befall upon our heads.

Micah yet aids another curse contained in the Law of Moses: "You will take hold but you will not deliver, and what you deliver I will destroy and put to the sword." The Jews interpret this statement to mean a woman in labor will not give birth and those who do will have their children put to the sword. But when we look closely at Micah's true intention, it is obvious he is saying, "You will take hold"; that is, however men lust after great wealth and however diligently they seek to acquire it, in the end everything will slip through their fingers and they will have absolutely nothing at all to show for all the great pain and anguish they put themselves through. Micah, however, is not just speaking here of gluttons who fail; for God's curse pertains to all men, so the rich and successful landowners are included here as well. Certainly when we look at the world today, we see that those who have successfully acquired wealth always manage to squander it one way or the other, some by negligence, others by living beyond their means, and still others by extravagant living. In the end, all their possessions up and vanish, and the wealthy fall into ruin and poverty.

So we see how our Lord has added yet an even greater curse: However men strive to acquire wealth, it will all slip through their fingers in the end. As it says in the Psalm, it is vain for a man to rise early, to sit up late, and to eat the bread of agony, unless God blesses his labors. When we have God's blessing upon us, we will profit more in sleeping than others do in waking. This does not mean that God intends the faithful to be idle; He wishes every man to work. However, the faithful will never have the daily struggle of the incredulous, who feel themselves to be on the brink of immanent disaster every moment of their waking life and who are continually asking themselves, "What will ever become of us? How are we ever going to make ends meet?" The faithful will never live in such extreme anxiety; for if they need something, they invoke the name of God and are content to put everything in His hands. As the Psalmist says, God will give rest to His own and will console His beloved; but the incredulous are in continual lust after worldly goods, and it does not matter to them how they come by them just as long as they have them.

It is very sad, indeed, that the vast majority of men lust after worldly goods and try to enrich themselves by rebelling against God. God has revealed to us the way in which we can enjoy all the goods we could ever hope for and not just for a day but throughout all our lives; indeed, He has shown us the way

379

even our children after us can enjoy our goods: We must walk in all humility before Him and treat our neighbors fairly and honestly. If we do these things, we will be content even if He gives us little; and if He gives us much, this will benefit not only ourselves but others as well. On the contrary, He has amply warned us that if we try to profit through fraudulency and violence, all that we may gain will flow through our fingers like water.

Nevertheless men stubbornly persist in their common train of thought: "I must get ahead. How? Just like everybody else does. I must run with the wolf pack and pillage everywhere." This is why God and men are in continual battle. True, to a certain extent, the Lord Himself encourages greed because He does not punish at once the gluttons who are striving to amass vast fortunes. But anyone with an ounce of common sense would heed Micah's warning that men will be able to save nothing of that which they have seized, which will all go up in smoke. Our Lord shows us examples of this curse every day; yet we are poor dumb beasts without an ounce of reason or intelligence; we are like sheep, as it says in the Psalm; and the Psalmist adds that it is important for us to realize that ill-gotten good will not be handed down from father to son. Nevertheless we will follow in the footsteps of our fathers and cling to our common train of thought, as if when one sheep jumped into the water, all the rest followed him. But God has clearly revealed that we must do otherwise, so the blame is squarely upon our shoulders if we are not sufficiently schooled in the will of God to follow it. It seems we deliberately wish to vex God and to prove ourselves totally incorrigible. So let us heed Micah's warning that all our efforts are in vain unless God blesses us and gives us the grace to use the creatures He has placed in our hands as He has so ordained.

Micah adds, "You will sow, but you will not reap; you will crush the olives, but you will not use the oil; you will trample upon the grapes, but you will not drink the wine." I have already said that these curses, which are found often in Scripture, are taken from Moses, specifically from Leviticus 27 and Deuteronomy 28, where he says those who obey God will be sustained in their persons, goods, houses, possessions, animals, fields, and villages. The prophets applied Moses to their time, just as we apply Moses to ours. So it is not enough merely to possess beautiful things which promise to bear great fruit. I say this to those who are quite fortunate in this regard. The fields can be sown and yet not reaped. We will see times in which our hopes run high because everything seems just right for a bountiful harvest; yet, in an instant, God will dash down all our hopes by sending a hailstorm that destroys everything.

That is a prime example of how our Lord will punish us if we do not heed His warnings. So if we have true faith in Him, we will fear His wrath and vengeance, which we are prone not to do. We are carnal beings and so we are prone to fixate upon things that we can see with our eyes. Consequently, we pay little attention to His threats. So let us remember that these are not scare stories for children, as the prevailing opinion would have it. Let us come to realize that it means absolutely nothing to have riches. All will be lost unless God blesses us and gives us the grace to harvest the grain and to profit from it.

Let us take care not to abuse the grace God gives us to harvest the earth, as we are prone to do. Whenever we have a good year, we make that the occasion to declare war on God. When things appear to be going well, we will say, "Let us rejoice, for we will have a good harvest and a good crop of grapes this year." So it seems we cannot rejoice unless we vex God. Indeed, the whole world is so perverse that it is unable to enjoy itself unless it offends and blasphemes God. So He has good reason to turn our joy into sorrow. When men abuse His grace, it is only just and fair He sends the pain upon them that they so well deserve; for they have used the good things God sends upon them as an occasion to declare war on Him, whereas these things were intended to inspire them to praise Him.

We should not find it in the least surprising, then, that our Lord will deprive us of an abundant harvest. The instant we expect to have goods in abundance, we will be deprived of everything. Just this year, everyone thought that there would not be enough graineries to store all our grain and that there would not be enough caves in which to store our wine. But when it came to harvest time, all we found were thistles. Our caves are nowhere near as full as we thought they would be. Yet everyone had said, "Judging by the way things appear, this is going to be a very good year." Now we see, of course, that precisely the opposite is the case. Whenever God gives us a good year, whenever He gives us the grace to harvest the fruits of the earth, He must also bless us, lest everything be lost. Even if we have the wheat in the grainery and the bread in our mouths, these will serve only to destroy us rather than sustain us unless God blesses them to our usage. So let us be thankful to God for all that He has given us. Let us pray that He continue to shed His grace upon us. Let us pray that the Holy Spirit bring us to recognize He is our Father and that He adopt us as His children.

Micah emphasizes that God is never cruel when He afflicts us. He says, "He will strike you." Why? "Because of your sins." He means that God has been very patient with us and overlooked our sins for a very long time. However, eventually we will be brought to account and our punishment will be so much the more grievous. Just because He delayed so long in punishing us, we must not assume we can flee His hand; there is no escaping it. We will feel the pain, however late it may come. So let us look far deeper into ourselves than we are accustomed to. Let us come to a fuller recognition of our sins. Then, we will realize that if we are afflicted, it is because of our offenses, which actually merit far more punishment that we receive. Let us remember that if we are afflicted once or twice, we can expect even greater punishment yet until we are fully converted to God.

When Micah is speaking of God's curses upon human sinfulness, he does not overlook the idolatries and superstitions that reigned in the land of Judah. He says, "You obey the statutes of Omri and you walk according to the laws of Ahab; therefore, I will send great desolation upon you." The reason why he speaks this way is that Omri became king of Israel after the two kingdoms were divided. The vast majority of the people, 10 1/2 tribes, followed Jeroboam, leaving only 1 1/2 tribes under Rehoboam. After Omri came Ahab, his son, who built an altar in Samaria, which further added to the superstitions dating back to Jeroboam. The latter, out of fear his subjects would go to Jerusalem to worship and therefore might be swayed to revolt against him by the house of Solomon, connived to have a temple built in Samaria, using as his excuse the argument that this temple must be built in order to show the world that God also dwelt among his people. Now, Ahab built a second temple, thereby augmenting the corruption that reigned throughout the land of Israel. Micah was commissioned to prophecy to the Jews who remained under the house of Solomon. They were supposed to ground themselves in the purity of God's Word, yet they were following in the idolatrous ways of the kings of Israel. Therefore Micah said to them, "When the kingdoms were divided, God blessed you by removing the idolatrous ones from your midst. This was to enable you to walk in the ways of the Lord. You have the Temple, which God ordained to be built; you have His promise to dwell in the midst of you; you have the assurance that you can worship Him in a way He finds acceptable; yet you have given in to the superstitions and idolatries of the Pagans."

Micah speaks of statutes and laws because men always wish to make their idolatry appear virtuous. Idolaters always think that they are serving God; their foolish piety has blinded them; the Devil has made them believe that God will find favorable whatever they do. We see today that those, such as the Papists, who serve God according to their own imagination are so blinded by their pride that they believe God will accept everything they do, whereas in point of fact they blaspheme and dishonor Him. The Papists will say, "Everything we do is done with the very best of intentions. So then, will not God find us acceptable?" They do not wish to comply with the will of God in any way whatsoever. Their sole aim is to make God comply with their own silly fantasies. Because the Jews were prone to such pride, Micah said in a very noble tone of voice, "You say that all you do is based upon laws, constitutions, and statutes, not to mention sound advice and wise counsel. You tell me what you do is the duty of any good citizen. Well, I will grant that you make an impressive case for yourself; but the fact remains that everything you do is an abomination before God. I say unto you that you are serving the Devil by believing to serve God according to your foolish fantasies." The point Micah is making is that we must totally subjugate ourselves to God, as He so commands through His Word, if we are to serve Him as we should. So he provides us with a lesson that should be of the utmost importance to us.

We can put on airs beyond count; we can make the most impressive possible case for ourselves; yet all of this will serve only to condemn us; for God demands to be served by complete obedience and total devotion. If we try and serve God otherwise, He will find us to be nothing but corrupt through and through.

Men may think themselves righteous and say of one another, "What a very devout man he is. What a very devout woman she is. Why, they are absolute bigots!" Men have I don't know what all ways of putting on a facade of righteousness. Provided that they mumble a lot, attend many masses, worship before the statue of a saint, put a candle on the altar, many will say of them, "These are truly righteous men!" Nevertheless God is grievously offended by them. So however we ourselves may be esteemed by other men, let us remember that we are all condemned before God unless we follow the commandments of His Word.

Micah, I emphasize, teaches us that we must take care to thoroughly ground ourselves in the pure simplicity of God's Word, for it takes almost nothing at all to turn us away from Him. True, when God gives us the grace to be instructed in His truth, we may not turn our backs upon Him at once; but it takes very little to lead us astray. Soon enough, the vast majority will take leave of their senses; some by their customary idolatries and superstitions; others by I don't know what all brutality and stupidity, by which they come to care no more for God of His Word than do beasts; others by a deep feeling of disgust and contempt for God's Word, which makes them rage against His teaching and those who profess it. This ingratitude in men means that we are in grave danger of falling down an abyss far more horrible and chaotic than the one from which our Lord delivered us by His infinite bounty. Although we are shown every day how we are to serve God, the vast majority of us wish to return to our old superstitions and customary ways of thinking.

For example, how many of you hold today, this Day of Kings, in great reverence and celebrate it as you are accustomed? I do not know where people came up with this idea. Scripture says that wise men came from the Orient to worship our Lord. But the Papists say that they were three kings who came from the south, the west, and the east. So they make the ignorant believe in something which was sanctioned neither by Scripture nor by any of the ancient doctors. What terrible theologians they are to make up something that is pleasing to themselves and then force the poor people to believe it! Even though we see this festival serves only to mock God and even though we see that the Papists revere this holiday simply because it gives them a convenient excuse to be wanton and intemperate, to get drunk and stuff themselves with food, if you asked a hundred, if you asked a thousand people in Geneva today if they thought we should observe this holiday, they would surely say, "Why not? What harm is there in so honoring God?" That is just the kind of response you would get from people who have been sufficiently instructed in the Word of God to know better. This is just the kind of thing

387

we must avoid. If we wish to serve God as He so desires, we must be stripped of all our silly superstitions and frivolous inventions, we must renounce all idolatry to worship God alone in spirit and truth, as He so commands, and we must live according to the simplicity we see in the Word.

Following this holy teaching, we prostrate ourselves before the face of our good God, acknowledging our sinfulness. We pray that it please Him to so open our eyes that we know what is good and agreeable to Him. We pray that we come to follow Him alone and reject all that He holds in abomination, such as the superstitions and idolatries we have invented out of our own heads. We pray that, having been given the grace to be instructed by our Lord, Jesus Christ, His Son, and by His Apostles, we so follow their instruction that we seek only to obey God. May we continue to profit in their instruction, until finally we come to know the joy and sovereign happiness, which the Lord has promised us in the heavens above. May God shed this grace not only on us but upon all the peoples and nations of the earth, etc.

All-powerful God, celestial Father, you call us so sweetly to yourself and you promise your aid and help will never fail us, provided we ourselves do not block the path. Give us the grace that however you may multiply your blessings upon us down here in great abundance, we do not come to trust in worldly things and abandon you. May we ground ourselves in your pure grace and bounty alone. If for a time we are deprived of all aid and support, may this serve to quicken our spirits and teach us to advance so that nothing will stand in our way. May we eagerly and with ardent desire give ourselves to you and comply fully with you. May we, having been delivered unto you, remain under the protection and safekeeping of your Son, whom you have constituted as the Guardian of our salvation. Amen.

* * *

(25) Wednesday, January 7, 1551

Woe is me! for I am as when the summer fruits are picked, as the grapes of the vine. There is no grape to eat, my soul desired firstripe fruit, etc. Micah 7

The prophet Micah, seeing how perverted is the land of Judah and seeing how poorly he is received, complains and laments. Indeed, these are very difficult things for God's servants to bear, who wish only the Church be well built and in good order. We know what charge God commissioned us when He commanded us to proclaim His Word. Seeing what ingratitude there is in the world, seeing how God's Word is held in contempt and rejected everywhere, what can we do save lament, groan, and be of heart? Micah laments the great destruction of the Church, when he cries out, "Alas!" But to make himself understood clearer, he uses a metaphor frequently found in Scripture; that is, he compares men to fruit, just as our Lord says that the Church is a field or vineyard He will cultivate. Now, the fruits God wishes to harvest after He has seeded this field by His Word and sent His prophets to work it is that men will return to Him, living in fear and obedience to Him.

Micah says that everything is damaged and ruined. "We are," he says, "like a field where all the fruit has been picked and only leaves remain. Yet my soul desires firstripe fruit. I have languished for a long time as a prophet sent by God. I hope that soon my teaching will have power among men to lead them to the Path of Righteousness. But my hope seems in vain, for the

390

season has passed. It is no longer summer. The time has passed for winning men over to God." So he is saying in effect, "I have waited but my waiting has been in vain. For a long time, I have hoped and I have diligently carried out my office, expecting to have some success. But the summer has passed; everything has become hardened again. There is no more hope that my teaching will lead men to salvation, for they are all abandoned to evil and perversity."

After this metaphor, he gives yet more ample testimony of the wickedness of his people: "There is no justice among them." The true sign that men fear and obey God is that they are fair and just with their neighbors. But he says his people are very cruel and crooked. Each strives to advance himself by harming his neighbor. What hope, then, could he have, seeing such wickedness among his people?

Micah speaks of the governors, saying, "The princes demand, and the judges accept bribes." Now, this passage may be interpreted one of two different ways: "They are wicked but they wish to appear righteous" or "They are very skilled in evil." Either way, his point is that those in authority are gluttons trying to swallow up everything. The judges are for sale; provided they are well paid off, they care not what one has done; they wish only to work for the rich, giving them license to do great evil. Men make nets to trap their poor brothers as fish and strip them to the bone. Yet their crimes remain unpunished, for they pay off the judges and go scott free. But those who have committed lesser offenses and cannot afford to pay off a judge are punished to the hilt.

He says that even the most righteous among his people are nothing but briars and thorns. He warns them, "Do not expect that God will come to you in mercy but in wrath. Do not expect the Lord will come to you for any other reason but to punish you severely, for you are all unworthy of His bounty."

Micah is a shinning example how dedicated and zealous must be those whom God calls to preach His Word, that is, to proclaim His mercy as well as His justice. We know that the Word of God has the power to convert men; we know that the Lord calls out ever so sweetly to men to return to Himself in order that God may adopt them as His children and be their Father; we recognize this is why God has given us salvific teaching; therefore, it is the responsibility of those of us called to preach to apply all our energies to lead men to salvation and to bring them to honor God. When we see that precisely the opposite is the case, we groan and cry out along with Micah. It is no small sorrow to see the Word of God, which contains all our life and goods, is held in such contempt that it is totally ignored, to see that God is dishonored, to see that men do not wish to obey Him, to see that the remedy given men to deliver them from death is in vain. When we see all this, we can hardly be nonchalant and shrug these matters off as mere trifles. When we see we have failed to win the world over to God, we cry out to Him, just as Micah did; for the Lord always hears the prayers of His preachers. Although we sadly failed, although we preached only to deaf ears, our Lord will not permit our efforts to be in vain. So whatever may come to pass, we must persevere in our calling, as God has so commanded. Although we may baptize only with water, as the expression goes, that is, although our teachings may be held in great contempt, we know our obedience is pleasing to God.

It is certain that God works in such a way that there is always a small number of men dedicated to honoring Him. Although the vast majority of men have gone mad, surrendering completely to Satan, nevertheless there will always be a small remnant of the Lord's people. He knows who they are, though they are invisible to us. God will make preaching bear fruit, although this may not be obvious to the naked eye. So we must persevere in our calling, despite all appearances. The seeds are hidden in the earth and will bear fruit at the opportune moment. The Lord works through preachers such that there is always someone who profits from their teaching. The Lord always so blesses the work of His preachers that their labors are never in vain. Even were the world to go to total rack and ruin, this would be to the glory of God; for God's justice is glorified in His damnation of the wicked and reprobate, just as He is glorified in His salvation of the elect. So let us remember that although God's teaching is in vain for the vast majority of men and indeed presents them with the opportunity to do even greater evil, still He wishes His Gospel to be preached. We should bear this point very carefully in mind; for it is very tempting today to

393

give up preaching, seeing that to the naked eye the world seems to get worse every day. Instead of the Gospel serving as a burning lamp to light the way to the Path of Righteousness, men more so than ever give free reign to evil and iniquity, as if the Gospel was a license to do evil.

Look at how the Papists shame our teaching, saying, "These men claim they wish to reform the world. But have they reformed themselves? Have they amended their ways? If anything, they seem to get worse." They take advantage of our situation to curse the Word of God. But we must not lose courage; we must remember that the Lord wishes His Gospel to be preached, despite the facts that it is poorly received and that many use it as an excuse to get worse rather than to amend their ways. We must not give up our ardent desire that all the world be led back to God; we must pray to God that He accomplish this task, for it is far beyond our strength and courage; we must live by faith; so if we see we have not borne fruit, we must not abandon our calling. Indeed, our preaching in itself is pleasing to God. Were the whole world destroyed, nevertheless God would be glorified, for the Word is a sweet scent to Him. So I say that we must persist in our calling, although things seem worse than chaotic.

However, we cannot help but gasp when we see that the world is so perverse that it rebels against God and refuses to return to Him. Seeing how the Devil has blinded men, we cannot help but be deeply saddened. It is no easy matter to see souls created in the image of God on the way to Hell. We cannot help but be deeply saddened and mourn when we see souls so dearly ransomed by the blood of Christ perish. Consider why our Lord ordained preaching: first, in order that men come to have faith, through which they obey God and honor Him, as Saint Paul says; secondly, in order that men be saved, for preaching is God's power to save all believers. Seeing how the malice of men frustrates God's intention, let us follow Micah's example and cry out; for he well reflects our own dilemma, when he says he looked forward to the first fruits of the year, as if to say, "I hoped that as soon as the Word of God was preached, it would bear good fruit, but precisely the opposite happened."

Note that Micah says, "I looked forward to." He means that the Word of God has the power to draw men to itself and to make them bear good fruit to the honor and glory of God. God, on His side, desires to be known by us only for the sake of our salvation. Seeing that God desires to govern and lead us solely for our own benefit, must we not allow Him complete and total authority over us? When we see that God cultivates us, that He is like a wine grower who does everything possible to make us fertile, but that we bear no fruit, is that not sufficient reason for Him to abandon and reject us because we are so useless? Micah had good reason to believe that his preaching would lead men to amend their ways, that it would cultivate them to bear good fruit. But his hope was not fulfilled. Our Lord speaks in a similar way in Isaiah and Jeremiah: "I made every effort to cultivate my vineyard; I overlooked nothing; I looked forward to a good crop of grapes, but my vineyard yielded only wild, sour grapes." And in Jeremiah, the Lord says He expected we would bear good fruit where the Word is preached but received in the end only very bitter, disagreeable fruit.

All preachers must share in this same hope and expectancy. When our expectancy is not met, when our desire is unfulfilled, we must not abandon our calling. We must realize, as I have already said, that we are not more privileged than the prophets, that God has called us to preach, though our teaching will not profit everyone. We must not abandon our desire to save the whole world; we must not become discouraged when we see clearly this is not the case; we must realize we are not better than the prophets; we must not be presumptuous enough to assume that men will be more receptive to our teaching than they were when taught by Jesus Christ Himself, the Son of God, and all His Apostles and prophets.

As I have said, we must ardently desire that men obey, honor, and serve God. Nevertheless, we should not be surprised that He will permit us to be tempted by seeing that all the pains we have taken to bring men to fear and obey Him are in vain. Micah is a perfect example of this; he laments and cries out, "Alas! I longed for firstripe fruits"; that is to say, "I felt assured that my preaching would bring men to honor God, but the season has passed." That servants of God fail is something very hard and very bitter for them to bear. At the beginning of this series of sermons, we saw that Micah persevered in his calling not just for one year or even ten, but for half a man's lifetime. At the end of his life, he says, "Summer has passed; my hopes are unfulfilled." So he has good reason to cry out, "Alas!" He is not at all like the many preachers today who think they have amply fulfilled their calling when they have preached but an hour. He knows well that to be a prophet requires that one have a deep paternal love toward those to whom one is sent, just as all ministers must be as fathers, mothers, and nurses to those whom they have been commissioned to serve, which is a point Saint Paul emphasizes. It is precisely because Micah has such ardent zeal to save those poor souls on the way to Hell that he cries out, "Alas!" when he sees his long efforts at preaching have been in vain.

When Micah says that men of mercy have disappeared from the face of the earth, he means that there is no justice among his people, who, refusing the yoke of God's teaching, have become cruel as savage beasts. Despite all the other vices that reigned in Jerusalem, he focuses exclusively on those covered under the second tablet of the Law, namely our duties to our neighbors, because there is no more telling example of our lack of fear in God than when we live like cats and dogs, when we are full of nothing but fraud and deceit, cruelty, and malice.

How true this is of us today! We boast of having the Gospel, but our lives are quite wicked. We worship God with our mouths but renounce Him with our lives, as Saint Paul says. Do we truly believe that God is content with our hypocrisy and impudence, by which we speak sugar-coated words, put on airs, and yet totally ignore Him in the way we live? If we wish to prove we are true and faithful servants of God, we must be fair and just with our neighbors. The word Micah uses here means merciful or full of pity, for this is the major characteristic that Scripture attributes to the Children of God. And with good reason; for nothing is more like God than to be kind and helpful to others. So if we wish to be in the image and likeness of God, if we wish Him to adopt us as His children, we must be merciful and full of pity.

Where is such charity and love as God demands of us to be found? Only by building a new world, for we treat each other as savage beasts. We are so preoccupied with our own self-interest that we have neither pity nor compassion for those who have failed us. However our mouths may claim God as our Father, our lives show we have completely renounced Him. So let us pay heed to Micah's admonition that "the merciful have disappeared from the earth, so there is no longer any justice in the world."

Next he adds that each is on the prowl after blood, each chasing after his brother. He is not speaking of robbers that cut the throats of men, but of those who wish to be reputed as honorable citizens; for they are worse thieves and murderers than those who prowl the roads. It is bad enough that you have to be on guard against highwaymen when you are out on the roads. But it is worse yet that though you think to be secure in your own hometown, right in the midst of you, the poor are sucked dry of their blood and stripped to the bone by rapine, loan sharking, fraud, and crooked deals, and widows and orphans are oppressed and also overburdened by debts. I say these crimes are worse and far crueller than being put on the wheel or tortured by some other device. Beware, I say, of these household pirates, of which Micah speaks, who hide behind a facade of righteousness and wish to be honored among men. Their traps are set and ready to snare the innocent by their cunning deceitfulness. "We are expert con artists," they boast. "We know exactly how to swindle so-and-so out of such-and-such." In brief, what are passed off as legitimate business practices today are nothing more than piratical acts that cut the throats of the poor, as well we should know.

God has passed sentence against all such practices, although men seek to justify them. So we say in vain, "We haven't wronged anybody; we're just using good business sense. Let the buyer beware. Every man for himself." No, no! These excuses will not vindicate us before God. Although men may resort to all sorts of facades to convince themselves they are not wronging their neighbors, God has condemned them all as pirates and will not rescind this sentence against them, for He is immutable. That, I say, is Micah's message for us today.

So let us be very careful how we act; let us recognize that God does not judge our faults according to our opinion or imagination. Although we may rationalize fraud as a very expedient way of making profits, God says we are cutting the throats of men. True, there is always someone who will argue, "Why does God feel that way? I never killed anybody. I never spilled one drop of blood, nor do I wish to. How can God say I cut the throats of men?" Because you are a pirate nevertheless. Let us stop fooling ourselves, as we are wont to do. These pirates are very skillful and cunning, so they easily throw one off guard. When they see some poor soul in dire need, they say, "He will listen to reason soon enough, once we get him trapped in our nets." He has no chance whatsoever to escape their hands. Yet he will say that they have done him a great favor. But how? In that they cut his throat. Although they suck out his very juices, still he will say to them, "You have done me a great favor." Nevertheless God has sentenced them as pirates. I emphasize that God's wrath and vengeance is upon all men; so whenever men feed upon one another, whenever they cheat and deceive one another, God's curse will be upon them regardless of their position.

This brings us to Micah's chastisement of the princes, judges, and governors. When he speaks of the princes, saying they are demanding, he is referring to those in charge of governing the people. At that time, Judah was under a king who governed through his council and officers principal, who were called princes, under whom were the judges or officers ordinary. These judges worked for the gain and profit of the princes, who were insatiable gluttons. The princes, then, were savage beasts who preyed upon the poor, exploiting them terribly. They were subject to no law and had free reign to do evil because those responsible for the administration of justice were themselves given to greed, rapine, and iniquity. This passage is important to bear in mind, for it makes clear that it is the height of all evil when the leaders are wicked. Never will the people be more oppressed. As it says in the Psalm, when the wicked reign, everything falls apart.

Micah, then, is saying in effect, "The principal cause of all disorder and chaos is the greed of leaders. If they prey upon others, if they seek only to enrich themselves, everything goes to rack and ruin." We see an intolerable number of examples of this truth every day; for men are so possessed by greed that the vast majority of today's leaders are savage beasts totally abandoned to impiety and dishonesty. Because the world is so perverted today, we have good reason to pray to God that He pity us and send us leaders who ardently desire to maintain law and order and who will therefore deliver us from the chaos of which Micah speaks.

So today it is especially important for us to heed his words that the source of all evil in the land of Judah is the avarice of the princes, which has warped their sense of justice, led them to prey upon men, and brought them to support and serve freely the wicked. Because he spoke out so strongly against the leaders, he received no support and his teachings were rejected. How this mirrors our own time. Many of our leaders wish to appear righteous, whereas in point of fact they battle against God.

401

They are terribly offended if they are given the least reproach. When they complain how ministers interfere with their business, it never occurs to them that they do not truly belong in the Church; rather, they will profess, "We are faithful men; everyone knows we are loyal members of the Church of God." Nevertheless they have nothing but spite and contempt for the Word of God. Rather than honoring God, they mock Him. They subvert justice. They support the wicked in their iniquities and they trample down the rights of the poor. I say that even a small child can see through their facade; yet we are like muzzled watchdogs, or they would not be getting away with what they do. So let us remember, as Micah's example makes clear, that the Word of God ordained us to spare no one in our preaching. Those in positions of power are not to be given special privileges over others. In fact, we should chastise them first, for they are the source of all evil. So let us follow Micah's example and have the courage to speak out against men in positions of power and authority, who are the ones responsible for the damnation of all others.

True, we have our tavern theologians who say, "I think it's a good idea that we have all this writing going on today, all these commentaries on Holy Scripture. But for my part, just a few simple words will do." They are very vexed that the prophets are preached, saying, "We are no longer under the Old Testament; we no longer need its teaching. Ministers who preach it are from Satan himself; they are adversaries of God, enemies of the truth!" They wish to see their own wickedness as righteousness. They desire ministers to flatter them, preaching I don't know what all corruptions of God's Word. But let us not fall sway to them. No, no! Let us recognize to what end God has called us and persevere in our vocation. Let us realize the necessity of remaining steadfast in our condemnation of all the many scandals in our midst, which would make us lose courage, were we not fortified by power from On High. We know that those who are supposed to maintain order and protect us from such scandals are the very ones who support the wicked in their iniquities and allow innocent, poor people to be oppressed. When we reproach them they say, "Don't blame us. We just don't know what to do; we just don't know how to maintain law and order." But God will well restore order, and He will not tolerate His Word being despised and rejected, without taking vengeance. On our part, when we see these things, let us carry out our calling as God has so ordained. I am finished now; but I will take up these matters again, at the pleasure of God, if things continue to go as they have been.

Following this holy teaching, we prostrate ourselves before the face of our good God, acknowledging our sinfulness. We pray that it please Him to so open our eyes that we, seeing the great poverty within ourselves, come to be more so displeased in ourselves than ever. May we be just, fair, merciful, and charitable toward our neighbors. May in this way we show throughout all our life that we are truly His children. May we

403

be so in His likeness that we rise to the immortal glory which He has prepared for us.  Thus we say all together:  "All-powerful God, celestial father, etc."

* * *

(26) Thursday, January 8, 1551

The best of them is like a briar; the most righteous is like a thorn. The day of your watchmen and visitation has come. Now will be their perplexity, etc. Micah 7

After Micah says that those who were responsible to maintain law and order are the most corrupt of all, he adds that those believed to be the most righteous men among his people are like briars and thorns, as if to say there is not one truly righteous man among them. He is taking poetic license here to emphasize that there is corruption everywhere. There are in point of fact some men among his people who serve God; but their number is so small and they are so thinly scattered that just when you think to have touched upon a righteous man, you are stabbed as if you had stuck your hand into a briar bush or a thorn hedge.

He says that the vast majority of his people are hypocrites who wish to appear righteous in all that they do, despite the fact their wickedness is more than obvious. True, some take this claim to mean that the majority of his people were quite adept at evil. But the more obvious and certain interpretation is that he is claiming they make every effort to appear righteous, despite the fact they do only evil. Word for word, he says, "Having evil between their hands, they wish to make it righteous," as if to say, "Their life shows what they truly are, for their wickedness is found in all their works. Their hearts are obvious to everyone. Nevertheless they wish to be esteemed as righteous men." In sum, he is saying that the vast majority of his people

405

are so impudent that they wish to be taken for men of honor, although their turpitude is quite obvious. They do not wish to be told what they really are; they wish to hear it said of themselves, "Here are the true pillars of the Church and justice!"

If we had no experience with what Micah is talking about, it would be necessary to go into a long exposition of this passage which would prove quite obscure. However, we do not have to look far to see what he is speaking of. Just take a look at ourselves today. We know of many judges and magistrates who are obviously impious men, given to all forms of evil, full of nothing but contempt for God's Word and yet who wish to be esteemed as leading Christians. If there is a quarrel, they are always ready to sustain it. They welcome the wicked with open arms. Provided that they are given gifts or that their palms are greased, they will support any and all forms of iniquity. Obvious as all this may be, still they wish to be esteemed as angels from Paradise. They are worse than the Devil, they glory in their evil, but still they wish to maintain an excellent reputation. When we see these things, we have no trouble understanding Micah; his words are by no means obscure. When we see how wicked the world is today, we know that what Micah had to say to his time goes for ours.

In order that we do not follow in the footsteps of these wicked officials, let us heed Micah's warning, "The day of your watchmen and visitation approaches. Then will you be perplexed."

Although some interpret this passage as a threat against the leaders, he is speaking specifically here of the false prophets. They give the people false hope by telling them everything will be just fine; they flatter the people and numb them to the reality of their own evil. So Micah warns them, "The day of your watchmen approaches." We saw this theme in an earlier passage, where he reproaches the wicked, who serve only to vex God more and more, glorify His name in vain, saying, "God will pity us; our hope is in Him!" "Do you truly think God will pity you?" he asks them. "What kind of a day do you expect? It will be a day of darkness and confusion for you. The coming of the Lord will not be a day of consolation for you; you have never searched for aid in Him but have continually provoked His wrath against you. So do not think that He will appear in order to comfort you, for He will destroy you. As up to this very hour you have been at war against God and as this war continues even at present, do you truly believe He will not visit horrible vengeance upon you?"

So in today's passage, Micah is warning of the destruction of the people, when he says, "The day has come for those who watch over you." In Holy Scriptures, the prophets are termed watchmen, for they watch over the people. As we read in Ezekiel, "I was ordained to be a watchman over my people." The prophet's task was to watch over the people in order to call their attention to evil and lead the fight against it. When they saw God was offended, they were like a trumpet to awaken those who sleep. That is why Scripture calls prophets watchmen. Likewise today ministers of the Word must be on the alert. When they see evil, they must cry out against it. They must awaken those who sleep in their sins and make them know they must not play with God.

Micah says, "The watchmen are the most corrupted and perverted of all people." Therefore, the day of their visitation will come, and they will be the first to be thrown into agony and perplexity. They will be in such great distress they will not know which way to turn. The rest of the people will also be afflicted, for the wrath of God will be everywhere." His point is that although God has been very patient and overlooked the evil of the people for a very long time, in the end we will be brought to account before Him. If He does not punish us at once, let us not assume that we have escaped His hand or have been acquitted by Him. Just as human judges assign dates for cases, so our Lord has set aside a day for our trial before Him. So let us bear in mind that if today we are at ease, tomorrow we may be before our Judge. Let us not be as the wicked, who are flattered by their own iniquities and who pay absolutely no attention to these warnings, thinking they will have an easy time of it with God. Let us take seriously Micah's warning and fear God. He has given the faithful sound advice: Although they do not yet see punishment befalling upon the heads of the God-haters, they must look forward by faith to what they cannot see with the naked eye. They must take great care not to associate with the wicked, for fear they will fall and be enveloped in their punishment. They must remember that all those who mock God's judgment and who think they will remain unpunished because they have abused His patience for such a long time will be without excuse before Him. To those mockers, Micah says, "Your day will come. Although God seems hidden now, in the end you will know Him as your Judge, for you refused to believe my words." So think hard upon how the wicked will come to know the hand of God as their destruction, although they pay attention neither to Him nor His Word.

Micah says that people will trust neither their friends nor their relatives, that all friendship will be gone, that a man will not trust the woman who sleeps in his arms, that the father will betray his son, and the son will betray his father. In brief, there will no longer be any trust in the world. Why? Because everything is corrupted and perverted. There is no kinship, love, congeniality, nothing of the sort. Men are such brutes that they lack any form of compassion; they wish only to poke out each other's eyes. True, this may not be obvious to us at first glance; but God sounds the depths of all hearts; He knows what is hidden; He reveals the truth; He is the Judge summoning us before the court to pass sentence upon us.

The question arises how Micah can proclaim this total lack of trust, when in fact charity is never suspicious. Saint Paul, in I Corinthians 13, says, "Charity is patient; it is kind; it is not jealous; it does nothing harmful; it means that we would rather be deceived than distrust a neighbor." Yet Micah says that there will be no trust among us, that we will be like savage beasts. But the issue here is not whether or not we should trust in one another. That is beside the point. Micah is not speaking of what we ought to do but realize how true it is we are unable to build lasting relationships among ourselves and so can enjoy neither friendship nor kinship. Micah, then, is chastising us, as if to say, "Were you taught nothing, still the fact that you recognize yourselves to be of one and the same nature should move you to live in harmony with one another." The word "humanity" means that we are all one, for the Lord has created all of us in His image. The wolves and other savage beasts do not harm one another; for they realize that they are all of one and the same nature, by virtue of the fact they all share the forests. Likewise, the fact that God created us all of one and the same nature should move us so much the more to live in mutual charity.

Nevertheless, the common bond of our humanity is not strong enough to guarantee that we will live in peace and harmony with one another. There is no intimate relationship that we will not betray. Family and marriage, which is a sacred alliance consecrated in the name of God, denote our strongest possible social ties. Here, I say, is where nature really holds sway, as we see in the love and affection between husband and wife, father and son. However cruel a father may be, he will regret having wronged his children and be moved by pity and compassion for them. However unfaithful a husband may be, his wife will remain loyal to him. One would expect, then, family and marriage to

410

inspire men to be loving and compassionate toward their neighbors, with whom they share one and the same nature. However, Micah says that there is such great corruption in his time that all these things are forgotten. "Men," he says, "are like brutal beasts who nibble and feed upon one another. The father does not feel secure with the son, nor the wife with the husband. The father betrays the son, and the son betrays the father. There is no more loyalty among husband and wife than there is among brutal beasts. Indeed, no matter where you look, you will find no trust, in the world."

When we see the corruption that reigned in Micah's time, we should take a long, hard look at ourselves; he is not speaking here of the reprobate, of savages unschooled in God; he is speaking here of the line of Abraham, of the people chosen above all others to be God's heirs, of the people who had been taught the law; yet he says there is less humanity in them than in savage beasts. What brought about such confusion? The people turned from God; they strayed from the Path of Righteousness; they held His salvific teaching in contempt. Therefore, God assigned them to the ranks of the reprobate; He turned them into brutes and made them forget what it means to be a human being. So let us take care, lest we abuse God's grace; for in the end, He will so blind us that we become brutes. Indeed, when men rebel against God, how much true humanity can they have had in the first place? If men are so rash as to rebel against their Creator and refuse to trust in Him, how much trust and loyalty can they have among themselves? By the same token, our Lord so punishes those who abandon Him and refuse the yoke of His obedience that in the end they bear the human form to their shame; for there will be nothing human left in them; in their minds and hearts they will be worse than savage beasts.

Already we see that part of this vengeance proclaimed by Micah has befallen upon us. If we were righteous and just, would we be living like cats and dogs, as we do today? There is not one among us who will not cheat his neighbor every chance he gets. We see that the world is so abandoned to evil that there is neither law and order nor trust among men. We see that fathers and sons do not share in the mutual affection they should. We see that children today are so wicked and perverse that they pay no mind to their parents; they no more honor their parents than if God had not commanded them to do so; they hold their parents in contempt, rebel against them, and torment them every chance they get. We see that marriage means nothing today. Although it is a sacred bond that God has consecrated in His name (as I have just said), it is everywhere trampled under foot today. Certainly the Word has taught us well that a husband must be one with his wife and that the wife must obey her husband. But this is all twisted round some other way today. Now, when we see all these things, do we not also see God's horrible punishment upon our heads? Is it not now or never that we recognize the fruits of our iniquities and return to God in true repentance? Does He not punish us because our transgressions are so enormous and detestable?  When we see God's punishment upon our heads, let us recognize this is the fruit of our sins.

True, as I have said, at first glance things may not seem to be so bad today.  But God has said otherwise, and we know He can see far more clearly than we.  Furthermore, when we look at things closely enough, we will find that Micah did not speak in vain.  We may have a general, overall impression that there is trust among men and that everything is in good order; but when we examine closely how each individual governs himself, we find there is not one man who is not totally corrupt, perverse, untrustworthy, and highly suspicious of others.  I am speaking here of the world in general today; for the Lord always has His own, as He did at the time of Micah and Isaiah, who were not at all like savage beasts.  But the number of the faithful is so small that we can say in general men are disloyal to one another today.  That is why the Lord tells Isaiah, "Hide my witness among my discipline," as if His teachings were to be secrets known only to the faithful.  When we look at things closely, we find the world is no better or more excellent of a place today than it was when the Lord thus spoke.  So let us be far more circumspect than we are accustomed; for the horrible vengeance of God is upon us. If we wish the Lord to accept us as His children, let us live in fraternal charity, as He has so strongly commanded us to do; let us be peaceful and friendly with one another; let us prove by our actions that we are governed by God's Spirit, which is the Spirit of truth, and which seeks not merely to reveal the truth to us but to bring us to live by it.

After Micah had spoken of the corruption in the lands of Judah and even in the city of Jerusalem, which was God's Holy City, he says, "I will hope in my Lord" or "I will trust in my God, and my God will hear me." This is a very important sentence for us to bear in mind; for bad examples easily lead men astray, drive them mad, corrupt and pervert them. Vices are a more than contagious pestilence. There is no disease, no infection in the world more dangerous than vices. Once they hold sway, it is impossible to protect yourself against them. We are inclined to follow bad examples rather than good ones; we cannot walk through thorns without being stabbed. That should be obvious; many of our common proverbs make this point. So let us follow Micah's example when he says he lives in a place like Hell and yet says, "I will hope in God; I will trust in the Lord." He is not merely showing what he will do; he is also teaching the faithful what they must do, as if to say, "My friends, it is true that we are naturally quite fragile. It is very easy to lead us astray. When evil reigns, when vice is taken to be virtue, there is grave danger each of us will fall. But that does not have to be the case. Let us be on our guard. However everything may be perverted and corrupted around us, let us not fail to walk in fear of our God. Let us hope in Him to care for us and sustain us in the midst of these horrible tempests. When we are near death, let us be assured we will live, for God cares for us. In sum, let us put all our trust in Him, obey Him, and rest assured that He will defend us against all assaults, no matter how grievous and bitter they may be."

To profit best from Micah's teaching, let us note that we cannot excuse ourselves before God by merely saying, "I couldn't help it that I went astray. I just didn't know which way to turn. The world was more perverted than it had ever been, and I just could not resist following the common train of thought." Was there ever a worse time than that of Micah, when men were incarnate devils? Not only had they buried all fear of God but they completely overlooked their natural sense of charity and equity. The whole order of nature was, then, reversed, with men acting as brutal beasts rather than as human beings. Nevertheless Micah says, "Let us hope in God." So we cannot excuse ourselves as we are wont to do by saying, "We cannot be angels in a world of devils; we have to run with the wolves." Such claims, I say, will gain us nothing before God; they will serve only to worsen rather than to help our case. Our Lord permits the world to be corrupted in order to test the perseverance and loyalty of His faithful, and in order to keep us on the alert and on our guard. So then, seeing how deeply troubled and confused the world is, we must hope in God more than ever, trust fully in Him to aid us; we must take great care not to follow the common train of thought. The goal of Micah's teaching is that we not be condemned before God by saying, "I just did what everybody else did; I'm no worse than my

415

neighbors." No, that kind of excuse will not work with God; we will be brought to account anyway.

Now, if this excuse will not work to pardon us for our offenses against our neighbors, do we think we can excuse ourselves from the offenses we have committed against God's majesty by saying that we merely did what everybody else does? Do we think that this excuse will truly serve as a shield against God's wrath, as do the many fools today who say, "I live according to custom"? When you reproach the Papists for their superstitions and actions, they say they are doing nothing more than following in the footsteps of their predecessors. They fail to realize that they are leading themselves and their neighbors to the exact same condemnation that befell upon their predecessors. These poor beasts think they are well armed against God; they think they will avoid all condemnation by merely saying, "I wish to live as I have been raised." But when we see that God will not pardon the sins we have committed against other men by our crooked dealings, do we honestly think that He will pardon us for having rebelled against Him, served Him in a perverse and twisted way, and robbed Him of His honor to lavish it upon idols and saints? Do we think He will accept what we do, when we wish to make vice virtue? No, certainly not! Even were we to walk around with our eyes closed, still it should be apparent to us that it is wrong for men to serve God by their own inventions. We should not at all be surprised that men do

416

such; we should realize that human nature is totally corrupt, so that men are naturally prone to evil.

But we should also note that when Micah says, "I hope in my God," he means that God will deliver us from all evil, provided, of course, that we place ourselves in His care and accept Him as our Protector. Even if we were thrown to the bottom of the earth's abysms, so to speak, God would rescue us, provided that we invoke His name.

Micah says next, "My God will hear me." He does not say merely, "I will invoke my God," although that alone would be sufficient to save him; for he is also teaching us what we must do, namely hope in God. In order that we would come to know that God is always ready to aid us, that we will never be frustrated in our hopes, he adds, "My God will hear me." If we are sometimes tempted to think that God does not hear our prayers, here is a passage to prove us wrong. If we were in the midst of Hell itself, if the Devil himself had a rope around our necks and complete control over us, still we would be delivered by invoking God's name. When he says, "God will hear me," he means that God will protect him in every way, that He will protect him against all enemies, spiritual as well as carnal. So then, let us recognize that if we are under God's wings, we are secure and in good safekeeping. Were Satan to rule everywhere and come against us with all his power, still God will deliver us; for it is said, "Whosoever invokes the name of God will be saved."

Let us apply this teaching to the evil we see in the world today. I have already said that vice is the common way of life, that we are inclined to follow the example of those who have no scruples. It seems we rival among ourselves to see who can be the master of offending God. This makes apparent the fact that by nature we are inclined to evil rather than goodness. Although we have the examples of the Patriarchs, prophets, Apostles, and Jesus Christ Himself, who is the Son of God, we refuse to follow in their footsteps; we renounce them and follow instead those whom we know by their conduct to be alienated from, and totally destitute of, God. So much the more, then, must we pay heed to Micah's teaching, in order to keep a tighter reign on ourselves and to insure that we walk in fear and obedience of God. However the world may reach the heights of all iniquity, let us say along with Micah, "I will hope in my God, and He will hear me."

When Micah says, "I will hope in God," he draws a hard-and-fast line between himself and the vast majority of men, as if to say, "It is very difficult to walk among thorns without being stabbed; however, I will not abandon my faith in God, and He will protect me from all evil." This is a point for us to bear carefully in mind; for whenever we walk among the infidels, we must remain steadfast in our faith and not be shaken by their Sacrilegious beliefs. If we trust in God, as we are exhorted to do in so many passages of Scripture, we will surmount all that might serve to turn us from the faith we have in His aid and help. Although the common opinion among the vast majority of men is that anything goes to get ahead, let us not follow in their footsteps. Although they seem to prosper and although it may seem that God favors them, let us remember that God does not take pleasure in our evil. If this teaching is firmly engraved in our hearts, the sacrilege will not lead us to stray from God. Let us pray that God so strengthen us in our faith that even if the world were turned upside down, even if the sky were to be mixed with the earth, we would follow Micah's example and say, "I will hope in my God, and He will hear me." Just as God has called us to know His truth and to serve Him, so, too, He has given us the grace to obey Him and to trust fully in Him. So when we invoke His name, we, along with Micah, can say in all honesty that God will hear us and so protect us that the Devil will not be able to destroy us, that God will lead us along the path to salvation and strengthen us such that by His grace we attain the goal to which He calls us.

Following this holy teaching, we prostrate ourselves before the face of our good God, acknowledging our sinfulness. We pray that it please Him to so open our eyes that we come to know our faults better than ever before. May we come to Him as our Savior. May we so renounce ourselves and our wicked desires that nothing blocks us from coming to Him all together, of common accord, to subjugate ourselves under His hand and to pay Him due homage and honor. May it please Him not to punish us with the rigor we deserve. May it please Him to discipline us gently, as our loving Father, until He has corrected all our faults. May He sustain us in our infirmities. May He shed this grace not only on us but upon all the peoples and nations of the earth.

All-powerful God, celestial Father, we live in a century that has given such free reign and horrible license to evil that only at great pain can we find one single spark of righteousness and kindness. Give us the grace that we remain intact among the thorns. May your Word sustain us in true piety and insure we are fair and just with our neighbors. Since we are powerless to maintain such integrity in ourselves, give us the grace that our Lord through the Holy Spirit will so strengthen us that we will be able to pursue our path until finally we reach the Kingdom of Heaven, which He won for us by His blood. Amen.

* * *

## (27) Friday, January 9, 1551

Rejoice not, my enemy, when I fall. I will rise up. When I will be seated in darkness, the Lord will be my light. I will bear the wrath of the Lord because I have sinned against Him, until He pleads my case and renders His verdict, etc. Micah 7

Yesterday we saw that Micah looks to God as his refuge in desperate times. Although his people have so abandoned themselves to evil that neither justice nor trust is to be found among them, he says he will hope in God, emphasizing this hope will not be in vain, for God will hear him. He is a shining example how we must remain invincible in the face of all scandals. Were sky and earth to be mixed together, we must remain steadfast in our faith; for if we invoke His name, He will take us in His mighty hand and so protect us that nothing we see happen in the world can conquer us.

Since he is setting an example for the faithful to follow, he says now that although they will be trodden down for a time, this will not be cause for rejoicing among the unfaithful. He speaks in a manner commonly found in Scripture, saying that the Church is his spouse, with whom he has become one. The Synagogue of Satan and the unfaithful wish to break up this marriage and throw the household into chaos, just as we see today how the wicked are always cooking up trouble and confusion in the Church of God. He compares the faithful to a woman who is temporarily separated from her husband for having committed an offense against him. On the other hand, he compares the unfaithful to a woman who delights in seducing a husband away from his wife and in turning his household upside down.

Micah, speaking for the faithful, says, "Rejoice not, my enemy. True, I have fallen, but I will get up again." Why? "Although that I am in darkness, the Lord will be my light," as if to say, "The wicked rejoice, believing they have triumphed over us. But pay no attention to their boasting. Although they oppress us, they have not dealt us a mortal blow. If God permits that we fall, He will rise us up again by His grace. Although it may seem we are destroyed, His bounty will deliver us; He will make us know that He has not forsaken being our God. Although they make us objects of great contempt and mock us, and although they believe they have vanquished us, let us trust in God to take pity upon us."

To best profit from Micah's teaching, note that we cannot help but have many enemies who rejoice in our calamities, as well we know from experience. We all bear the name Christian, but the bad are mixed in with the good. Whenever God's hand strikes one of the faithful, those who call themselves Christians but are really from Satan will rejoice and exploit this situation to their advantage. We must be well armed against all such sacrilege. Worse yet, we are confronted with this diabolical see of Rome, which is nothing but a whore seeking to corrupt and pervert the Church of God. Whenever some evil befalls upon the poor Christians, this wicked whore, Rome, rejoices, thinking that we are destroyed. So let us heed Micah's words in order that we are not taken by surprise when, being chastised by the hand of God, the infidels mock us, thinking to have vanquished us when they see us in such a pitiable condition. When we are assailed from all sides, let us remember this has been the condition of the Church from all time; let us also remember these assailants can do us no real harm; for God has bestowed an inestimable honor upon us by becoming one with us through a sacred bond, so that He is our spouse and we live in obedience to Him, just as the wife is one with her husband. So, seeing what marvelous grace God has shed upon us, let us be content and patiently endure all the assaults, all the mockery, ridicule, and shame that the wicked and the infidels heap upon us.

Whenever God releases us from His hand, we fall. We remain in our present state solely because it pleases God to sustain us. True, Scripture often uses the word "fall" to denote sin, just as when we do not attend to our God-given calling and stray from the path He has ordained for us, in brief when we offend Him, we are said to have fallen. But Micah is using the word "fall" in a different way; he means the affliction God sends upon people to correct their ways. He says, then, "I will rise up, however I have been destroyed and ruined." I emphasize that we will sometimes see the Church to be so desolate that it seems to be totally destroyed. Indeed, Micah's point is that we must be surprised by the fact that God will so punish His Church that it will seem all is lost, all is destroyed, and there is no remedy in sight. When such troubled times befall upon us, let us not abandon our hope that God will always preserve a small remnant which will have their refuge in Him. God's promises are intended to lift us above the heavens to see what is hidden. Consequently, Micah say, "I will rise up," meaning that the faithful will never be destroyed, however they may fall. As it says in the Psalm, "A just man will fall seven times in a day, but He will be raised up by the hand of God."

So when Micah speaks of falling, he is not speaking of our offenses against God; rather, he is saying that God will permit us to suffer great poverty and many afflictions. The Psalm says seven times in a day. This means that the Children of God will be afflicted in many ways, that we will never be comfortable in this world, that we will be struck with one rod and then another, so that it will seem God is making a spectacle out of us for the whole world to say of us: "Look at those poor dumb clucks." But just as we will fall seven times in a day, just as God will send many trials and tribulations upon us, so, too, He always has His hand out to protect us so we do not fall and break our arms, legs, or necks. Our Lord will sustain us always. However the Lord may bring us to fall many times, He will always turn our afflictions into something good and make them serve to the benefit of our salvation.

So let us remember well Micah's words: "I have fallen, but I will rise up." He is not speaking just of himself alone; he is showing the faithful how all God's afflictions contain consolations. Provided that we invoke God's name with total and

424

complete faith and trust in Him, He will be our place of refuge. However times may be so troubled that it seems earth and sky will be destroyed, the hand of our good Father will deliver us, provided we put all our trust in Him. We will never be disappointed in our hope that God will deliver us from our afflictions. Scripture says that while God corrects our ways by afflicting us only for a minute of time, His bounty and mercy are shed upon us forever and ever. Does not such knowledge cause us to rejoice in the midst of our sorrows? In sum, let us realize that all our afflictions will have a happy ending and serve to the benefit of our salvation, provided that we believe with all our heart that God will raise us up if we have fallen.

Consequently Micah says that although the Church be in darkness, God will be its light. This is a very important point to bear in mind. Although God may not pick us up the instant we have fallen and leave us to languish for a time, we must not become desperate and say, "We're wiped out. Scripture says that God will stand His children back on their feet. But how, when? We see nothing of this. Since He has not kept His promise, we can assume only that we mean nothing to Him, that He has rejected us." That kind of attitude, I emphasize, is precisely what would lead us astray from God. So instead, let us remember that it is through His promises that He is a light to the faithful. If these promises are sealed in our hearts by the Holy Spirit, we will rejoice, although He chastises us; for we will recognize

425

that however severe His chastisement, still He will reveal to us how deeply He cares for our salvation.

If we have these promises firmly engraved in our souls, we will fear nothing, for they will console us and give us light in the midst of darkness. David says, "Were I to walk in the shadow of death, that is, in the darkness of the tomb, I would be certain of life and salvation. I would fear nothing, for God is my guide." Listen to Job, who says, "Even if God were to murder me, I would hope in Him." Where does the confidence and surety come from to say, "In death I will have life; in the darkest dark, I will have light"? It comes from the fact that all God's promises are guaranteed and therefore bring rejoicing. If we trust in the Lord to be our Father and Savior we will be consoled by His promises. Then, even if we were lost in the deepest abysms of the earth and on the verge of death, without any aid or hope in sight, still we would not give up hope; for we would trust that God, that is to say, the good will of God, of which we are made certain by the Word, will lead us to salvation. So we see how Micah's passage is something very important for us to meditate long and hard upon. It is wanting only of our careful attention and not of further exposition, for it is obvious enough in itself: God will be my light, though I am in darkness.

No matter what all may be said of this passage, it all comes down to one point: We live in a very dark, shadowy world. And what is the cause of this darkness? Our affliction, which totally obscures our view of God. The clouds, the fumes, and all the things the earth throws skyward because it does not need them do not half as much obscure our view of the sun as our afflictions do God. We are naturally inclined to be distrustful; so the very instant God's hand strikes us, we think we are totally alienated from Him and no longer have any real access to Him. That is the darkness which eclipses the face of God. On the contrary, when we feel certain that God loves us and attends to our salvation, then His face shines upon us. When we know God's grace, it is obvious to us that He is close at hand, as if our salvation were shining down upon us. On the contrary, when we are afflicted, it seems God is far from us and we can no longer see His face. Thus, it is not without reason Scripture says we are most often in darkness in this world; for we are continually preyed upon by all kinds of troubles, torments, and temptations from all directions. They are like a dark cloud hovering over us; they are like a dark pit in which we are trapped. So what should we do? Let us receive God's light as He has presented it to us; that is, let us go to the Word. Our human senses can perceive nothing at all of God's bounty, by which He will sweeten our afflictions. But when we hear the Lord speak to us and say that He will never abandon us but wishes to assist us in every way, then we find the light.

Do we wish to be struck down in the midst of our afflictions? Then, we must arm ourselves with the promises of Holy Scripture. Why is it that these promises are not more deeply ingrained in us and that we do not profit more from them?

427

Because the Devil finds us disarmed and so catches us napping. Instead of drilling ourselves in Scripture, which Saint Paul says is our shield, helmet, and armor, we totally ignore it. That is why we have nothing to defend ourselves with. So let us remember that God trains us in this world through everlasting battle. We should not be upset because we are afflicted, for God knows when the time is right to deliver us and by what means. In the meantime, He is training and testing our sense of patience. On the one hand, our afflictions are the fruits of our sins, which our Lord will transform into something good, as will be more amply explained shortly. On the other, as I have just said, God is training our sense of patience; so afflictions serve the benefit of our salvation because they teach us to be very patient and therefore help us become more and more like Jesus Christ, who is our Chief, who is the Son of God, who shows us the way, and who, by patiently enduring so many afflictions, entered into immortal celestial glory, to which He now wishes to lead us. I emphasize, then, that if we bear all these things in mind, we will not be upset because we have to suffer in this world; for it is a sure sign that God loves us, when He chastises us, provided, that is, we patiently bear the afflictions He is pleased to send upon us. So the very first thing Micah says we must do is to humble ourselves before the mighty hand of God and confess our sins, saying, "I am shameful and condemnable, for I have offended my God." Until we do this, it will be impossible for us to glorify God by confessing that He is just and fair with us; it

428

will be impossible to know Him as a gentle and loving God; for we must honor and glorify Him if we wish to enjoy His grace upon us. So Micah's lesson is very important to bear in mind; indeed, it should be our starting point.

Micah says, "I will bear the wrath of God, for I have offended Him"; for the first step on the path to repentance is to confess, "I have sinned against God." Until we acknowledge our faults, we can never be patient. We can only grumble and be very vexed with God, just as we see the vast majority of men gnash their teeth whenever God corrects their ways. Why? They think God has done them a great wrong by chastising them. This comes from the fact that men wish to be flattered and so do not wish to acknowledge their vices and sins, saying, "Alas! I have offended my God. I deserve very severe punishment. Indeed, I deserve far more grievous punishment than I receive from Him." True, there are many who will confess their sins without any heartfelt contrition. They are so audacious they think it is merely enough to mouth the words in order to gain an easy acquittal. Indeed, there is nothing but hypocrisy in many who confess their sins. It is not an easy thing for men to become displeased in their vices and condemn themselves, as does Micah; for we must be dead to ourselves in order to have the spirit of contrition and humility, of which the Psalm speaks. The sacrifice God demands is that we humble ourselves, recognize the evil we have done, and confess, "Alas! What has it profited me to rebel against God, to refuse to obey Him, to serve the Devil, my mortal enemy, rather than Him who created and made me?" I emphasize that when we realize the enormity of the offense we have committed by declaring war on the living God, we will be deeply saddened, being deeply displeased how grievously we have offended our God. that is what Micah means when he says, "I have sinned." By no means is this just a confession of the mouth, so that one may obtain an easy acquittal merely by saying, "I am a sinner," without his heart being deeply touched. No, no! His heart must speak before God. It is not just a simple matter of making some gesture of repentance before men and resting content with that; we must recognize with whom we have business. In truly confessing our sins, we will actually feel the insupportable weight of God's wrath and vengeance upon us, which is sufficient to send us to Hell.

Knowing our sins teaches us to be patient in our afflictions and to bear them with steadfast courage. However, it is not enough just to know our sins. Why? Judas makes an ample confession of his sins; he acknowledges his offense, saying, "I have sinned by betraying innocent blood." But why does he do this? Is it because he is patient? Does he realize it is necessary to humble himself before the mighty hand of God? Does he take seriously enough his own sinfulness that he truly repents? No, quite the contrary. Cain was unable to flee from his trial, by which God found him guilty of murdering his brother. He was very enraged against God: "The punishment you impose on me is more than I can bear." Although he saw himself as in Hell, he never humbled himself to say, "Alas! Lord, since you punish me for my iniquity, I must bear the sentence you have pronounced against me." It is not enough that a man confesses his sins; he must also add, "until God pleads my case and renders His verdict," as if to say, "I have sinned, I have provoked God's wrath, but I hope He will be merciful with me." In acknowledging our sins, we must also appeal to God's mercy. Knowledge of our sins must go hand in hand with knowledge of the condemnation we have merited. In addition, we must be fully confident that God will receive us in mercy. If we meet these conditions, then we have true patience.

The unfaithful, deep inside themselves, are compelled to recognize that they are sinful and that God's judgment is upon them because they have provoked His wrath against them; but they refuse to accept their sinfulness; they flatter themselves in their vices rather than repenting for their sins. If you ask a wicked man if he is a sinner, he will say yes, without the least hesitation; yet he will not turn to God, repent, and ask for forgiveness. The thought of having to appear before his Judge frightens him off. The iniquitous wish to lead an easy, comfortable life; they say there is no point in thinking about their sins because all that does is make people very upset and gloomy. However that the wicked may recognize their sins, they do not come willingly to this recognition. On the contrary, the man of faith will examine himself closely; he will look deep within his conscience and ask, "Alas! How have I lived?" That

431

is how the faithful come to a true recognition of their sins. But, as I have said, it is not enough we know our own sinfulness; we must also come to know the mercy of God, by which He sweetens all our afflictions. Oil must be mixed with the vinegar, as the saying goes. When we come to know God's rod and chastisement, when we come to realize His judgment and condemnation against us, we must also realize that He sweetens them by the oil of His mercy and that He will forgive our sins. That is what Micah means when he says, "until God pleads my case and renders His verdict."

He is teaching us that the afflictions suffered by the faithful are only momentary; they will not last forever. This is far from the case with the reprobate. Although God may grant them periodic rest periods from punishment, He will incessantly afflict them, for He is their complete opposite. But the Children of God know that their afflictions are merely momentary and that God will see to it they always have a happy ending, as Saint Paul says. However downtrodden is Micah by his afflictions, still he continues to hope in God to deliver him; so he says, "until He pleads my case," to which he adds, "God will bring me forth to the light, though I am in darkness." Here are words that serve as great consolation to sweeten the most horrible afflictions we can suffer. True, God is our Judge and so will punish us. For this reason, Micah says, "I bear the wrath of God." But God has also revealed that He is not angry with us, that He chastises us for our own good, that it is to our own benefit we feel His rod upon us.  So we have good reason to be consoled and rejoice in Him.  As we must recognize that God's chastisements are the fruits of our sins, so we must also recognize that He cares deeply for our salvation.  So let us remember always Micah's teaching:  Whenever God afflicts us, it is only momentary.  Why?  In the end, He will plead our case.  As Saint Paul says, we are chastised by God in order that we do not perish with the world.

When Micah says that God will bring him into the light, he means that He will deliver him from all afflictions.  However, this is only one way in which the Lord shines His light upon His own.  The other is that when the Lord leads His people and delivers them from all evil, He lifts them above themselves and their world in order that they may come to trust and ground themselves in Him alone.  Now, this light will never be seen fully as long as we are in this world; for God lives in an inaccessible light, which is the true light.  But if we wish to share in Micah's consolation, we must look to the heavens above, we must look On High, to catch a glimpse of the light which awaits us.  In this world, there will always be dark clouds, although God's face shines upon us; for we are subject to so much great misery.  Nevertheless God will bring us to the light, in our present life.  When He delivers us from evil, when He frees us, when He sweetens our chastisement by pardoning our fault, He brings us into the light, though we were in darkness, as Micah says.  When He does all these good things for us, we must look beyond this world; for these things are merely sparks of the true light, which will be revealed to us when we finally arrive at the Kingdom of Heaven. We must recognize that the grace and bounty God sheds upon us in this world are foretastes of what awaits us in Heaven after our deaths.

Micah adds, "And I will see His righteousness." He is not speaking for himself but for all the Church. But how can we look upon God's righteousness when we live in such a shameful, chaotic world? As I have said, God's light shines upon us in two ways; so, likewise, there are two ways we may come to view it: Faith and hope, those are the ways we come to see what is hidden. When horrible afflictions befall us, we cannot see God's bounty, which seems hidden away from us; and we are unable to see His face, so He seems far away from us. Indeed, it seems God is our complete opposite. But when He gives us the grace to know His chastisements are for our benefit, then by our faith we have been brought to see what is hidden, as we have already noted. When God fulfills the promises He has made through the Word, then by our hope we have been brought to see what is hidden. That is what Micah means when he says, "I will look upon the righteousness of God." We know of God's righteousness, through His promises; but we come to experience it as an actual, living reality when He delivers us from evil. Then, having glimpsed God's bounty, we are assured that our hope in Him is not in vain and that He makes every effort possible to redeem us. So, aside from knowing God's righteousness by faith and hope, we have firsthand knowledge that He will fulfill all His promises. Let us, then, patiently wait upon God to manifest His righteousness. However we may be afflicted, let us glorify His righteousness. However we may be afflicted, let us be guided by our faith; for through it, God is bringing us to a full and direct revelation of Himself.

Following this holy teaching, we prostrate ourselves before the face of our good God, acknowledging our sinfulness. We pray that He touch us deeper than ever before. We pray that in this way we come to humble ourselves in total obedience to Him. We pray that knowledge of His bounty bring us to overcome our stubbornness and rebelliousness, by which we are like savage beasts, and therefore enable us to come to Him freely, without having to be forced. We pray that we bear in patience all the afflictions He sends upon us. We pray that we be governed by our Lord, Jesus Christ. We pray that the light of the Holy Spirit so illuminate us that we never turn from the Gospel but become more and more thoroughly grounded in it. We pray that in the end we come to share in the immortal celestial glory Christ has promised us, being made one with Him in true perfection. May God shed this grace not only on us but on all the peoples and nations of the earth, etc.

All-powerful God, celestial Father, we live in a world full of evil. Every place we turn, we see an infinite number of evils, all of which are signs of your great wrath. Give us the grace that in truly humbling ourselves before you, we may fix our eyes upon your promise to be bountiful and loving toward us, which you made through your Son. May, in this way, we come to be assured you are gentle and kind, that you have truly adopted us as your people. Because our enemies are so well armed and equipped, so cruel, and continue to fight against us so fiercely, give us the grace that we be assured you will sustain and protect us; for you know it is wrong and unreasonable for them to so torment us. Give us the grace that we may march ever confident of your bounty. Give us the grace that we may come to groan under the burden of our sins and to confess incessantly and boldly we would be deserving of a thousand deaths, had you not condescended out of your infinite mercy and bounty to receive us and gather us through our Lord, Jesus Christ. Amen.

* * *

And my enemy will see it, and she will be shamed, she who said to me, "Where is the Lord, your God?" I will look upon her and see her trampled down as mud in the streets, etc. Micah 7

Micah, having said that the faithful will see God's righteousness and have their heritage restored to them, now adds that their enemies will also see God's righteousness. God overlooks punishing the wicked only in order to train the patience of the faithful. For a time, the unfaithful think they have triumphed, seeing the afflictions of the faithful; but in the end they will be shamed; for they will realize that God chastises His own only to make them obedient and that He uses His rod with great moderation to insure His chastisements are brief and always have a happy ending. But on the contrary, Micah says, our eyes will see God punish the unfaithful in a radically different way; He will use His rod to plough them into the earth.

Let us not be unhappy when the wicked mock us so boldly; let us bear our afflictions in patience; for in the end God will squelch all their hopes and desires. Because they are so cruel, they wish to exterminate us, and they believe they are already halfway there when they see God's wrath upon us, as indeed it is for having offended Him. God will never permit them to triumph over us. For a time they will enjoy great prosperity, and we will be tempted to think that God is on their side, aiding and favoring them. Nevertheless, Micah tells us we will live to see the day when they are punished, trampled down like mud, which is

437

a common way the Holy Spirit speaks of God's punishment, through the Scriptures.

Our Lord does not use severe punishment upon His children, as we have already seen; He sustains them, treats them gently, and sweetens all their afflictions, although they deserve to be punished severely. But the wicked and reprobate will be trampled down like mud, without any relief in sight. Although we are in the midst of our adversaries, who are like a dark cloud, let us look to the light God shines upon us, namely His promise of our salvation. Let us ground ourselves thoroughly in this promise, so that we do not lose courage. Seeing the great prosperity of the wicked, who seem to be the happiest men in the world, let us be patient and wait for God to carry out His sentence against them. Let us remember that we cannot judge by the naked eye whether or not God loves or hates someone. Anyone who judges by the naked eye is a fool who will think everything happens by chance, says Solomon. Indeed, when the wicked see that afflictions are common to both good men and bad, they are encouraged to give free reign to evil because they think everything is purely a matter of luck. So we must not judge according to what we see at present by the naked eye; we must wait patiently for the time to come when God will reveal Himself as Judge and punish all those who have rebelled against Him. Rest assured He will do so but not as soon as we might like. So let us, then, live by faith. As Micah says, "My eyes will see." However that we may see the wicked prosper, let us not be tempted to envy them. As it says in Psalm 37, the prosperity of the wicked does not mean that they have escaped the hand of God, that He has forgotten their sins and will leave them unpunished. Our hope must look to the future. When we are in the midst of chaos and nothing seems to go our way, let us remember that God will put everything back in order. I emphasize that everything destroyed will be repaired and restored. Our eyes will see what we cannot even imagine now. So let us never lose faith in the facts that there is a God in Heaven and that He will put all things back together again into such excellent working order that this will be beyond anything we could have ever hoped for.

Now the question arises: How can the faithful rejoice when they see God punish the unfaithful? Should we not desire the salvation of all the world? Since we are reproached for rejoicing in the torments the wicked suffer according to the flesh, is this not ample reason why we should not rejoice in the damnation of all souls? We must bear in mind that Micah is speaking form the viewpoint of God's Spirit, whereas our own viewpoint is a deeply troubled one; our natural senses and passions are totally chaotic; there is no temperance within us. That is why we have no business demanding the damnation of the unfaithful. However, if the Holy Spirit so works within us that all our desires conform to the will of God, then we have true zeal and can in fact rejoice in the condemnation of the iniquitous; that is to say, we may rejoice, provided that our eyes are fixed upon God's judgment and that we are not driven by our own carnal appetites for vengeance, as we are prone to be. That is the first major point to note in the exposition of this passage.

The second major point to note is that Micah is not saying we should rejoice in the evil per se that befalls the iniquitous but that we should rejoice because we look beyond it to the Kingdom of God. Although we should desire the salvation of all men and work as hard as possible to bring it about, nevertheless we must forget all about men when we look to the Kingdom. We have a far more important consideration in mind, namely that God put down all His enemies, who will become His footstool, that He be glorified by His vengeance upon all those who are rebellious, disobedient, and hold His Word in contempt. In knowing God, we must forget about men, except, of course, those whom God calls to Himself, those who are His flock, through whom His glory shines. But in regard to all the rest of men, we can well rejoice in their afflictions; for the Kingdom of God, I say, becomes more and more perfected to the extent the wicked are put down and rejected.

In sum, Micah is saying that we, who are the Children of God, are entitled to rejoice in the damnation of the wicked. However, he makes it clear that we are not entitled to do so on the basis of our own point of view, which is deeply warped. Rather, God and His Word must be our light, so that we are guided by purity and righteousness rather than being driven by our carnal appetites. Our zeal must be to glorify God's

440

righteousness and not to revenge ourselves. Our faith must lead us to God, so that we overcome all human emotion. We must come to recognize that the wicked are the enemies of God, that there is no remedy for them, that they are the reprobate, and that it is necessary for God to damn them in order that His glory be known and His majesty be exalted. If we meet these conditions, then we can rejoice in the damnation of the wicked, indeed even in the damnation of the Devil himself. But as long as we are dominated by the flesh, we must keep a tight rein on our appetite for vengeance, by which we wish that whosoever we hate be destroyed. I emphasize that we must guard against such desire; for our emotions run to wild extremes. Therefore, let us pray to God and ask Him to tame our passions and bring them into conformity with His will; let us ask Him to deliver us from our vengeful appetites, so that we may do everything possible for the salvation of all and will be able to pray that He pity those whom He ransomed by the blood of His Son. Indeed, let us so pray; for Scripture warns against our recklessness, when it says that if we see a wicked man, we cannot tell whether or not God will succeed in converting him and rendering him obedient in the end.

Micah says next, "Behold my enemy who said to me, 'Where is the Lord, your God?'" There is no doubt God takes pity on us when our adversaries mock us, saying, "What good has come from all this hope and faith you have in your God?" When they speak this way, they are not making war on us but on God; for they are accusing Him of lying, of failing to fulfill His promise to be our Savior. If we honor God by trusting fully in the Word, we recognize that He will afflict us either to test our patience or to punish us for our sins, as we must be prodded along by blows of the rod to return to Him. So when the wicked mock us in our afflictions, they vex God because they are accusing Him of lying through His promises. Do not think that God will let such blasphemy go unpunished.

The more our adversaries mock us and rejoice in our afflictions, the stronger must become our faith, as we see in the example of Micah. That is why good King Hezekiah, hearing Sennacherib and Rabshakeh mock God by claiming He has gone back on His promise to save Jerusalem, says, "Lord, hear how they blaspheme you; hear how they mock your promise to save the city. Lord, will you tolerate such blasphemy?" Hezekiah has shown us a way to pray that should become a rule of thumb for us. The more the wicked and the adversaries of the truth, blinded by their pride and arrogance, rejoice in our sufferings and blaspheme, saying, "We see well what kind of a God you trust in!" the more steadfast we must become in our faith, for that is our major weapon against them.

Let us not be as the many who are tempted and led astray whenever the wicked hold great sway; let us remember the wicked are the enemies of God, who reject His truth and wage war on Him. Will this not be to their shame in the end? Will God permit Himself to be blasphemed and not raise a hand to show He is sincere in His promise to save His people?" Let us note well

Micah's words:  "Behold my enemy who said to me, 'Where is your God?'"  Let us arm ourselves against such temptation, by realizing that it is nothing new for the wicked to mock us, saying our faith is deceitful.  This is the age-old way the Devil tries to drive men to despair.  The same thing was said to David, who was a foreshadow of the Son of God.  When Christ was on the cross, the wicked mocked Him, saying, "He trusted in God, so let God help Him now."  When we see that the wicked mocked the faith of David and even of our Lord, Jesus Christ, we should not be surprised if God tests us in this way.

Micah says that after God's people have suffered great affliction, He will restore them, console them, and return their rightful heritage to them.  On the contrary, he says, the wicked, who have totally abandoned themselves to evil, will feel the heavy hand of God upon them.  Having so spoken, he now adds, "In that day, the walls will be rebuilt."  Now, he is speaking here metaphorically; for the Church is like a house and has always been said to be His temple.  Furthermore, Jerusalem at that time was the living image of the Church of God.  So when he says that the day will come to rebuild the walls and gates of Jerusalem, he means that God wishes to restore His Church, that He will not permit it to remain in rack and ruin, as it has been.

Next he says, "In that day, tribute shall be far removed" or "in that day, the edict shall be proclaimed."  The Jews interpret this passage to mean that their ancestors would no longer have to pay tribute to Babylon once God destroyed that city.  However,

443

this is a forced interpretation that does not at all fit Micah's intention. The Jews see well the letter of the Scriptures; but as they are blind and totally destitute of God's Spirit, they have no real understanding what it means. On the contrary, Micah is continuing his consolation of the Church, as if to say, "True, you will undergo great destruction, but the day will come when you will be restored." He means that this promise will not be fulfilled until the coming of the Lord, as will be more amply explained in due course.

The noun Micah used in this passage can be interpreted in two ways. On one hand, it can be taken to mean ordinance, law, commandant. On the other, it can be taken to mean tribute, insofar as people were summoned to pay tribute, through public edicts and ordinances. Either meaning fits well with this passage; for Micah's intent is to console the Church of God by telling the people their period of oppression by the Chaldeans will one day come to an end. "The day will come," he says, "when you will be set free from your slavery and rebuild the walls." In that day the edict will be proclaimed, that is, the edict of Cyrus, who commanded that the Jews be set free and given the means to return home and rebuild the Temple. But, as I have said, this promise does not hold just for that time period; for Micah is speaking of all the redemptive work of our Lord from the time He delivered His people from Babylon to the time Jesus Christ appeared on earth to redeem all men, when the Gospel was proclaimed throughout all the world.

444

In sum, Micah is saying that the enemies of the Church must not make us lose courage when it seems they have triumphed over us. So today, when things are extremely chaotic and hardly go our way, let us remain steadfast in our faith that God will deliver His Church from its desolation. This point is amply made in the Psalm where we read: "Lord, remember the rocks of Jerusalem, for the time to rebuild has come." The "rocks of Jerusalem" signify God's own people, and the Psalm means that God will take pity upon them and not allow His Church to go to rack and ruin, that He will not allow His rocks to be strewn about the highways and byways. Why? The time to rebuild has come. This Psalm is actually a prayer made by the faithful during their period of captivity, when they looked to the promises made them. This Psalm was not composed by David but by the faithful in exile, who, through the inspiration of Jeremiah and Micah, knew to pray, saying, "Lord, you said that our captivity would only be for a time. May it please you now to fulfill what you promised by your Word."

That is how we must hope and pray today; for we live in terrible desolation, and our situation seems hopeless; indeed, wherever our Lord seemed to have gained a foothold, things have gotten worse instead of better. So let us pray to God that He not permit us, who are the ruins of His Church, to languish in desolation. Indeed, He has already fulfilled part of this promise by giving us the grace to have the pure teaching of His Gospel. So let us not be upset and discouraged when we see how

445

confused and troubled are our times; let us wait patiently upon God to restore the Church, for we know it is His office to put everything back in order again.

If we interpret Micah to mean tribute, then, according to what Isaiah tells us, he means God will deliver His people from servitude; for Isaiah, speaking of the deliverance from Babylon and the coming of the Lord, says that God will break the yoke of His people. In spelling this out, he says, "You will undergo cruel servitude for a time. Edicts and ordinances will be sent to you demanding tribute," as if to say, "You will be in continual terror during your time of servitude under the Chaldeans. Messengers will come to demand tribute. The officials of this tyrant will come to sack and pillage you. But in the end God will deliver you." So when Micah says that "tribute shall be far removed," he means that God's people will no longer be trampled down as they have been.

It was in virtue of this promise that we were delivered from our awful servitude under Papism. God delivered us from the yoke that not only oppressed us physically but submitted us to such cruel tyranny that our souls were in grave danger of being destroyed by the incessant torments of the Devil. He took pity upon us and did not merely lift a great burden from us but freed us from all the shackles of the world. We have been liberated from all the traditions and inventions of men. Although we are no longer in spiritual custody, we do bear the yoke of God's Word; but it is sweeter and more gracious to us than all the

446

freedoms of the world, for through it we obtain the remission of our sins. So let us realize what great love God has shown us when He delivered us from the yoke of Papism; let us recognize how deeply He wishes us to invoke His name willingly and sincerely, and to obey His Word, in order that He may dwell among us.

When we realize these things, we will see readily that we were delivered neither through human intervention nor because of our merits but solely through the gracious bounty of God in order to fulfill His promise made through Micah. Consequently we should recognize that God delivered us from the tyranny of the Devil and of men and their shackles in order that we would be free to come to Him. Therefore, if we disobey God, He will throw us back into servitude. Why are men slaves to the Devil and oppressed by one another? They do not obey God. As Saint Paul says, "Is it not fair that those who do not wish to serve their Creator serve creatures?" The Devil, indeed all creatures, will oppress us if we disobey God. So let us pray to God He keep tight enough rein on us so we do not act like wild horses that have to be given over to Satan to be tamed; let us beg Him not to destroy us when He sees that we are totally incorrigible, that we are full of nothing but stubbornness and rebellion.

If God has demonstrated such terrific power in the past that through a pagan king, Cyrus, He was able to deliver His people and rebuild the Temple in Jerusalem, know, I say, that the Gospel has even greater power and efficiency. If our Lord has such power that He could deliver His people through the edict of a poor, blind pagan, how much yet even greater power does He make available to us because He descended to earth to speak to us face to face and proclaim the truth of God, His Father? Since Christ, in whom is the power of God, speaks to us and since we have the Gospel, which is the salvific power of God, there is no doubt that He can and will deliver us, provided we do not destroy ourselves by our ingratitude. That is what Micah means when he says the day will come that God has ordained for the walls to be rebuilt and the edict to be proclaimed, as if to say, "My friends, expect that God will one day visit you. Since it is His will that you remain in captivity for a time, you have to go along with this. So be patient and have faith that He will one day deliver you, provided that you truly believe in His promises." That is Micah's message for us today.

So let us wait patiently upon God; let us never give up hope that He will turn all evil into good. Let us not be upset and discouraged by the fact we live in such a deeply troubled world. Let us remember that if God does not put things into good working order as soon as we would like, we must not give up hope in Him; for in the end He will turn all evil to our benefit, provided that we obey His Word and follow Him wherever He may call us.

Following this holy teaching, we prostrate ourselves before the face of our good God, acknowledging our innumerable sins, by which we incessantly provoke His wrath against us. We pray that it please Him to so open our eyes that we may behold Him and therefore keep our courage up when we are in the midst of our afflictions, indeed even when we are lost in the deepest abysms. We pray that we may come to behold Him as our Protector and Guardian, who will protect us against all that may come to pass. We pray that He so strengthen us in our faith that we are able to successfully resist against all the assaults of the Devil, the world, and our flesh, in order to serve Him in a way He finds fitting and agreeable. May He take pity and have mercy not only upon us but upon all the peoples and nations of the earth, etc.

All-powerful God, celestial Father, our sins have so provoked your wrath against us that there is horrible desolation everywhere. In ancient times, you gave memorable proof of your salvific power, through your people. May you shed this same grace upon us today so that your Church rises up, true religion flourishes, your name is honored and glorified, and we are able to continually call upon your aid. Do this for our sake so that we do not come to doubt that Christ will put back together again this miserable, broken world. May the Lord now shed the power upon us that you have given Him to save the whole world, so that we have the confidence to continue our battle, knowing through living proof that our hope in you is not in vain and that our prayers do not go unanswered. Amen.

* * *

# TEXTS AND STUDIES IN RELIGION